AYANA

Happiness is impossible.

scope and without

RON THOM
ARCHITECT

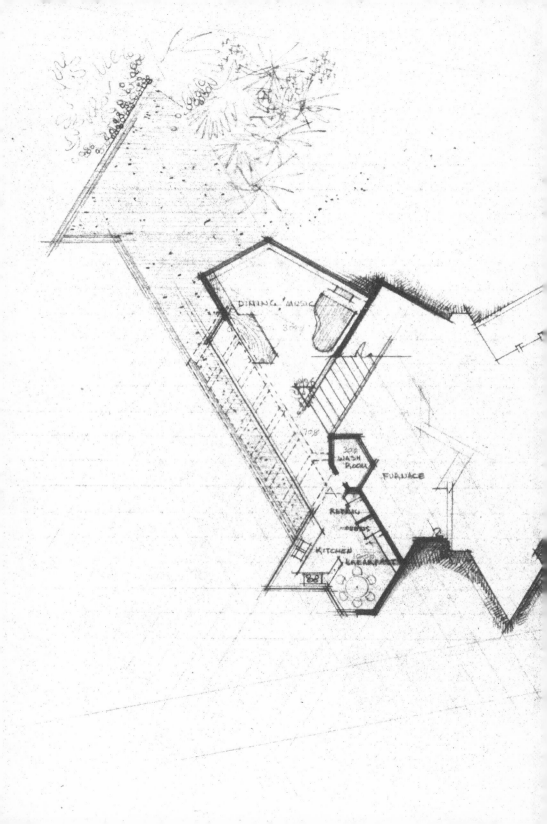

DINING MUSIC

WASH ROOM

FURNACE

KITCHEN

BREAKFAST

ADELE WEDER

RON THOM
ARCHITECT

THE LIFE OF A CREATIVE MODERNIST

GREYSTONE BOOKS
Vancouver/Berkeley/London

Greystone Books Ltd.
greystonebooks.com

Cataloguing data available from Library and Archives Canada
ISBN 978-1-77164-322-1 (cloth)
ISBN 978-1-77164-323-8 (epub)

Editing by Derek Fairbridge
Copy editing by James Penco
Proofreading by Jennifer Stewart

Jacket and interior design by Jessica Sullivan
Front jacket photograph of the Case House, West Vancouver. Courtesy of Anne
Ferries, photographer unknown.
Back jacket image of the Case House, West Vancouver, main floor plan. Design by
Ron Thom; drawing by Paul Merrick. Courtesy of the West Vancouver Art Museum.
Interior photographs as credited
Front Endsheets: Ondaatje Hall, Massey College, Toronto. Photo by Steven Evans.
Front door (detail), Carmichael House, West Vancouver. Photo by Josh Nychuk.
Back Endsheets: Window with tinted egg-crate flats, Dodek House, Vancouver.
Photo by Carla Dodek. Champlain College dining hall ceiling, Trent University,
Peterborough. Photo by Alexi Hobbs.

Printed and bound in Canada on FSC® certified paper at Friesens. The FSC® label
means that materials used for the product have been responsibly sourced.

Every attempt has been made to trace ownership of copyrighted material. Information
that will allow the publisher to rectify any credit or reference is welcome.

Greystone Books thanks the Canada Council for the Arts, the British Columbia Arts
Council, the Province of British Columbia through the Book Publishing Tax Credit,
and the Government of Canada for supporting our publishing activities.

Canadä

Greystone Books gratefully acknowledges the xʷməθkʷəy̓əm (Musqueam),
Sḵwx̱wú7mesh (Squamish), and səl̓ílwətaʔɬ (Tsleil-Waututh) peoples on
whose land our Vancouver head office is located.

is there a rhythm drumming from vision?

shall we tower into art   or ashes?

it is our dreams will decide

& we are their Shapers

EARLE BIRNEY,
from "the shapers: Vancouver," 1958

CONTENTS

PART TWO: EAST

AUTHOR'S
NOTE

WHEN I FIRST STARTED researching this biography over a decade ago, I had yet to recognize the difficulty and complexity of the subject matter. As an artist and architect, Ron Thom worked intuitively, expressing his thoughts in images and gestures more often than in words, which has made his own beliefs and design approach hard to pin down. I never had the opportunity to meet him in person, and the number of surviving friends, colleagues, clients, and other witnesses had already dwindled by the turn of the millennium.

Yet so many people across the country had known him, worked with him, and been deeply touched by him that more than a hundred key witnesses were still alive and lucid. I tracked down his surviving family members, close friends, and significant colleagues; most stood ready to share what they knew of this unique human being. Their recollections were recorded and transcribed, and offered a wealth of insightful thoughts and revelations. As I cross-referenced these interviews with architectural pilgrimages, historic texts, and archival research, a rough picture of his inner creative life slowly emerged.

This methodology involved two major challenges. The first is the passage of time. As his dear friend Molly Bobak told me, "Memories don't fade, but they alter." Confirmation of some events and comments required follow-up interviews, phone calls, and emails to double-check certain details, cross-check with historic documents, and compare one individual's memories with another's. With an eye to improving accuracy, I have sent pertinent manuscript excerpts to Bill Lett, Paul Merrick, Murray Beynon, Denis Smith, and Sherry McKay. When I've quoted individuals, I've sent them the specific sentence or paragraph to check. Three individuals who knew Ron Thom for most of his adult life—Morton Dodek, Barry Downs, and Dick Sai-Chew—saw late-stage drafts of the entire manuscript and provided me with feedback on context, facts, and tone.

Citations from speeches, letters, and other text documents are quoted verbatim. Comments by Ron Thom and other individuals that have been recalled by second parties are in most cases paraphrased, but a small number are in quotations if they are remembered with clarion certainty, if they align with incontrovertible facts from primary sources, *and* if they are in keeping with the character of the person and the context of the times. When the memory has been hazy, I have paraphrased or omitted the recollection entirely.

In a few cases, the quotations from interview subjects may seem jarring to our contemporary ears. The twentieth-century vernacular included derisive ways to describe people of short height, men of refined grooming, and male-female relationships. That language—along with the gender-specific word "draftsman" and the general marginalization of women, Indigenous people, and minorities—reflects the irreverence and non-inclusivity of an era. By the time the architectural profession welcomed a critical mass of female designers into its fold, the computer had already taken over the draftsman's work and the term became anachronistic. This is a book about how things were, not how they should have been; the quotations relay how people spoke, not how they should have spoken.

Family members have previewed the most sensitive and detailed passages that pertain to their own individual memories of a husband

and father. Ron's first and second wives and all six of his children generously offered access to a great volume of photographs and letters, as well as their own recollections. From this well of deeply personal information, I have chosen to cite certain anecdotes and comments that help illuminate an aspect of the character, talent, demons, and humanity that also informed his career and his architecture. Therein lies the value of reading about the lives of artists and architects: the life beyond the workplace can help us understand the work.

That brings us to the second major challenge to writing a biography of Ron Thom: how to deal with the issue of the alcohol dependence that dogged him and ultimately destroyed him. We do his memory no favours by ignoring its pernicious effects on his life and career. For many years recognized as one of the greatest architects in Canada, he seemed destined to progress into one of the greatest in North America, until his addiction tightened into a stranglehold. In the words of Trent University founder Tom Symons, "That was a great loss to the nation." And though some may find the details of his final days disturbing and gratuitous, I've included them to dismantle the even more disturbing—and false—rumours that festered after his death.

But human beings are more than the sum of their demons. Typical of his closest friends, Molly and Bruno Bobak remembered him not only as tormented, hotheaded, and self-destructive but also as brilliant, gifted, funny, generous, magnetic, loveable, and unforgettable. In 2011, as I wrapped up my two-day series of interviews in Fredericton with this nonagenarian couple, I told them that I would do my best to check back with them about any quotes or comments that might end up in this book. Molly replied with cheerful nonchalance, "Oh, we don't care what you write. By the time you finish your book, we'll both be dead!"

Her prediction turned out to be sadly true. Bruno died in 2012; Molly, two years later. As with several other sources in this book, they left us before I could extend the courtesy of sending them the quotations and anecdotes I wished to use from our recorded conversations. In these cases, when the subject is no longer there to check information or quotations gleaned from our interview, I have applied diligence and discretion in ascertaining which comments to use. Throughout this process, I have tried my best to catch and correct erroneous recollections on matters large and small. Whatever errors remain are entirely my own.

—AW

PROLOGUE:
THE ROYAL BLESSING

HIS ROYAL HIGHNESS Prince Philip, the Duke of Edinburgh, is standing midway between a construction crew and a lineup of elaborately dressed men. The Prince has been invited to lay the official cornerstone of a landmark building at the University of Toronto. The day—May 25, 1962—is balmy, to the relief of the event planners. With the structure a year behind schedule and still bereft of a roof, it would be unseemly to welcome the Prince in a downpour.

Beyond the cordoned-off roadway in front of them stands an audience of gawkers and paparazzi, while four trumpeters in full military dress sound the fanfare.[1] With the builders on wooden scaffolding in the background, and besuited VIPs in the foreground, the scene resembles a dress rehearsal for a soundless opera.[2] Metaphorically speaking, that's exactly what it is. The building under construction is Massey College, destined to be a kind of grand plot twist in the story of modern Canadian architecture.

For the previous fifteen years, the city around this building site—the entire continent, in fact—has been transforming. To this point, North American architecture has largely mimicked that of neoclassical Britain. Now, the postwar generation is designing an entirely new built landscape.

1

Prince Philip addresses the crowd in front of the Massey College construction site, while Vincent Massey and Robertson Davies (standing behind the Prince) and Ron Thom (far right) look on.

The cast of characters in this operatic tale includes the cream of Toronto society: Canadian aristocrats; business mandarins; sharp-eyed high modernists trained at Harvard, McGill, and the University of Toronto. All men, many of them draped in silver and gold regalia or coloured stoles, signalling their social or academic standing. "This is an occasion where the men far outshine the women," jokes the Prince as he surveys the glittering lineup.[3]

Among the front-line guests: Robertson Davies—playwright, novelist, and inaugural Master of Massey College; Claude Bissell—president of the University of Toronto; and the most elevated Canadian of the group, the Right Honourable Vincent Massey—recently retired governor general and the founder, benefactor, and namesake of Massey College.

Vincent's brother Raymond, sons Lionel and Hart, and nephew Geoffrey stand alongside him in the front line—Canada's own brand of royal family. As the writer and magazine editor B.K. Sandwell has famously proclaimed, "Toronto has no social classes / Only the Masseys and the masses."[4]

Also in the lineup is the architect of the building: Ron Thom. He belongs to none of these vaunted cliques or fine old families. He's an artist-turned-architect from the West Coast who has broken into their world. He glows with pride as Prince Philip addresses him, but he is wearing no academic regalia himself. Alone among this phalanx of high-powered men, he has never attended university.

Why all the fuss over a smallish college residence—a building that only a tiny sliver of the population can access? Why does *this* building warrant the blessing of a visiting royal? Because its brick walls are poised to carry a symbolic load hugely disproportionate to the actual purpose of the building. Both the Masseys and the masses have been slow to embrace the sleek juggernaut of modernism now taking over the world. For many, the unadorned, high-functioning glass-and-steel buildings lack the dignity, grace, beauty, and warmth of the best traditional architecture. Vincent Massey

Left to right: Prince Philip, Claude Bissell, Ron Thom, Vincent Massey. May 25, 1962, Massey College construction site, Toronto.

endorsed those four qualities so ardently that he had written them right into the original competition brief for the building.

The seductive concept of a sanctuary, encouraging thoughtful exchanges and intimate friendships, shielded from the boisterous world outside its walls: this is what Ron Thom's architecture is offering, and what so many people are craving. The building is already becoming a conceptual paradigm, an inspiration for others seeking ways to address the human need for beauty and intimacy in an age of modernity and mayhem.

As architecture seems to have evolved into a choice of either stark, unadorned boxes or fusty pseudo-historical mimicry, Massey College will offer a third way. Contemporary and yet crafted, like a jewel box of brick, wood, leather, ceramic, and wrought iron. A geode, with an inscrutable brick exterior sheltering the magic within. It will be unlike any other building, old or new.

The Prince places the cornerstone as instructed by Robertson Davies: not in an outside wall at ground level, as Mr. Thom had wanted, but inside and aboveground. As Master Davies had warned the architect: such a densely symbolic building component must not be placed where roving dogs could pee on it.[5]

MR. THOM doesn't even live in Toronto—at least, not yet. He toils over his drafting table in a large Vancouver firm run by other men. Over the next few years, he'll break free of that firm and make his name across the country. But nothing could ever feel quite like this moment of royal affirmation. Now, as His Royal Highness shakes his hand before a throng of reporters and photographers, Ron Thom's status crystallizes into that of a national star.

In a few days, he will fly back to Vancouver—back to an empty apartment, since his wife has left him. But he can share the news of this great day with his mother. Elena Thom, once determined to make her firstborn child into a famous pianist, has instead watched him transform into a famous architect. Surely the accolades pouring in for her son must soothe any lingering disappointment, especially at this exultant moment.

If only the moment could last forever.

SOFFIT FRAMI

PART ONE

WEST

1

A FOUNDATION
IN MUSIC

AT THE DAWN of the twentieth century, a young woman in rural Ontario had few career opportunities, other than farmwife or teacher. Elena Fennell, who grew up south of Ottawa in the village of Kars, chose teaching. While her Irish-immigrant parents tilled the soil on the nearby family farm, Elena taught schoolchildren in Kars, while gestating her ambition for a grander career. In 1907, at age twenty-three, she enrolled at Victoria College at the University of Toronto.

Four years later, bachelor of arts degree in hand, Elena looked around for work. A new career befitting her advanced education proved elusive, however. She looked westward, travelling to Estevan, Saskatchewan, where she had relatives. In this prairie town of two thousand residents, Elena finally found a job—once again, as a teacher.[1]

In Estevan, Elena joined the Methodist Church, maintaining the religion of her Protestant-Irish upbringing. She played the piano and organ for the church's Sunday school, and immersed herself in Methodist ideology. At that time and place, the Church supported the then-radical notion of minimum wage, sickness and disability insurance, and old-age pensions—all of which aligned with the

Elena Fennell, graduation photo
from Victoria College, Toronto.

Prairies' agrarian socialism.[2] Elena would promote these values and policies for the rest of her life.

Growing restless after four more years of teaching, Elena embarked on becoming a lawyer. In 1915, she secured an apprenticeship at the law office of William J. Jolly in the nearby town of Weyburn. At that time, only men were allowed to practise law, but Elena had reason to be hopeful. Just two years earlier, an amendment to Saskatchewan's Legal Profession Act allowed for the admission of women. The provincial society confirmed the first female lawyer in its history, Mary Cathcart, in 1917. Soon afterward, the second and third women were called to the bar, and then Elena Myrtle Fennell became the fourth.[3]

After logging several hundred articling hours and toiling through days of exams, Elena registered with the Law Society of Saskatchewan as a barrister-solicitor in 1919. There is no record of Elena ever setting foot in a law school, though. In those days, five years of articling—or three years following a university degree in any field—sufficed to apply to the bar.[4] Elena rose through the apprenticeship system and became one of the female trailblazers in her profession by the very fact that she was able to practise it.

A town of roughly three thousand people, Weyburn served as a way station for farmers and westbound fortune-seekers as well as its base of permanent residents. Craftsman homes, a department store, two English-Gothic-style churches, and the stone-clad Royal Hotel projected the image of a comfortable, prosperous town. For an ambitious young barrister, however, the professional milieu was limited; the town wouldn't have a purpose-built courthouse for another decade.[5]

With Saskatchewan's Prohibition in full force, Weyburn didn't have many social offerings for young singles. But it did have a Methodist church with a choir. Here, before long, she met a young baritone named James Anderson Thom.[6]

JAMES THOM was born in Scotland to a long line of craftsmen. His grandfather, John Thom, was a journeyman cabinetmaker in mid-nineteenth-century Aberdeen.[7] His father, George Thom, moved to Glasgow and became a stonemason, shaping craggy rock into the geometrically formed building blocks for villas on the outskirts of the city. As soon as James reached his teens, he dropped out of school to apprentice at his father's business. Very soon afterward, the youth's life changed abruptly when his father contracted silicosis—the occupational hazard of a stonemason. After two years of gasping for breath, George Thom succumbed to the disease in 1898, at age forty-two. His distraught widow immediately pulled James out of the apprenticeship and found him a job as a quantity surveyor in a builder's office, where he would learn to help builders cost out their projects and keep their spending in line. She felt determined to keep her son out of the trade that had killed his father.[8]

After several uneventful years in Glasgow poring over balance sheets, James immigrated to Canada in 1907, enticed by a pal who was resettling in Winnipeg and convinced James to accompany him. In Winnipeg, James took whatever work he could get. His first employment, in this era before electric refrigerators: cutting blocks of ice out of the Red River for household iceboxes.

He returned to England from 1917 to 1919 to work in the Royal Air Force payroll office.[9] Not a particularly adventurous position, but likely more comfortable than spending his days hacking into a frozen river.

With the Great War over, James returned to Winnipeg, and strung together a series of temporary jobs in bookkeeping, farming, and door-to-door insurance sales.[10] After another year living with the region's brutal winter weather, he made plans to resettle on the country's more temperate West Coast.[11]

In 1920, mid-journey, he stopped in Weyburn for a short-term job. After a long slump, the local economy was booming, powered by the construction of the Weyburn Mental Hospital, a 260,000-square-foot brick leviathan sprawling along the outskirts of town.

The plethora of job opportunities made it viable for James to extend his stay in Weyburn, and other attractions beckoned. James loved music and singing, and he joined the town's Methodist church. There, during choir practice, he met the volunteer organist—Elena Fennell.[12]

They wed in 1922, and Elena's life changed again. After logging only three years of practice, she abandoned her law career to take on her new role of wife. In the early months of 1923, James and Elena moved even further west, to Penticton, in the British Columbia Interior. On May 15, she gave birth to their first child, a son. They named him Ronald James Thom.

A YEAR LATER, the Thoms continued westward to James's original destination, arriving at a grand neoclassical railway station and a spectacular setting of forests, mountains, and ocean. Vancouver owed its nickname—Terminal City—to the virtue of being the last stop of the national railway. The moniker also evoked a sense of mortality, an elegy to the forests that had been cut down to clear land on which to build the city.

By the time Elena and James Thom arrived in the city in 1924, that clear-cut land had evolved into a quilt of vacant lots alternating with blocks of hybrid architectural styles. The majority of the area's Indigenous population, which had settled in the area thousands of years before, had been moved to reserves outside the periphery of the city. Now, in the Roaring Twenties, affluent residents dwelled in turreted mansions in the West End, just a few blocks away from ramshackle wooden pitched-roof houses inhabited by threadbare

James Thom
with baby
Ron and pup.

families. Middle-class couples ordered arts-and-craft house kits from catalogues and built them in the south end of the city.

James soon landed a job as a bookkeeper at a sheet metal plant. Elena folded up her professional ambitions and stayed at home to devote herself to their infant son.[13]

James does not appear to have had much of a direct role in young Ron's life.[14] The father-son emotional distance seems visible from the start, in a formal family portrait of James Thom holding his infant son in one arm and a bulldog puppy in the other. The father is regarding both of the small creatures with apparent indifference, as though he is holding a couple of interchangeable ten-pound sacks of potatoes. The baby looks dismayed.

Ron Thom, age five.

The Thoms purchased a two-storey cedar-shingled house in Marpole, a working-class neighbourhood at the southern edge of the city. Their new home stood five hundred yards east of Granville Street, the boundary line between Marpole and the more affluent neighbourhoods of Shaughnessy and Kerrisdale. By bourgeois standards, they still lived on the wrong side of the tracks, literally, but their address fell into the same catchment area as the adjacent neighbourhoods' well-regarded public schools. And the electric streetcar on Granville Street could whisk them all downtown in minutes.

THE NEXT FEW YEARS brought two more children to the family: Mavis, and then Heather. They received the trappings of an aspiring-middle-class childhood, including occasional professional photography in their Sunday best. But Elena continued to devote most of her attention and vicarious ambition to her firstborn son.[15] At age five, Ronny smiles beatifically in a formal white shirt, dark cravat, knickerbockers, cuffed knee-high stockings, and leather shoes buffed to a shine.

That same year, his mother enrolled her son in piano lessons. At the piano keyboard, Ronny showed himself to be highly adept—gifted, possibly. She also ensured that he took swimming lessons and joined the Young Worshippers League at the United Church, which had been created in 1925 when the Methodists merged with other Protestant congregations. But she prioritized his piano lessons beyond all other activities.

Clockwise from left: Heather, Ron, Mavis, Elena, and James Thom.

Elena's sense of nurturing extended beyond her immediate family. When the prosperous 1920s plunged into the Depression of the 1930s, her compassion extended to the desperate men who were "riding the rails" in search of work. One or two at a time would occasionally show up at her back door, bedraggled and starving. Elena would prepare meals for them and spend time listening to their stories before sending them on their way, well-fed and comforted.

Throughout his life, Ron rarely mentioned his father but spoke frequently of his mother. To friends, colleagues, and his own children, he exuded pride in her pioneering law career and her socialist values. Paradoxically, he resented those rail-riders that his mother had nourished. As a young boy, he had found them distasteful in their bedraggled state, strange and hirsute and unwashed. He would have preferred to keep the family home just for themselves.[16]

AT HIS MOTHER'S DIRECTIVE, Ronny grew steadily more serious about the piano. Throughout elementary school, he pounded the keys several hours a day, every day, after school and into the evening.

Ron, age twelve, with trophy from provincial piano competition win.

Following the lessons and exhortations of his private teacher, the child learned the sonatas of Beethoven, the fugues of Bach, and much else. He progressed, winning regional accolades. At age eleven, he passed the Trinity College intermediate exam with honours. The following year, he reached first place in the 1936 Victoria Musical Festival, not only in his age division—"junior boys"—but among all contestants in the entire festival.[17]

And so he practised and practised and practised. He won medals and trophies and local newspaper coverage, and his future career as a concert pianist seemed on track. However, the competition judges often expressed reservations about his playing style in their stern written evaluations. While many judges noted his unique "expression," most of them noted that his playing was "a little fast," with the fustiest among them even calling his touch "a little violent on the forte passages... hardly graceful and fastidious enough to catch the old-world flavour."[18]

Despite his certificates and trophies, it seemed that Ronny's musical prowess could not reach the ultra-high level required to make a profession of it. He could not reliably heed the old-world penchant for a gentle, even, predictable tempo. Or perhaps this signalled his innate creativity, wanting to inflect the composition with his own tempo rather than slavishly follow a score.

Still, he spent almost every spare hour at the keyboard, following his mother's non-negotiable scheduling. But as he approached his teens, other priorities emerged, along with a growing sense of independence. And when he began high school at Magee Secondary, a bevy of interesting new subjects and activities awaited him.

He enrolled in drafting class. There, he learned how to create detailed renderings of everyday objects. Simple things like boxes, and then more complex objects, like threaded bolts. At the behest of their strict and demanding teacher, the students learned how to work with adjustable drafting pens, which they dipped in ink and periodically wiped off as they worked.

They learned the proper use of tools: #2 lead pencil, gum eraser, drafting pen. They learned to brace a T square against the side of the drafting table so that they could slide a ninety-degree-angle triangle along its edge, or glide the T square up and down the edge of their slanted tabletop to draw perfect horizontal and vertical and angled lines, as precise as a machine. They learned to use a protractor or a French curve to replicate a complex angle or rounded shape. And they learned to draw "sections" of objects and shapes, by determining how the inside of the object would look if it were cut in half.[19]

The act of drafting trains the mind not only to replicate precisely but also to understand space—how to order one's mind to simultaneously read and reconfigure an image in different dimensions. Ron and the other students transformed two-dimensional images into their axonometric drawings, which simulate a three-dimensional view. Although the process does not allow creative flights of fancy, it instills not only an improved rendering skill but also a higher realm of spatial understanding.

His attention soon turned to another subject: art. The art teacher at Magee Secondary told him he had a strong natural talent, and she encouraged him to develop it.[20] Ron inhaled the praise and felt spellbound by the creative possibilities of drawing and painting. He now shunned the provincial competitions at which he had once excelled.[21]

One more distraction emerged in high school. "I'll never forget the day I looked out the kitchen window and saw my girlfriend playing baseball with a whole bunch of boys," he recalled, decades later. From that point on, he concluded, "Practising piano didn't mean a damn thing to me."[22]

After life-devouring years of practice and a series of very good but imperfect evaluations, he shut the piano lid and never took a lesson or played in public again.

Ron's abandonment of music dismayed Elena. It violated her Protestant sensibility and defied one of her favourite sayings: "Always finish what you start."[23] Plus, it meant that her only son would not become a concert pianist. He would have to find some other means of earning a living and making his mark.

2

BUILDING
A CULTURE

IN JANUARY OF 1941, after a morning of grade twelve classes, Ron Thom stepped onto the Granville streetcar and journeyed all the way downtown, to a three-storey brick building at the corner of Cambie and Dunsmuir Streets. A mashup of Gothic and Victorian styles, the building sprouted gables that tapered into finial-topped points like the peaks of a circus tent roof. Ron walked up the steps and through its porticoed front entrance. The letters arching around its curved lintel spelled out its name and purpose: the Vancouver School of Art. He would now begin his training as a visual artist—part-time while he finished off this final year of high school, and then full-time beginning in the fall of 1941.[1]

Though music had been a precarious career choice, art would be no safer. In wartime Vancouver, a small scattering of artists had managed to fashion comfortable lives for themselves, travelling and exhibiting regularly. Most of these men and women came from a different world, with financial support available from wealthy fathers and grandfathers who had profited from the land and quarries and forests in British Columbia and beyond. Lawren Harris, co-founder and main funder of the Group of Seven art collective, rode on a family fortune derived from Massey-Harris Company Ltd., the largest manufacturer of farm machinery in the British Empire. Artist and cultural philanthropist Harold Mortimer-Lamb had grown rich in the mining industry, which bankrolled his painting, photography, and art collecting.[2]

Ron Thom had no such fortune or social network to buoy his ambitions. He would have to rely solely on talent and discipline to carve out a career as an artist.

THE ART SCHOOL presented something of an anomaly in a young city whose society was still financed by shipping, mining, and logging. The school's founder, Charles Hepburn Scott, had trained at the Glasgow School of Art and emigrated from Scotland to Canada in 1912. Two years later, he joined the Vancouver School Board as art supervisor. He stood out among the education system bureaucrats, not only on account of his voluminous black monobrow hedged above his spectacles but also because of his singular passion for transforming his adopted city into a cultural epicentre.

In Vancouver, Charles Scott saw not a barren field but a blank slate. Resettling in a city bereft of cultural infrastructure, he had embarked on creating it. To this end, in 1920 he formed the British Columbia Art League, a society whose aim was to build an art gallery and open an art school. Five years later, the Vancouver School of Decorative and Applied Arts opened on the second floor of the municipal school board, which operated the school. During its first year, its sole staff member was its director: architect George Lister Thornton Sharp, co-founder of Sharp & Thompson Architects.[3] The syllabus did not yet offer any courses in architectural design, but that would come soon enough.

For the second year, George Sharp returned to the full-time job of running his busy architectural practice with Charles Thompson. Charles Scott assumed the directorship and lobbied the city and public for continued support. In his public talks and his guest spots on local radio, he emphasized not just the school's cultural value but

Some of the instructors and staff on the steps of the Vancouver School of Decorative and Applied Arts. *From left to right*: Charles Marega, Charles Scott, Kate Adeline Smith, George Thornton Sharp, and Theodore Frederick Korner.

also its practical benefit. The School of Decorative and Applied Arts would train future artists and designers to transform Vancouver into what he called "the City Beautiful."[4]

"There may be art in the order and tidiness of our streets, the quality of our civic buildings, the condition of our shop fronts and interiors, our boulevards, our front gardens and our back gardens, our parks, and our beaches," he asserted. "Art flourishes on canvas too, but it would be a mistake to sequester it there."[5]

Scott injected the school with instant prestige by recruiting as faculty Group of Seven member Fred Varley from Toronto and future Painters Eleven member Jock Macdonald from Edinburgh. They taught several future notable painters, among them Vera Weatherbie, Fred Amess, and Bert (B.C.) Binning. The "decorative and applied arts" aspect of the school's name and mandate bent to the city's utilitarian spirit by promoting the school as a means of creating useful design technicians.[6]

By 1933, the Depression threatened to bankrupt the school as revenues and enrollment fell and municipal revenues evaporated. Charles Scott saved it by slashing faculty wages by sixty per cent. The fact that he reduced his own director's pay by just one-third enraged Varley and Macdonald; they resigned in protest and started their own institution, called the British Columbia College of Arts. With little tuition revenue and no public funding, the Varley-Macdonald rival school limped along for two years before folding.[7]

Scott continued to nurture the original school, its name now condensed to "Vancouver School of Art"—or vsa, for short. The economy remained miserable, but the city now had not only an art school but also, since its 1931 opening, a public art gallery from the template he had created. Both were still small in size and scope, but together they produced a tangible cultural infrastructure, and the genesis of something much larger to come.

After completing his studies in 1932 under Scott, Bert Binning had spent time studying sculpture in Eugene, Oregon, before joining the permanent faculty the following year.[8] In 1938, he sailed overseas with his wife Jessie for a sabbatical in London under the tutelage of important artists, most significantly Henry Moore. The British sculptor, then on the brink of international renown, offered a seismically different view of spatial expression, with his drawings, and later his sculptures, exhibiting organic, canted perspectives and forms.

The Binnings returned to North America in mid-1939 and landed in New York, where they viewed the exhibition *Art in Our Time* at the Museum of Modern Art. There, in addition to painting, sculpture, and industrial design, Bert and Jessie saw the most exemplary new works of the European modernist diaspora now resettled in America, including Le Corbusier, Ludwig Mies van der Rohe, Walter Gropius, Richard Neutra, Berthold Lubetkin, and Frank Lloyd Wright.

Jessie and Bert Binning, relaxing at the inside-outside border of their landmark modernist house.

Bert Binning brought back to Vancouver a trove of ideas, along with the thick exhibition catalogue. With renewed enthusiasm, he resumed his teaching position at the Vancouver School of Art. And then he built a small house on a West Vancouver slope for himself and Jessie, a house that would serve as a living showroom for avant-garde art and architecture. In pencil and ink, Binning sketched out the house plans and elevations himself: a highly unusual, slightly asymmetric version of the sort of modernist houses he had viewed in London and New York. He drew up a canted hallway to create optical foreshortening effects and spatial excitement.

Upon the completion of his house in 1941, Binning began welcoming a critical mass of the city's emerging cultural leaders: artists, architects, professors, students, dancers, musicians, poets. The Binning House had become a semi-public gallery and gathering space.

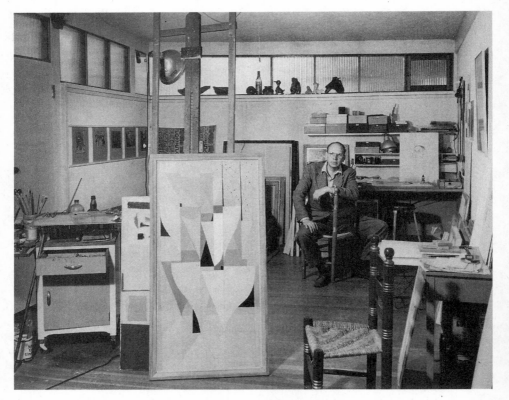

B.C. Binning in the painting studio of his 1941 self-designed modernist house in West Vancouver.

He had created his own manifesto—not with words, but with a small house that showcased contemporary art, architecture, and design in daily living.[9]

The instructors of this cohort now included Charles Scott, Grace Melvin, Jack Shadbolt, Bert Binning, and Fred Amess. Within a decade or two, they would see their works hanging in the National Gallery of Canada on the other side of the country. For now, they taught a roomful of teenagers, including a few who whose talent—like their own—would soon be recognized across the country, and beyond.

Ron (centre) drawing during a Vancouver School of Art outing.

Like the staff, the male students wore tweed jackets and ties, and the female students wore skirts. Their shoes were polished, as were their manners: they addressed their teachers with honorifics. Mr. Scott taught painting and drawing; Miss Melvin taught calligraphy, graphic design, and decorative arts; Mr. Shadbolt, an abstract expressionist, taught painting and drawing; Mr. Binning taught painting, drawing, and, in Ron's senior year, architectural design.

The compact student body grew to know each other fast, forging strong friendships, rivalries, and romances. Here, in stark contrast to his years of solitary afternoons hunched over a piano, Ron found kindred spirits and a social life. After class and studio, students and faculty often headed to the blinking neon of Granville Street, or would simply amble across the street to the bar at the Alcazar Hotel.[10]

Ron grew exceptionally close to several of his classmates, especially Molly Lamb and Don Jarvis, who became Ron's best friends.

Most important was Christine Millard—Chris, as everyone called her—and she became everything else to him.

Chris first met Ron at the art school's annual Beaux-Arts Ball, a bacchanalian costume party held every year at the Commodore Ballroom on Granville Street. She could only attend school part-time, but her beauty and boisterous personality enthralled several of her classmates, especially the men.[11] Among those enthralled was skinny, soft-spoken Ron.

Chris lived with her parents in a modest apartment in the West End, a residential enclave on the other side of downtown. On his first visits there, Ron showed up each time with an armful of cedar boughs, which he then carefully arranged around their apartment until it looked like a small conservatory. An unusual courtship ritual—but it worked: she fell hard for him, too.

Ron and Chris spent their extracurricular hours strolling down the city streets or walking in Stanley Park. When they could scrape up enough money, they would join their classmates at the Alcazar. They both held jobs while attending art school—Chris selling car parts at an automotive outlet, and Ron working as a stock boy at a nearby shoe store.[12] Their shared obsession and common vocation was the creation of art.

Girded by ocean and islands and forest and snowcapped mountain peaks, the city offered the perfect backdrop for both courtship and artmaking. Mr. Scott believed in painting from life, rather than pictures, and he periodically ordered the students to walk down to the beach, park, or railway station. There, after claiming a spot on a washed-up log, or the grass, or a bench, each student would spend a half-day drawing and painting.

Inside the walls of the school, the lessons themselves received mixed reactions from Ron. He found Mr. Amess, Miss Melvin, and Mr. Scott to be dreadfully boring. Their students endured rigorous lessons in the depiction of natural materials and the human form. Mr. Scott hired live models and arranged the still-life compositions himself. Whether he was discussing a jug of flowers or the naked human figure, Mr. Scott talked about the subjects in similar scientific terms, as conflations of botanical or anatomical parts. As his students sat bug-eyed before a nude model, his dry pedagogy desexualized the context. "Note the triangle from the nipple of the breast to the umbilicus," he would flatly exhort.[13]

Ron's sketchbook soon filled with anatomical drawings, a source of pride for him, though little understood by the world outside. One day, while working at the shoe store, he encountered his boss thumbing through the sketchbook and leering at his drawings of nude women. On another day, he endured his father's lay critique of his sketches. James Thom could not imagine any practical reason for learning to draw a bunch of naked humans, and he told his son as much.[14]

Jack Shadbolt taught in an entirely different way from Charles Scott. Like Binning, he had studied in London and Paris and for a year at the Art Students League in New York, which immersed him in avant-garde ideas. He subsequently introduced his students to the then-new concept of abstract expressionism. He inflected his talks with fiery enthusiasm that captivated certain students in a way that Mr. Scott never could.[15] For Mr. Shadbolt, a flower was not the sum of its botanical parts, but a tumescent symbol of growth.

Bert Binning's approach lay somewhere between Mr. Shadbolt's and Mr. Scott's. He drew and painted in a semiabstract way, bending and inflecting his perspective lines. Whatever he depicted—a sailboat, a city street, a woman with a tea tray on her lap—seemed to exist in a kind of gently warped space.

Mr. Binning soon took a focused interest in Ron Thom, one of his first-year drawing and painting students. As Ron later recalled:

> We would be sitting at our easels around the studio, facing the model we were drawing. I can remember one day when I was drawing, and I sensed this person standing behind me. He leaned over, pointed at the face on the drawing and said: "Now look, Ron, you have to pretend that you're a little fly, with short little legs

walking down this nose, over this big bump, then down-over-up-and-down around the bottom." In plain language, we were being instructed to look at everything meticulously—to be sure we saw every nuance.[16]

Mr. Binning also showed his students black-and-white slides of the art and architecture he had seen firsthand in England, Europe, and New York. He showed them images of the narrow lanes of Venice, medieval cathedrals, and Renaissance paintings. Not direct observation, but the next best thing to travelling there.[17] And although Mr. Binning proclaimed himself a "modern" artist and had just built the region's first modernist house, he saw no contradiction in this historic subject matter and his directive to be contemporary. "When I say that a new approach must be found," he later explained, "what I have in mind has already [happened] in the past." He cited the Gothic era and the first part of the Renaissance, when societies shifted to the new approach of treating art and architecture as a continuum, "in dynamic unity; when sculpture fused with architecture... when painting and decoration seemed the flowering of the building from which it grew; when, indeed, the Artist was very often the Architect."[18]

3

THE SHADOW
OF CONFLICT

TO DIE IN BATTLE is horrific. But the least horrible way to go is in the air, as a fighter pilot, flying a thousand feet above the Earth. Or so Ron Thom thought as he prepared to go to war. He imagined ground troops skewered by bayonets and marines drowning in icy waters. As he would later tell his offspring, he *assumed* he would die, and preferred to go fast and mercifully, in an exploding plane.[1] That's when his ambition to fly a plane first took hold.

The young men of Ron's generation had known for years that sooner or later they would head to the battlefield. Prime Minister William Lyon Mackenzie King laid bare the existentialist threat fermenting on other continents. "For months, indeed for years, the shadow of impending conflict in Europe has been ever present," he declared in his September 1939 House of Commons speech announcing the recommendation to declare war. "Unhappily for the world, Herr Hitler and the Nazi regime in Germany have persisted in their attempt to extend their control over other peoples and countries, and to pursue their aggressive designs in wanton disregard of all treaty obligations, and peaceful methods of adjusting international disputes."[2]

Ron was nineteen and had logged a year of art school when he registered to join the Royal Canadian Air Force (RCAF) in October

Ron Thom in uniform.

of 1942, citing Charles Scott as one of his four character references. He hoped to rise higher in the ranks and in the air than his father, whose wartime service had been mostly spent on the ground. Military service had its advantages, though. The federal government offered full post-secondary tuition and living expenses for all who served and came back alive.

Although Ron wanted to fly, he feared the possibility of being recruited as a tail gunner—the crewman who would strap himself into a glass capsule at the back of the plane in order to return enemy fire.[3] "I didn't want to be bullet-bait," he later told his children.[4] Tail gunners were the first targets of anti-aircraft fire. The main criterion for exemption was size: tall men couldn't fit into that tiny capsule. According to an initial military physical examination, Ron weighed 132 pounds and stood five-foot-ten—a little too compact for comfort.

In preparation for his interview and a follow-up physical exam, he made a few spurious attempts to extend that recorded height. After attaching a pulley device around his head and neck, recalled Chris, he suspended himself from the doorway header at his home, in a bid to stretch out his spine.[5] Some of the prospective recruits, he later told his children, actually smashed their heads against the wall, in the hopes that the resulting bump would nudge their heights past the tail-gunner maximum height limit. Nobody wanted to get blown up in the aircraft tail.[6]

The attestation of Registrant #192943, as he was catalogued, described him as "physically fit, emotionally stable, well-motivated, slightly tense." The report noted his future intentions: finishing his studies at the Vancouver School of Art, and then teaching art to others. It also charted his height: five feet, ten-and-a-half inches—and, in the next report, five-foot-eleven. By the third and final examination, he would chart in at six feet tall. Either all that spine-stretching paid off, or his examiners used discretion in their measurements.

In the end, Ron avoided the tail gunner's cage, but didn't get his much-desired pilot training either. The RCAF instead assigned him to train as an aero engine mechanic, or AEM.[7]

For his AEM training, the RCAF first sent him to Lachine, Quebec, and then to St. Thomas, Ontario. He next headed to his one and only overseas station. In August of 1943, having completed his coursework, the RCAF shipped him and his squadron out to a U.S. military base in Alaska. The American forces had recaptured the Aleutian Islands from the Japanese earlier that year. After the active battles ended, the Canadian contingent served as airborne sentries, on the lookout for the possible return of the Japanese army. During their overhead patrols, the squadron had to brace for possible attack at any moment, but the enemy forces never returned. One member of the Canadian contingent, Flying Officer David Francis Griffin, kept a diary of the daily tension and tedium. "Canadians back in civilization from the Aleutians are often asked: 'How did you live? What did you do for amusement?'" wrote Griffin. "Answer to the first one is: 'As best we could.' Answer to the second one: 'Not much.'"[8]

BACK AT THE BASE, most men killed off the hours with card games and liquor. Day after day, for all thirty-six days of Ron's time in the Aleutians, the islands remained as quiet as a tomb. Meanwhile, Ron continued in his mechanic role while fervently hoping for an opportunity to switch to navigation training.

Ron left Alaska and the Aleutians in late September 1943, a little over a month later, and headed to his next round of postings in

Boundary Bay, B.C. In November, Ron applied to be "remustered," the air force term for reassignment to another duty. A commanding officer signed the recommendation for aircrew training. Following a series of interviews and examinations, the RCAF education officer who reviewed his application described him as "above average" aircrew material; the subordinate commander noted how he seemed "quite keen on remustering."

A month later, his application for aircrew training was approved. Now, all he had to do was wait. After a short break in Vancouver for Christmas, his squadron headed off to Tofino and then to Edmonton, where he continued working in engine maintenance.

Meanwhile, Chris waited patiently back at her parents' house on Comox Street. The war that raged on the other side of the world continued to shadow their daily lives. Rationing continued for everything from food to nylons, and Chris used her drawing skills to pen a trompe-l'oeil "seam" down the back of each leg, to make her bare legs appear sheathed in nylons.

The war permeated the physical landscape as well. On the University of British Columbia's waterfront campus, the Department of National Defence had built three circular gun emplacements of reinforced concrete, with underground magazines and ammunition hoists and a network of tunnels to connect them. Across the water, in West Vancouver's Lighthouse Park, military contractors installed additional concrete gun emplacements and converted the park's Point Atkinson Lighthouse into a surveillance lantern for spotting enemy vessels.

In late August of 1944, Ron procured a military leave marked "special" on the request form, returning to Vancouver for a fortnight. On September 1, 1944, he and Chris entered Marpole United Church and exchanged wedding vows.

For their honeymoon, the newlyweds embarked on a canoe trip in Banff, snapping dozens of photos of each other as they paddled and hiked, beaming with happiness.[9]

Then, one week later, Registrant #192943 set off to the Prairies—finally approved to train as a flight navigator.

Ron headed to the flatlands of Regina and Portage la Prairie to commence his training. Over five months, he logged just over one hundred hours of flying time during which he was the navigator—and many additional hundreds of hours of theory, meteorology, aircraft-recognition training, log keeping, and all the other knowledge required for the role. His final report described him as "a keen and enthusiastic worker; inclined to be erratic; lacks powers of concentration. He has a neat

Ron and Chris on their wedding day.

clean-cut appearance; is extremely co-operative and of friendly disposition. He is not impressive as a leader but should crew up well and do his job well."

On February 2, 1945, Sgt. Ronald J. Thom became a qualified flight navigator ready for airborne action. It was too late, though. With the Aleutians campaign over, and with no new hostilities in the region, his newly acquired skills as a flight navigator were no longer needed. Sgt. Ron Thom received an honourable discharge on March 8, 1945.

He had learned how to load, mount, and fire a Browning .50-calibre machine gun, a weapon capable of firing over five hundred rounds a minute from the air, and acquired knowledge of engine mechanics and flight navigation. But he never secured the opportunity to fly or even guide a plane in an actual theatre of war.

RON CAME BACK to Vancouver with a veteran's allowance to bankroll the rest of his art education. The skinny teenager who had enlisted three years earlier now presented as a young man, weighing in at a healthier 145 pounds. Chris did notice one other change in him, though. He had started his military service as a sober man—a "social drinker," as he described himself on his enlistment form. When he and Don Jarvis each returned home from their concurrent years of service, she recalled, "they came back soused."[10]

AFTER WRAPPING UP their military duties, Ron and Don Jarvis and his other classmates-turned-soldiers plunged back into their civilian lives, ready to shift their focus back to art and design. The distance between the two realms is not as great as you might think. Around 30 B.C., the Roman architect-engineer Marcus Vitruvius Pollio had written a landmark treatise, *De architectura*, defining the primordial qualities of architecture as *firmitas*, *utilitas*, and *venustas*—stability, utility, and beauty.[11] Architecture as defined by Vitruvius included not just houses and temples but also military equipment: catapults, ballistic carts, and siege engines—beautiful killing machines.

Two millennia later, the bloodiest conflict in human history would also help undergird modern architecture. The two World Wars had galvanized western nations to modernize their manufacturing industries on a grand scale, spurring technical innovations in plywood, steel, and tempered glass—newly essential materials for fighter aircraft and other military machinery. In a neatly inverted "grave-to-cradle" design cycle, the technological advances from a deadly war would later help supply houses and schools for the postwar baby boom.

The efficient mechanization of sheet glass allowed manufacturers to make large mullion-free windows for homes and workplaces.

Larger windows could offer a larger view. Since most architects and builders designed every house with its picture window facing the street, that view would usually turn out to be a random street scene: a parked car, fire hydrant, sidewalk, pavement, sporadic traffic, and the same kind of house right across the street—with its own picture window blankly staring back. But it didn't have to be that way. Astute and talented architects could configure their window locations, sizes, and shapes in such a way that the residents inside might see a picturesque landscape or bands of sunlight instead.

ARCHITECTURE BENEFITED not only from wartime technological advances, but postwar wealth. The expanded and improved infrastructure of the mining, logging, and hydroelectric industries had first been essential to win battles and now would be part of the spoils of war, generating far greater wealth than before. British Columbia's ocean, forests, and rivers would provide the lush settings for the new architecture, while simultaneously being ravaged in order to heat, illuminate, and pay the bills for the region's ambitious postwar life.

The war experience also shaped the individual lives of the generation set to create this new architecture. On a practical level, their education bursaries—along with a new school of architecture fermenting at the University of British Columbia—made it more viable than ever for Canadians to pursue a career in architecture. Up to this point, the profession had been dominated by architects born and educated in the United Kingdom. Now, the young Canadians returning home from war included many aspiring architects and builders, swelling with ambition to make something new of their world.

They would no longer need British practitioners and British traditions to design postwar Canada. The war helped spur the transition—and they would definitely need the natural-resource industries to bankroll it all.

The future looked glorious. But the price would be enormous.

BACK AT ART SCHOOL, Ron encountered some old and new faces. His friend Molly Lamb had also just returned from the war, where she had served overseas for three years as Canada's first female war artist, accompanied by her fellow war artist and now-husband, Bruno Bobak. Bruno secured a VSA teaching position and, by way of Molly, joined Ron's circle of close friends.

Molly came from a highly cultured and romantically compli-cated household. Her father, the wealthy art titan Harold Mortimer-Lamb, had begat Molly with his housekeeper, who lived together with Harold and his sickly wife while raising Molly.[12] Group of Seven co-founders Lawren Harris, Fred Varley, and Alexander Young (A.Y.) Jackson were all family friends. A.Y. Jackson grew so close to young Molly that for the rest of his life he signed off his many letters to her as "Uncle Alex."

Despite the unconventionality of the household arrangement—or because of it—Molly Lamb turned out to be outgoing, funny, crea-tive, productive, and irreverent. Charles Scott's turgid academic style of teaching bored her, whereas she exulted in Jack Shadbolt's vibrant, expressionist work and his dynamic teaching approach. "He set me on fire," she recalled of the Shadbolt studio lectures.

Ron also became acquainted with a new student, Gordon Smith, who joined them in senior year. At twenty-four, a few years older than most of his classmates, Gordon had come to the school at the behest of Charles Scott, who proposed that he spend a year in art school before joining the school as a teacher.[13]

Gordon had already studied at the Winnipeg School of Art before heading off to war. He had been seriously injured in Sicily and spent a year recovering in Winnipeg. And now he stood out amid the ragtag art students at the VSA. Tall and poised, he came to school immaculately dressed, spoke eloquently with a subtle British accent, and listened attentively in class. And while most of his classmates casually threw their dirty brushes and palette knives into a tin and wiped their paint-smeared hands on their smocks, Gordon handled

At the Fair Grounds, painting by Ron Thom, as featured in the November 1946 edition of *Canadian Art*.

them like surgical tools, cleansing and wiping them carefully and re-slotting them in their case at the end of each studio session.

Watching Gordon, Chris rolled her eyes—*this* methodical, buttoned-down guy, obsessed with decorum and order and cleaning, in *their* freewheeling world? "He'll never make it as an artist," she guffawed to her classmates.[14] She turned out to be quite wrong about that, as she would later acknowledge with a laugh.[15]

And yet it was Ron and his small circle whom Jack Shadbolt cited as the most likely candidates to shake up the art world. "Ronald Thom, Don Jarvis, Bruce Boyd, Joan Wright, Dorothy Mount, Peter Aspell: This group might justly be regarded as one of the most significant creative groups in Canada today," wrote Shadbolt in the November 1946 edition of *Canadian Art*.[16] "These younger artists know how to draw, they know the traditions and the craft of art and most important, they go on location and face the implications of the social scene." Illustrating his report in *Canadian Art* was a reproduction of Ron's painting *At the Fair Grounds*. This impressionistic depiction of a crowd at an amusement park displays overtly broad brushstrokes tilting dynamically toward the centre of the canvas. Its centrifugal composition would eventually become Ron's signature approach in architecture as well as art.

In the 1947 edition of *Behind the Palette*, the VSA journal edited by his friend and fellow student Don Jarvis, Ron harnessed the language of an aspiring revolutionary. "Art and architecture are the reflectors of a degrading class struggle, between one class—bourgeois, machine-made aristocracy seeking the mirage of grandeur behind classical facades and soft, sumptuous, sensual idioms of art—and the other class—an ignorant, impoverished mass seeking comfort in religion and a sentimental art."[17]

And then, defending the modern movement's rightfulness in superseding it, Ron unpacked a précis of his future career. Just as the contemporary artist extends these elements into abstraction to express ideas, the architect makes use of them, "not by adding superficial ornamentation, but by honestly making the organic structure of the building or structure be the expressive vehicle," wrote Ron. Like the artist, "the architect has the same problems of control and articulation of space and volume, control of light, relationship of surface texture, transparency, translucency and opacity, patterning, etc."[18]

All of those assertions can also be turned around into the basic questions that postwar designers were now debating: What defines our shelter? All those structures that we live in, work in, play in, pray in—what should they look like? What kind of social expectations or constraints do they create?

The most useful social offerings of modern design were both more humble and more tangible than the exalted theorizing of Ron and his art school peers. Within the Victorian and other traditional paradigms, families lived in clearly demarcated spaces, with kitchens and dining rooms walled off and their inhabitants and activities sequestered from one another. This longstanding design approach kept housewives away from the home's central conversation sites. Modernist house design offered greater power and comfort to the people who spent most of the day at home—society's underserved groups: women and children. Kitchens opened into dining rooms, which in turn merged with living rooms. Larger windows would bring in light and a greater sense of connection to the outside world. The reduction or elimination of attics, crannies, overstuffed upholstery ornaments, and brocaded curtains would reduce dusting and cleaning requirements.

All of these concepts had emerged thirty years earlier in Europe, and they would be embraced across the western world by the late twentieth century. When Ron concluded his senior year at the Vancouver School of Art, such ideas still seemed radical.

As graduation drew near, Ron had yet to choose his means of making a living, and professional protocol required a label—artist or architect? Jack Shadbolt encouraged him to become a visual artist; Bert Binning urged him to become an architect. Ron thus found himself in the enviable position as the protégé of two of the school's most prominent instructors. Their endorsements carried weight. And they each saw in Ron the signs of a future star, but in different fields.

For the moment, Ron could see himself straddling both realms. He stood poised to graduate into a world that supported this united view of the arts. *Canadian Art* magazine had begun life in 1943 with a masthead dedication to "Fine Arts, Architecture, Graphic Arts, Design." Articles on retail window displays and West Coast houses were published alongside essays by Lawren Harris and A.Y. Jackson. *Canadian Art*'s West Coast correspondent was Charles Scott, who had argued that all of the arts—whether applied or "pure"—enriched the public realm.

In this spirit, the school prepared its graduates to break new ground—metaphorically in painting, literally in architecture and urban design. Just as Charles Scott had argued a quarter century earlier, studying art would be as useful as studying engineering or politics, in terms of preparing students to plan their future communities. Art existed within a continuum that included architecture, industrial design, craft, and artisanship of all kinds. In Ron's mind, this did not diminish the lofty status of art but elevated it to that of craft.

By graduation day, about half the students remained in Ron's Vancouver School of Art cohort, from the dozen or so who had started out. After receiving their certificates, they repaired to Charles Scott's house for dinner, washed down with dandelion wine.[19] The freshly minted graduates floated on a sense of optimism throughout the evening: the art school had plenty of teaching jobs for their alumni. The outside world—barren and artless after years of depression and war—seemed ready to welcome them too.

Mr. Shadbolt and Mr. Binning, as all their students had addressed them, soon became "Jack" and "Bert" to Ron. They evolved into friends and peers, to whom he would forever feel close. Binning, more than any other teacher, influenced Ron's architectural approach at the deepest level. "Binning taught me to see, and he taught me to think," Ron would later write. "The strongest thing he taught us, which has had a profound influence on everything I've done in architecture since, was that every aspect of the design had to respond directly to the world around it, whether it be colour or form, or where the light came in, or the views looking out."[20]

Ron and his Vancouver School of Art cohort had lucked out in having the best teachers they could have possibly wished for, at the best time to learn from them. Decades later, after the work of Jack Shadbolt and B.C. Binning filled scholarly monographs and hallowed galleries, Ron would still be exchanging trenchant views on art, architecture, and society with them both. He would never forget Binning's confidence-building directive, the words shifting in various retellings:[21] "Okay now, come on: you're a little fly and you're walking over that thing, and think of what all the ups and downs mean to him. You're a little tiny fly. Now, go get your pencil, kid!"

4

REBUILDING

WORLD WAR II had razed half of Europe, but the European pioneers of the modern movement unfurled reams of plans for building things up again. From his Paris base, the Swiss architect Le Corbusier projected the dominant influence. Other Europeans, like Bauhaus leaders Walter Gropius and Marcel Breuer, had already crossed the ocean and resettled in Ivy League universities in the northeastern United States. Viennese architects Richard Neutra and Rudolph Schindler had migrated to California after stints in the Midwest with Frank Lloyd Wright.

In the ensuing years, Toronto architects and academics developed strong ties with the hard-edged modernists to the south. Vancouver architects felt closer to their own southern counterparts in California, and proceeded to make pilgrimages to the works of Neutra, Schindler, and Bernard Maybeck for inspiration.

The postwar building boom coincided with newly restored attention to the arts, now including the budding culture of the West Coast. The October 1947 edition of *Canadian Art* contained a report on the region's visual arts, opening with an Emily Carr landscape painting and concluding with a Ron Thom portrait.[1] Ron's painting, titled *Seated Figure*, features a woman sitting tensely, hands clasped together on her lap as though in handcuffs, as the surrounding space

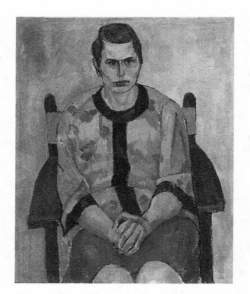

Seated Figure, by Ron Thom,
permanent collection,
Vancouver Art Gallery.

seems to enclose her.[2] Its organizing lines and composition draw the viewer away from the edges and toward the centre of the canvas, a centrifugal composition that by this time had become strongly characteristic of Ron's art. The model and subject in the painting is Chris Thom, just three years into married life, her furrowed brow and scowl suggesting a trapped and unhappy creature.

The portrait of a brooding Chris abutted an essay on West Coast architecture written by Fred Lasserre, the director of the architecture department at the University of British Columbia. In his essay, Lasserre decried the architectural indifference to the region's distinctive qualities, and he called on architects to move beyond the city's existing "distorted traditions" that had produced its "depressing, ugly, and chaotic array of buildings."

The architecture of the Canadian West Coast, wrote Lasserre, should be designed with large windows to bring in as much of the region's subdued light as possible. Its houses would benefit from large overhangs to shield both the house and occupants from the fierce winter rains. In other seasons, the temperate climate called for generous outdoor spaces. The nearby forests offered plenty of wood to build with; the ocean and mountains offered beauty. "The breath-taking view which almost every home and building can have before them demands that screening walls be pierced to the utmost and that entrance or lounging terraces open out to it."[3] This regional arm of the new modern movement would soon acquire its own name: West Coast Modernism.

Lasserre had seen enough of the world already to make the call. Born in Switzerland, he moved with his family to Canada at age ten. After studies at the University of Toronto's architecture school and then in Zurich, he worked in London with Berthold Lubetkin. He came back to Canada—first to McGill University as an associate professor, and then to Vancouver to become the founding director of UBC's architecture school.

As part of his overall ambitions for design education and the improvement of local architecture, Lasserre brought with him a firm commitment "to bring to the campus more fine art, particularly visual art."[4] He enlisted Ron's mentor, Bert Binning, to teach Introduction to Art and Art History, and then painter and muralist Lionel Thomas to teach Visual Design and Theory. Both men taught at the university's visual arts faculty as well, and the two faculties commingled on campus and off.

Meanwhile, Ron pondered his options for earning a living. He taught sessions of Architectural Design at the Vancouver School of Art and, in the spring of 1948, joined artist Lionel Thomas and former VSA classmate Peter Aspell to teach Saturday morning art classes in Stanley Park.[5] By the following year, Chris was pregnant with their first child. Ron now had a family to support, and he needed a more reliable income than he could glean from part-time teaching and sporadic sales of his paintings.

Bert Binning encouraged Ron to think about a career in architecture—and then he introduced his former student to the man now steering the most important firm in town, Ned Pratt.

Tall, well-educated, well-tailored, and exuding confidence, Ned could have forged his career in any Canadian city of his choosing. But Vancouver, for Ned, was home. After graduating with a general arts degree from UBC in 1933, he had entered the University of Toronto to study engineering. His plans changed when his pal Bob

Berwick convinced him to join him at the university's architecture school instead. The transition wasn't that much of a stretch; at that time, the architecture school was part of the university's Faculty of Applied Science and Engineering. Its fifth-year classes emphasized practicality over creativity: Town Planning, Architectural Programs, Heating and Ventilating, Professional Practice, Structural Design, and either Architectural Design *or* Architectural Engineering.[6]

When Ned and Bob graduated in 1937, they both headed west, and Sharp & Thompson stood ready to employ them. Having honed a reputation for its Beaux-Arts style of architecture, Sharp & Thompson had begun to creak with age, along with its founders. Both men became partners shortly after their arrival, and the firm became Sharp & Thompson, Berwick, Pratt.

By the mid-1940s, the very principals who had founded the firm—George Sharp and Charles Thompson—would find their influence fading as Ned Pratt and Bob Berwick shifted the firm's direction from classical revival to modernist architecture.

Sharp stepped back in good time, retiring in the early 1950s to return to his early livelihood of painting. Thompson, on the other hand, clung to both his partnership and to the Beaux-Arts approach for as long as he could. Meanwhile, clients in business, governments, and even the university—his landmark project—all lined up for modernist buildings.[7]

Some of the younger associates saw Thompson as a spectre, the spirit of the nineteenth century haunting the brave new firm. Now, in the mid-twentieth century, he hovered around the office like a ghost, seeking here and there to maintain some vestige of the firm's neoclassical beginnings.[8] Like a grandfather clock in a new house, Thompson served as a symbolic fixture: his physical presence bespoke veneration more than the ability to get the time right.

Bob Berwick and Ned Pratt knew that the years of replicating historic styles were over. The region no longer had the craftspeople or the collective will to construct buildings with heavy stone arches

Ned Pratt (left)
with Arthur
Erickson.

and intricately carved pediments and friezes. Nor did most design firms have the means or motivation to do so, since their schools, houses, banks, retail outlets, and office buildings could be built much faster and cheaper with unadorned concrete, steel, and glass.

Even so, Ned and his fellow modernists still hobnobbed in one of the city's most unabashedly neoclassical enclaves: the Vancouver Club. Located near the north edge of downtown, a few blocks away from the firm's Pender Street headquarters, the all-male private club served as the power centre for the city's decision makers, within walls quilted with historic mimicry. Sharp & Thompson had designed its 1914 five-storey brick building with an Edwardian facade, English Renaissance wainscotting, Corinthian pilasters, and Palladian windows.

The region's politicians, lumber barons, mining magnates, and other corporate titans convened there regularly to eat, drink, smoke, gossip, and conjure up the region's future. Architects invested in its high-priced memberships, which paid off handsomely in relationships and design commissions. For the senior partners at Sharp & Thompson, Berwick, Pratt, the Vancouver Club served as the incubator for many a commission. The club overseers expected its members to look sharp and dress smartly, which Ned and his coterie always did. Two of Vancouver's finest men's clothiers, Edward Chapman and Arnold & Quigley, stood on nearby Granville Street to serve this growing market of aspiring professionals.[9]

Ned recognized something else—that even when people wanted efficiency, they still wanted beauty. They especially liked it when someone could show them a beautiful house in a beautiful landscape. The limited graphic technology of the age required architects and designers to create their work manually, with a sheaf of pencils and rolls of drafting paper. For client and public presentations, the team needed to come up with a detailed colour version of their scheme.

For one West Vancouver house on a complex waterfront site, Ned asked a young draftsman named Doug Shadbolt to do the perspectival drawings. Doug knew he didn't have the talent to give Pratt what he needed, so he asked his brother, Jack Shadbolt, to suggest an illustrator. Jack recommended his former student, Ron Thom. With a joint endorsement from Bert and Jack, Ron procured his first assignment at the headquarters of Sharp & Thompson, Berwick, Pratt.

When Ron returned a couple of days later, his 24"×30" watercolour astounded everyone in the room.[10] He had rendered the scene from the perspective of a boat out on the water looking back at the house. The watercolour captured the vista of cliff, trees, beach, and sea, with a tiny image of a barely visible house. This was not what Pratt wanted; client presentations focused on the building, not the landscape. But it showcased Ron's singular talent as a great illustrator—an artist, even.

On June 1, 1949, Ron began his apprenticeship at Sharp & Thompson, Berwick, Pratt, as it was still formally called. For now, he would still just be the delineator of other people's designs.

That would change soon enough.

BY 1950, the firm had condensed its name to Thompson, Berwick, Pratt & Partners—usually called by its acronym, TBP, in everyday conversation. With Ned and Bob the de facto leaders of the firm, the TBP headquarters moved from its neoclassical building on Pender Street to a newly built concrete modernist low-rise a few blocks away, at 1553 Robson Street. To some draftsmen and partners working all hours, their building seemed to be a world unto itself—which, in so many ways, it was. A few blocks to the east, merchants plied sausages and dry cleaning from small family-run shops. To the west lay the thousand acres of old-growth forest known as Stanley Park. And between them, the most important architectural firm in town.

Ned's forte was not art but acumen. He knew what art and artists could achieve. He understood the same principles that had been espoused by Charles Scott in his mid-1920s argument for the creation of the Vancouver School of Art, that the city needed professionally trained artists to grow a socially healthy and economically strong society.

Nobody at the firm could draw and paint as skilfully as Ron, or apply such imagination to the shape and feel of a structure as this quiet young art school graduate. What's more, Ron quickly showed himself to be far more than an illustrator. He began to conjure up his own designs, and with the same speed and skill that had impressed his new bosses. Ned soon assigned Ron as the design lead or co-designer on projects that needed an artist's eye.

THE POWER OF ART extended beyond city boundaries. In the post-war years, the federal government had pondered how to strengthen the country's cultural identity, now that Canada lay adjacent to the world's new dominant power.

In 1949, Prime Minister Louis St. Laurent had asked Vincent Massey, at that time the chancellor of the University of Toronto, to oversee a major study called the Royal Commission on National Development in the Arts, Letters and Sciences. For brevity, every-one called it the Massey Commission and, upon its release two years later, the Massey Report. Vincent assembled a team of intellectuals who spent two years on the report. Its four hundred pages would help codify Canadian culture for the next half century.

Informed by several hundred interviews across the country, the Massey Report laid out the case for a government-supported arts infrastructure, paving the way for the National Gallery of Canada, Library and Archives Canada, Canada Council for the Arts, and major expansion of the Canadian Broadcasting Corporation. It pro-moted a system of awards and funding for artists, architects, writ-ers, curators, and other arts professionals; and it called for massive federal government funding for public and university buildings. A decade later, the UBC School of Architecture, still housed in rot-ting wooden military huts, would be one of many entities to receive funds for a permanent building as a result of this recommendation.

About architecture itself, the Massey Report had plenty to say. Its architect-informants who had travelled elsewhere noted that the building industry's new mode of mass production had affected architecture in Canada more than in other countries, wiping out regional characteristics that would have developed naturally. As a result, the most influential of the arts on our manner of living, archi-tecture, was largely ignored by the public, resulting in "row upon row of architectural monstrosities" in some communities. Cana-dian architecture was cleaving into two camps that presented the worst of both worlds: a "cult of the extinct" that created knockoffs of old Europe, and "the inevitable striving for form in building of a country without architectural roots." The Massey Report cited British Columbia alone as the one region with architects responding to local materials and settings. "No such experiments are yet apparent elsewhere. It has been stated to us that a true Canadian architecture must develop in this way."[11]

The country actually did have architectural roots, albeit unrecognized by the Massey Report, in the building traditions of its first inhabitants. The post and beam longhouse, plank house, pit house, tipi, igloo, and other housing forms had been an unheralded part of architectural history for millennia.[12] Until Indigenous cultures were brutally uprooted by colonization and then suppressed by government decree, Indigenous architectures exemplified the regional design approach that the Massey Report called for. Some of the West Coast's emerging architects and designers, such as Rudy Kovach, acknowledged that underpinning,[13] but much of society would misperceive West Coast Modernism as something entirely new.

When the Massey Report boosted architecture's profile within Canadian culture, the nation's overall cultural awareness grew in tandem, expanding beyond a self-identification as a British colony. Japan—North America's enemy in war—became its cultural avatar in peacetime, at least among architects. Young architects across North America—and particularly on the West Coast—read and talked about Japan and its building culture. They studied the wood joinery and post and beam construction of Japanese houses. They learned about the beauty of exposing the supporting posts and beams. They looked closely at domestic floor plans and their different way of dividing up household space. They travelled to the studio of world-renowned potter Shōji Hamada—and they brought back all the news to their students and instructors and colleagues.[14]

Ron Thom had indirectly absorbed forms of Japanese culture at the Vancouver School of Art through Bert Binning's teachings. In his architectural design course, Binning emphasized the virtues of Japanese design, and of Frank Lloyd Wright.[15] Wright himself had extolled Japanese culture as "extraordinary" and "the only genuine culture," uncolonized and authentic. Images of Wright's 1923 Imperial Hotel in Tokyo, with its deep eaves and interlocking volumes, made a particularly strong impression on Ron. But Ron experienced this and so many other landmarks only through lectures and books and journals. With a young family, a career in its infancy, and endless workloads, he didn't ever seem to have the time, cash, or inclination for the overseas pilgrimages that some of his peers were making.

As though some invisible leash tethered him to the Vancouver region, he rarely ventured more than a few hundred miles beyond the city limits. His favourite journeys transpired close to home: driving through the Fraser Valley or the pine-dotted hills of the Okanagan, or ferrying to one of the Gulf Islands on the other side of the Strait of Georgia—or, when time allowed, further north on Vancouver Island to take a short ferry trek to Hornby Island, his favourite place on Earth.

In any case, Ron Thom's short journeys and cerebral promenades usually brought more creative dividends than the grandiose adventures of his well-travelled peers. His strolls along Hornby's bluffs and stone beaches proved more illuminating than visiting the Louvre; his treks around the contours of his own mind proved more revelatory than travels to the other side of the world.

5

ACROSS
THE WATER

PRIOR TO 1938, the sloped landscape north of Vancouver had seemed a world away from the city, moated by the waters of Burrard Inlet. Its ragged shoreline meandered over twenty miles, jutting out near its westernmost edge into a promontory. Atop that rocky bluff, the sixty-foot-high Point Atkinson Lighthouse lorded over the inlet, blasting its foghorn and winking at passing vessels before they fanned out into the Pacific Ocean. East of the lighthouse, the Squamish and Tsleil-Waututh communities dwelled near the jagged coastline and worked intensely at lumber longshoring, hauling raw logs and milled timber onto barges. Elsewhere, the half-logged, half-wild hillsides were randomly stippled with tiny wooden squats and weekend cabins.

To reach the shores of North and West Vancouver, Vancouverites needed a skiff or ferry. And then came the Guinness family, who changed everything. The Ireland-based clan had made a fortune in banking, politics, and dark stout beer. Through the family-owned British Pacific Properties corporation, it would soon make another fortune by purchasing a thousand acres of land across the upper slopes of West Vancouver. As part of the deal with the municipality, the corporation committed to building a bridge from Stanley Park to West Vancouver.[1]

Bruno and Molly Bobak, c. 1950.

The completion of the Lions Gate Bridge in 1938 instantly transformed the entire North Shore from cottage country to suburb, consolidating the shrewdest real-estate manoeuvre in the region's history. Joining the throng of new buyers, Bert and Jessie Binning paid $600 for their tiny wedge-shaped West Vancouver lot in 1939, buying just in time. Land prices skyrocketed after that.[2]

The newly accessible region welcomed a new generation of families—at least, those that were white. Prospective residents of other skin colours were legally excluded, as Article 7 of the 1931 British Properties' land title regulations stated: "No person of the African or Asiatic race or of African or Asiatic Descent (except servants of the occupier of the premises in residence) shall reside or be allowed to remain on the premises."[3]

That discriminatory policy did not dissuade those whose ethnicity allowed them to buy and build there. For ocean views, few sites could compare with West Vancouver and its expansive water views, especially around the lush, 182-acre Lighthouse Park.

By the mid-1940s, lot values there had already climbed beyond the budgets of most young architects and artists, who looked instead to North Vancouver. Many chose to purchase the new and inexpensive lots in the Lynn Valley neighbourhood. Molly and Bruno Bobak bought a groomed and plumbed lot on Peters Road, a cul-de-sac abutting Lynn Canyon Park. The Bobaks lived on Galiano Island during construction, hauling in timber from the island and then doing most of the construction work themselves in the few pockets of time available between ferry crossings.[4]

Soon after, Chris and Ron Thom bought the Peters Road lot immediately adjacent to the Bobaks for one hundred dollars, and started drawing up their first home together. Now they would be just a few steps away from close friends and the near-wilderness of Lynn Canyon.[5]

RON DESIGNED their house in the post and beam style learned from Binning and Pratt but inflected with his own idiosyncratic flair. The bedroom windows, for instance, abutted each other, so that the wall separating the rooms was also the window mullion—an unusual feature for a house, then as now.[6] He

Ron Thom outside of his not-quite-finished self-designed house on Peters Road, North Vancouver, with the Bobaks' house, designed by Doug Shadbolt, in the background.

did most of the construction work himself, with sporadic help from friends; it was the only affordable way. But the work exhausted them all. More than once, Bruno came over to check up on Ron or help with construction—and found him slumped in a chair on the deck, fast asleep and with hammer in hand.[7]

As Doug Shadbolt had done with the Bobaks' house plan, Ron Thom arranged the rooms of the small house with little wall separation. He fitted two of the walls with floor-to-ceiling glass, frosted for privacy, which generated the magical effect of a lightbox show of plant shadows.

For the rest of the vacant lots on Peters Road, Ron approached as many of their owners as he could find, begging them to let him design their houses free of charge. He dreamed of transforming the entire street into a panoply of modernism and offered his architectural philanthropy in the hopes of making it happen. Four property

owners took Ron up on his offer, and soon Peters Road was punctuated with avant-garde Ron Thom–designed houses, standing out
like rebels in a lineup of uniformed soldiers.

He also designed homes for many of his former art school classmates, including Don Jarvis, Peter Aspell, Bruce and Joan Boyd,
John Grinnell, and Rudy Kovach—in exchange for artworks, or just
as a favour. He didn't seem to care much about extracting money for
his work.[8]

IN 1949, Chris and Ron welcomed their first child: a son, whom
they named Robin. He had a rough birth: a forceps-assisted breech
delivery. Apart from that, it seemed like a bucolic paradise awaited
this newborn, in this new suburb designed for young families.

Ron's professional life and social life grew in tandem during
this time. He forged an important friendship with Jack Shadbolt's
brother, Doug, the architect who designed the Bobaks' house. Doug
was embarking on a career in design education; he and Ron found
they had much to talk about.[9] Chris, housebound with a toddler and
expecting a second child, found herself limited to the North Shore
house parties, when she was able to join them.[10]

The Bobaks, Shadbolts, and Thoms met up frequently at their
homes for spirited conversations about art and architecture.[11] Bruno
and Molly would forever afterward remember these nights of fun,
wit, and revelry.

They would also remember on other nights how, while sitting
quietly in their living room, they could hear Chris and Ron next door,
screaming at each other.

BERT AND JESSIE BINNING, by contrast, got along beautifully, and
the Binning House usually presented an oasis of joy. Their weekly
fireside salons roared with conversation and laughter. Bert invited
artists and architects to the salons, and he also brought in luminar-
ies from other disciplines.[12] Poet Earle Birney, who began teaching

at UBC in 1948, became a regular. Among the discreet minor trib-
utes that the poet bestowed on the painter were the allusions to his
name within two of his pseudonyms: Earle Binning, B.C. Birney.[13]
Birney had bolted to fame in 1942 with 184 lines of free verse, titled
"David." First published in the journal *Canadian Forum* and then in
the collection *David and Other Poems*, the poem relays the tale of a
life-affirming mountain climb that ends in a lethal fall. The poem's
evocation of the natural world as an anthropomorphic continuation
of humankind dovetailed with the views of the West Coast artists
and architects.

In 1947, after joining UBC as the inaugural head of its fine arts
department, Binning had tendered an invitation to Richard Neutra,
the Viennese émigré now resettled in Los Angeles, to visit Vancouver and give a public presentation of his work. Neutra's reputation
had grown tremendously since immigrating to America in 1923.
After working briefly with Frank Lloyd Wright, he left to join his
friend and university classmate Rudolph Schindler in California.
There, Neutra designed landmarks like the 1929 Lovell House, a
monument in architectural history.

In midcentury Vancouver, public talks by visiting architects were
rare, and almost every ambitious architect trod through the doors
of the Vancouver Art Gallery to hear him. Binning invited him to
return in 1953, this time to present the contents of his recently published book *Mystery and Realities of the Site*. The architect, argued
Neutra, should harness the bedrock, boulders, and plant growth he
finds at the building site—and defer to them. "Trees are wonderful—
even though they may drop leaves or seeds and give you the chore of
tidying up the place," he argued. "But who would want to forfeit his
teeth, just to avoid brushing them? If there are trees granted you by
fate, can you conceive a layout to conserve them? Never sacrifice a
tree if you can help it."[14]

Ron would listen to Neutra with rapt attention—first within the
packed hall of the Vancouver Art Gallery, and then at Bert's small

Richard Neutra (extended hand) holds forth at the 1956 Banff Session conference, with Ron Thom (centre right) and John C. Parkin (to the right of Ron) in the small audience.

post-lecture gatherings at the Binning House, and then a few years later at the Banff Session architectural conference in Alberta.[15] Neutra's lectures and conferences resonated throughout the Vancouver design community. Here stood one of the world's most important architects, describing landscape as a primordial element of architecture rather than a contextual nuisance or an afterthought. The book *Mystery and Realities of the Site* transformed into something of a West Coast manifesto.[16]

Ron's earliest houses in leafy North Vancouver brought him a healthy dose of media attention. The Thom house, Bobak house, and a third house that Ron designed for Chris's parents were featured in the December 1950 issue of *Canadian Homes and Gardens* magazine alongside a chirpy headline: "Three Young Families

Build Their Own—on a Shoestring!" With their Peters Road family homes, both Doug and Ron aimed to fuse the concept of a custom home with modernity and economy of construction. "Families with one child will find this little place a 'dream house,'" concluded the *Canadian Homes and Gardens* article.

Ron had settled into his house and surrounding greenery for the seemingly ideal suburban postwar life: wife, toddler son, and, in 1951, a baby daughter, Sidney. Rounding out the nuclear family, they acquired a golden lab named Taffy.

Town planners conceived the area as both family-friendly and car-friendly: the perfectly planned neighbourhood for the new modern era. The men of the North Shore drove south across the Lions Gate Bridge to work downtown every morning; the women shopped and gardened and cleaned house and raised children amid trees and parks and the good new schools.

The city planners and engineers could do little to plan or engineer life behind closed doors, though. Ron spent ever-longer hours at the workplace or socializing after work without Chris, who now felt imprisoned and abandoned. She had been able to complete only two years at the Vancouver School of Art and lost touch with their mutual friends once she married and moved to the other side of the water. The combination of social isolation, creative annihilation, and an absentee husband strained her mental health. When Chris sought medical help, she received little verbal support but loads of sedatives and other pharmaceuticals. They didn't help; they just amplified her anxieties to the breaking point.[17]

In any case, Chris had another person to blame for her anguish. Her name was Marya.

Marya Fiamengo, an aspiring poet, worked at the city's main library at Hastings and Main Streets, an ornate Romanesque building sponsored by philanthropist Andrew Carnegie. The library served as a hangout for artists, and Marya grew close to Vancouver School of Art alumni Joe Plaskett and Molly Bobak.

One day, Joe and Molly introduced Marya to their mutual friend Ron Thom.[18] And that was that.

Marya knew full well Ron's marital status, but she fell irrevocably in love almost instantly upon meeting him.[19] Their first outing, at Ron's suggestion, was a picnic lunch in Lighthouse Park. After that languid afternoon on the North Shore, he suggested that they explore the countryside together.

A striking brunette, Marya bore an uncanny resemblance to Ron's wife Chris—though without the relentless familiarity and the drudgery of a shared domestic life. Single, creative, and unfettered, Marya evoked "the earth goddess, radiating a sort of primal feminine wisdom, and exuding sparks of wit and fires of passion from a great well of creative exuberance!" as Joe later reflected to Molly. "Alas, but that way it seems far from reality and yet that illusion was what we adored in Marya."[20]

Ron began spending occasional evenings with Marya. Meanwhile, Chris remained trapped on Peters Road in the never-quite-finished house. Her loneliness and exhaustion combusted into fiery rage when she learned about Marya. Days later, Chris abruptly fled the family home, heading first to Nanaimo and then to Penticton—alone, mentally strained, and without a plan. She left a message for Ron that their two children, a two-year-old toddler and a six-week-old baby, were now *his* responsibility.[21]

Ron panicked. He still had to drive to work every day, and he had no idea what to do with a toddler and an infant. He first asked Molly and Bruno if they could take care of his children. Busy with jobs and a young child of their own, they gently but firmly told Ron that they could not. He then called on his mother, Elena, who couldn't take them in but helped arrange foster care.[22]

Outside of that, Ron plunged into his swelling workload, and worried openly within his inner circle about Chris and their children, although seemingly unable to connect with or take care of any of them. He continued to see Marya, their time together now extending into weekends, since he was a temporary bachelor. During most of their meetings, he drove eastward with her along the Fraser Highway to the flame-coloured grasslands of the Okanagan Valley. They talked about art and architecture, about history and poetry and pottery, or just appreciated the silence and the shifting landscape.[23]

Marya Fiamengo, late 1940s.

For Marya, it developed into the most intense love affair of her life, though she recognized the relationship as lopsided. She wrote him love letters, but didn't receive any in return. He told her he loved her, but never in writing. And despite his chafing at the constraints of marriage, it turned out that he had no desire to actively leave it.

Several months after her abrupt departure, Chris returned, ready to give their marriage a second chance. Ron could barely contain his overwhelming sense of relief, while Marya slumped into grief.

Marya sank her feelings about Ron into several poems of her first published poetry collection, *The Quality of Halves*:

> I had an Icon once when I was young.
> I swallowed it
> To be companion to my heart
> I hear it murmuring now,
> A portent in the blood.[24]

NEWLY REUNITED with Chris, Ron immediately embarked on making a new home for his family. He bought a new property several miles to the west, in the Capilano Highlands neighbourhood of

North Vancouver. Here, he designed and built a modernist bungalow, eager to take advantage of newly available building materials
and methods.

For the media, Ron aptly called the new Thom family quarters
the "Experimental House."

FOR THE TIMES, "experimental" served as the right adjective. By
this time, architects, engineers, and builders had figured out how
to use new materials—plywood sheathing, glue-laminated wood
supporting posts and beams, and drywall—as new staples for mass
construction of ordinary houses and buildings. But the provincial
building codes—in British Columbia and elsewhere—did not reflect
the new capabilities of either the materials or the architects. Drywall
didn't exist in the general building materials market or in the building code, and so plaster still served as the default interior cladding.
Conventionally built houses of the era relied on interior walls for
structural support, and so their rooms tended to be small and closed
off from one another. The post and beam construction methodology
espoused by Ron and the other West Coast Modernists would soon
change that.

The whole package of materials arrived at the site on a single flatbed truck. With some assistance from builders, Ron then assembled
the 1,300-square-foot post and beam skeleton on a slab of concrete,
filling in the walls with two-inch-thick plywood panels connected
with wood splines.

The Experimental House joined the roster of new housing paradigms in the West Coast architectural community, conceptually
expanding on the prototype created by Ned Pratt two years earlier
with the modular plywood construction of Ned's own self-designed
family home.

Ron finished construction of the Experimental House in 1952;
the Thom family reunited and moved in. The transition seemed
to mark a new start to his relationship with Chris, or at least an

attempt at one, though their friends felt their main issues remained unresolved.[25]

A few years later, *Western Homes and Living* featured a generous spread on the Experimental House. Sandwiched between the magazine's coverage of neocolonial and country-kitchen house styles, the Experimental House looked unabashedly avant-garde. The concrete slab of the foundation, sanded down and waxed, also served as the floor. Le Corbusier had championed concrete slab floors in his landmark 1915 Dom-Ino conceptual house scheme, and concrete flooring would eventually become a signature feature of cutting-edge domestic architecture. But in early 1950s Canada, Ron's concrete floor did not just seem audacious; it seemed downright odd.

Its factory-made plywood walls were also unusual. Then as now, plywood was not a practical choice for an exterior cladding, given its vulnerability to the elements. The concept of interchangeable wall panels of different sizes, however, offered ideas for the future. "Although the house is prefabricated, which might denote a stock plan, the design is flexible as frame construction due to the varying size of the panels," assured the *Western Homes and Living* report. "As designer Thom explains, 'the panels influence the character of the house but don't fetter the design, since they are so flexible. The same type of prefabrication could be applied to any other plan.'"

Swiftly fastened together on the site like a Meccano set, it could be replicated and customized at a low cost—in theory. At this point, long before the age of big-box retail building supply outlets, the panels Ron used were not yet available to the general public. For the infill between the post and beam framework, he tried a new system of prestressed plywood panels.[26]

This spirit of experimentation, by Ron and Ned and other architects along the West Coast of North America, would soon be ubiquitous across the continent. The plans reflected the need in a modest house for the kitchen to be contiguous with the living and dining areas, where the family could play and dine, and the matriarch could

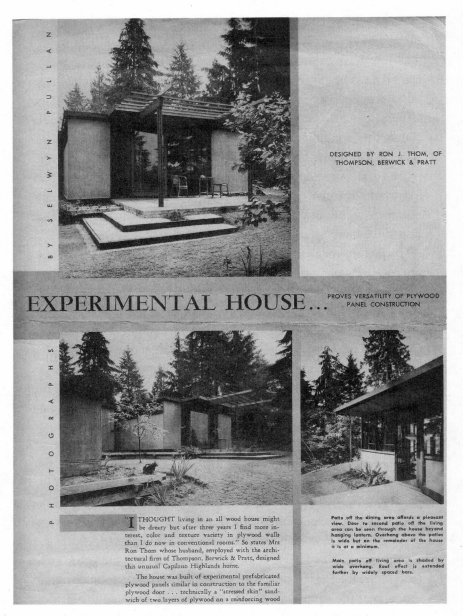

BY SELWYN PULLAN

DESIGNED BY RON J. THOM, OF
THOMPSON, BERWICK & PRATT

EXPERIMENTAL HOUSE...

PROVES VERSATILITY OF PLYWOOD
PANEL CONSTRUCTION

PHOTOGRAPHS

"I THOUGHT living in an all wood house might be dreary but after three years I find more interest, color and texture variety in plywood walls than I do now in conventional rooms." So states Mrs Ron Thom whose husband, employed with the architectural firm of Thompson, Berwick & Pratt, designed this unusual Capilano Highlands home.

The house was built of experimental prefabricated plywood panels similar in construction to the familiar plywood door . . . technically a "stressed skin" sandwich of two layers of plywood on a reinforcing wood

Patio off the dining area affords a pleasant view. Door to second patio off the living area can be seen through the house beyond hanging lantern. Overhang above the patios is wide but on the remainder of the house it is at a minimum.

Main patio off living area is shaded by wide overhang. Roof effect is extended further by widely spaced bars.

Opening page of the 1956 *Western Homes and Living* coverage of the Experimental House.

supervise or participate from the kitchen. Though still largely tethered to the stove, the woman of the house could at least see part of
the world around her: the blur of a running child, or a cedar bough
waving through the window glass.

Chris Thom obligingly described their home's tiny galley kitchen
as "a joy to work in." And the magazine coverage read as follows:

> Mrs. Thom has no complaints about the cleaning and mainte-
> nance of this house of plywood, concrete, and glass. The dark con-
> crete floors show up footprints but are very easy to clean. Waxed
> and buffed to a gloss, the floors need only be wiped with a damp
> cloth... Mrs. Thom is emphatic in her appreciation of the play
> area or family room near the kitchen. "The children are never in
> the way," she relates. "Even the toddler is perfectly happy in there
> with only a gate to keep him out of the kitchen."[27]

WESTERN HOMES AND LIVING's utopian report underplayed the
challenge of living in experimental architecture—which tends to be,
almost by definition, suffused with shortcomings. Their Glenview
Crescent experiment *was* hard to cook in, hard to clean—and, like
their previous home on Peters Road, its plywood walls and single-
glazed windows brought in the winter chill. The purported easy
maintenance of the home's revolutionary concrete floors proved to be
as propagandistic as any revolution: they were *not* easy to clean, they
required periodic re-waxing, and they chilled her feet to the bone.[28]

Great innovators in all fields often find their families paying the
price for their work, not only in terms of their reduced time at home,
but also, in some cases, using that very home as their research prototype. Such has been the case with many architects, whose first clients
are often their blood relations for reasons of both ideology and necessity—and Ron Thom followed in this tradition. The "experiment"
of his second home sought a breakthrough in the age-old struggle of minding the children while getting other tasks done in life.

The lessons Ron learned from his family home's attributes and shortcomings helped burnish his insights and confidence in his subsequent design of hundreds of West Coast houses over the next decade. For other architects and home builders, his house showcased the ease and economy of modular construction for everyday homes, and it brought attention to plywood as a mainstream building material. And it *looked* good: avant-garde for its day, its aesthetics would turn out to be timeless. One could see the identical house in a present-day shelter magazine and consider it to be perfectly contemporary.

Within fifty years, the once-radical open plan showcased by Ron Thom and other midcentury architects would become ubiquitous. An open plan allows easier and more continuous communication with family members and dinner guests; it does not, unfortunately, guarantee the efficacy and quality of that communication.

According to *Western Homes and Living*, the Experiment succeeded—though according to Chris Thom, privately at least, it failed. Decades later, when asked what she thought of her own long-ago comments published in the magazine, Chris offered a two-word assessment: "What crap."[29]

6

BOLD BOYS
ON BLUEPRINTS

IN MIDCENTURY VANCOUVER, the future shone like gold. A newly accessible North Shore promised bright and affordable homes for burgeoning families. On the western edge of the city, the university recommenced its massive expansion plans. Families, individuals, and businesses needed schools, churches, restaurants, and office buildings. For all these, the West Coast could offer plenty of inexpensive land, ready to build on.

By 1950, the West Coast Modernists—as they were now called—were drawing national media attention. The April 18 edition of *Saturday Night*, the nation's premier news and culture magazine, featured Ned Pratt on its cover. He was wearing a finely tailored suit and looking off-camera with an expression of immense seriousness, like a politician during wartime. The cover story itself, titled, "Bold Boys on Blueprints," offered a rare focus on a West Coast subject:

> It's a return to the "Go West" policy and a reversal of recent migrations East. Easterners like Ned Pratt are finding scope, freedom, and clients in Vancouver for their new "contemporary" houses.[1]

The magazine's odd reference to Ned Pratt as an "Easterner" reflected the Toronto media's perception of Vancouver. Ned had lived in Vancouver from the age of ten onwards, moving away from the city just for the four-year duration of his architectural studies. But *Saturday Night* and other Toronto-based cultural arbiters presented the West Coast not as a region or the site of a growing city, but as an exotic hinterland in which to make one's fortune.

COGNIZANT OF Ron Thom's growing stature, the partners placed a rotating lineup of young graduates to work under him. Some would always remain draftsmen, relegated to the useful but largely uncreative work of drawing plans and details under the direction of the senior staff. Others would show early indications of creative talent, and either rise in the ranks, or get bored and move on. Among this latter group was Arthur Erickson, who had recently joined the firm.

Ready to service the postwar building boom, TBP won commissions to design hundreds of public schools, along with large-scale, big-budget buildings for UBC and other institutions. With the approval of their bosses, Ron, Arthur, and many other TBP draftsmen worked after-hours on house designs for individual clients' homes that would be too small-scale for such a large firm. Before long, the house type emanating from these late-night sessions acquired a natural nickname: the "2 AM special."

After sundown, during the moonlighting hours, Ron could stickhandle a half-dozen house designs at once, stopping at tables to tell the draftsman or junior designer to elongate this window here, pull that wing there out a little, expand the hearth.

Almost everyone at the firm soon recognized Ron as the fastest and most gifted of the bunch. He would sketch out a rough floor plan with lightning speed, and then within a half hour draw up an exterior and an interior rendering. For most of these moonlighting jobs, Ron kept things simple: a basic modular prototype, usually a rectilinear massing made sculptural by large windows and a jogged roofline with a clerestory window.

These nighttime ventures served the young TBP architects well, like jazz musicians trying out new riffs at an after-hours club. In many houses, the architects positioned the supporting posts away from the corners of the building and let the windows elide almost seamlessly, without frame or mullion—a gesture known as "butt joint." Or they would avoid mullions by specifying "jalousie" windows, composed of horizontal slats of unframed glass. The approach dissolved the visual boundaries between the inner lives of humans and the outer life of the rest of the world. Younger draftsmen would often work overtime with no pay just to be part of this great experiment in housing. If they were lucky, Ned Pratt might wander in at midnight and give them a pat on the back. Neither the bosses nor the underlings seemed to mind these ungodly hours, for it kept the creative minds active and brought the firm indirect glory and renown.[2]

In collaboration with other draftsmen at the firm, Ron could easily design up to ten houses at a time. By his eye alone, he could finesse a plan or elevation until the proportions seemed just right—perfectly harmonious. And somehow, he knew exactly how to manipulate the fenestration pattern—the positions of the doors, skylights, and windows—so that the views would be perfectly framed and the incoming light would sweep around the interior space in magical ways. It was as though he were channelling Bert Binning's proverbial fly on the drawing paper, jogging the lines of each floor plan and elevation, creating uncanny light wells and shadowy niches, and thinking all the while of what all the ups and downs meant to him.[3]

While Ron's hand helped shape hundreds of TBP houses, the collaborative nature of these designs made for ambiguous authorship. In many North Shore homes, Ron Thom's gestures, sense of proportion, and overall spirit lurk throughout the space, even when his actual signature is absent.[4] He established ruthlessly high standards for every team project he worked on, raising the bar for colleagues who had grown accustomed to more formulaic modes of designing.

The staff watched in shock one evening as Ron, on the cusp of a team deadline, plunged the elaborate watercolour of the project in the office bathtub, swishing it back and forth in the water until all the fine pencil detailing and pigments leached from the paper into the filled tub. "It's not good enough," Ron explained.[5]

His colleagues slogged home, appalled that he would destroy an elaborate rendering the day before a presentation, and baffled as to how he would explain to his bosses. When they returned to the office at dawn, they saw that he had spent the night completely redoing the entire rendering, intricate detailing, and perfectly hued water-colours. In Ron's eyes, it was now finally "good enough."

Among others, Ron's brilliance impressed Geoff Massey, a young Harvard graduate who started at the firm in 1953, and who would prove to be immensely important to the trajectories of both Ron Thom and Arthur Erickson. Born in London and raised mostly in New England, Geoff had a cache of fine-old-family connections. His uncle, Vincent Massey, had been sworn in as the first Canadian-born governor general of Canada in 1952. His father, Raymond Massey, was a high-flying Hollywood actor.[6] With prominent relatives in so many fields, Geoff had access to many career opportunities, but he had chosen architecture. To him, it seemed to be the profession of the future.

During his student years at Harvard Graduate School of Design, he and his classmates felt "like revolutionaries, at the forefront of everything."[7] The talk focused on the new cities of Chandigarh in India by Le Corbusier and Aluminum City Terrace in Pennsylvania by Walter Gropius and Marcel Breuer—brand-new cities planned and designed entirely from scratch.

This is when Geoff had first learned that in Vancouver, a firm called Thompson Berwick Pratt would be designing a new smelter town too, Kitimat, for the Aluminum Company of Canada—Alcan, as everyone called it. TBP would design everything: the master plan, the stores, the houses for all the workers and their families. Like Aluminum City Terrace, Kitimat promised the utopian notion of affordable worker housing in a model city. At least, that's what Geoff presumed. It seemed to him that there could be no better place to build his career than at the firm making Canada's own city of the future.

Once hired, though, Geoff saw the pitfalls of a modernist revolution in a corporate world.

The master plan and architecture of Kitimat were already schematically designed when he arrived, and Geoff then realized the truth. This wasn't going to be Le Corbusier's Chandigarh, with its great sweeping curves and subtly textured surfaces, or even Aluminum City Terrace, with its modest but distinctive row housing.[8] The Kitimat plan displayed a huge grid of nearly identical conventional pitched roofs plopped on shoebox forms with minor variations in shape. "Kitimat was a lost opportunity," according to Geoff. Like most of the firm's big clients, Alcan just wanted to build everything as simply and cheaply as possible.

When constructing for the masses, they could benefit from architecture's new functionality while ignoring its creative ideals. Former student revolutionaries like Geoff felt a discomfiting pull into the corporate maw.

The work at TBP struck Geoff, and Arthur, as painfully dull. Now living together in the West End, the two men saved their sanity by designing their own projects on the side, including a post and beam house for Ron's former classmate, artist Gordon Smith.[9] But at TBP, Geoff felt creatively moribund. When he wasn't tediously replicating Kitimat details, he would draft formulaic layouts for retail bank outlets. In Geoff's eyes, nobody at the firm was creating anything exceptional—except for Ron Thom.[10]

Ron seemed fireproof. Even better, he seemed immune to the firm's monotonous design directives that seemed to straitjacket other creative hands in the firm. As awareness grew of his artistic talent, and its importance to the firm's marquee projects, Ned treated Ron as his protégé, one of the few designers in the firm who was irreplaceable.

The 1958 West Vancouver house for local jeweller Karl Stittgen is unsigned but likely one of Ron Thom's "2 AM specials."

Ned saw architects as falling into one of two categories, which he called "neck-up" and "neck-down."[11] The coolheaded thinkers were neck-up people. They calculated their way through design problems, weighing each decision on a rational basis. These were practical men like Bob Berwick, the partner who managed the day-to-day logistics; Roy Jessiman, who surveilled the projects and the balance sheets; and Dick Sai-Chew, the unflappable project coordinator. The methodical neck-up designers thought their way around the design process, making sure that blueprints transpired, entrances and exits made practical sense, plumbing and mechanicals were properly placed, contractors stayed on track, and that projects wouldn't collapse.

Then there were the "neck-down" architects; they were more like artists, who felt their way around the design process and relied on gut feelings for a lot of decisions. Their creative flair energized the other draftsmen and buffed up the firm's name and reputation. The neck-down architects included Fred Hollingsworth—sax player,

Frank Lloyd Wright devotee, sculptor who transformed industrial pipe into lanterns; Zoltan Kiss, expat Hungarian gifted in drawing and ceramics, who joined in 1952; Dick Mann, wizard of intricately detailed woodwork and metalwork; and Bob Boal—like Dick, an artisan who designed many of the exquisite wooden lanterns in Ron's houses and greatest buildings.[12]

Ned himself, like Fred Lasserre, was a staunchly methodical neck-up architect. In a 1947 edition of the *Journal of the Royal Architectural Institute of Canada*, Ned had penned a five-point treatise that echoed Lasserre's essay in *Canadian Art*. Two years later, Ned manifested his five points within the Vancouver Art Gallery's 1949 *Design for Living* exhibition. The regional considerations, asserted Ned, are rainfall (hence, design generous roof overhangs); muted sunshine (large windows to bring more natural light into the house); view (shift perspective from the street to nature); exterior treatment (showcase the beauty of locally sourced, unpainted wood); and plan (maximize its flexibility with few interior partitions).

In a young city still developing a sense of identity, the *Design for Living* exhibition offered a homegrown alternative. To the modernists, a contemporary architect clinging to historic building styles would be akin to a contemporary doctor practising medicine by bloodletting or phrenology; it just didn't make sense. The Lasserre-Pratt checklists carried the air of hard-edged authority.

In 1950, Ned designed his own family home in West Vancouver. Its flat roof, open living-dining area, and rectilinear L-shaped plan provided him with a physical expression of his *Design for Living* manifesto. He included one delightfully idiosyncratic note, relating to none of his five points: an interior wall demarcating the foyer from the main living space, composed of translucent multicoloured ovoid cells, like a stained-glass window. For this, he needed an artist. He needed Ron Thom.

Ron created this wall, and others, out of industrial egg cartons—the dimpled fiberglass sheets used to transport eggs from wholesale

Ned Pratt with family at his self-designed home, with the Ron Thom–designed translucent egg-carton wall panel in the background.

distributors to retailers and restaurants. He flattened the crates and filled the area within their ovoid wells with dye, evoking the stained-glass cloisonné of a medieval cathedral. Nobody, including Ned, could ever have conceived anything quite as beautiful and creative, and Ned was smart enough to know that.

IN 1953, Vincent Massey launched the Massey Medals for Architecture, following the spirit and recommendations of his eponymous report. In material terms, the new awards were modest, a series of inscribed pewter discs accompanied by a modest cash prize. But their value went far beyond that: now Canadian architects could vie for something that could mark them as exceptional, something that could make a few of them into stars.

Midcentury architects owed much of their new prestige and many of their clients to the Massey Medals, and to the media that covered them. Design magazines and architectural photography proliferated. They would fuel the essential tasks of explanation and name-making.

Ron Thom owed much of his growing fame to the design press, both as a reader and a subject. Having not had the benefit of architecture school or international travel, much of his design education derived from these specialty publications. The TBP library shelves bulged with books and journals showing new architecture from California, Scandinavia, Italy, and other far-flung corners of the world. The partners received a number of international journals, including *Domus*, *Arkkitehti*, *Architectural Review*, *Dansk Form*, and many more.[13] Architects of ambition pored over them religiously.

As the pages of these shelter magazines swelled, so did the status of the architects within them. *Canadian Architect* launched in 1955, connecting architects across Canada to the work of their peers. Everyday consumer magazines—*Western Homes and Living* and *Canadian Homes and Gardens*—were even more helpful; they reached the new groundswell of prospective house clients.

This would be a major transition in the way many Canadians thought about their family homes. For most middle-class couples, modernist houses still seemed a little strange. The cheerful texts, simple floor plans, and dramatic photography in shelter magazines helped demystify them.

Graham Warrington and Selwyn Pullan became the two most important photographers for the West Cost Modernists. Their work would be crucial to promoting the new architecture. Selwyn had studied under Ansel Adams in California and brought back to Canada a rare breadth of technique and tools. He worked with a Hasselblad 5×7 camera, with a then-rare innovation: a super-wide-angle lens. This large-format camera afforded him both the delicate aim of a sniper and the rapid-fire capacity of an infantry gunner.

Self-portrait of Selwyn Pullan, c. 1960.

Selwyn presented the modernist house as a place where you would want to raise your family and spend languid evenings with friends. Setting up the composition and snapping the pictures comprised just half the job. The other half was the alchemy of transforming it all into images. He spent long nights in a bathroom at the back of the house, where he had fashioned a makeshift darkroom. There, in the glow of an infrared lamp, he would plunge the plastic film into trays of chemical baths to create the final 8″×10″ print photographs.

On Friday afternoons, Selwyn hauled his work to TBP's Robson Street office, often arriving at happy hour, when the craps games were getting under way. He would zigzag between splayed limbs and clouds of tobacco smoke to reach Ned's office and deposit his contact sheets and invoice.[14] And then, despite the open invitation to join the game, he would pack up his gear, climb into his Jaguar, and drive back across the Lions Gate Bridge to his North Vancouver home.

7

HIGHER
LEARNING

THE REGION'S EMERGING design culture permeated the academic community. Harold Copp, head of the new Department of Physiology, enlisted Thompson Berwick Pratt to design his family home. Harold and his wife Winnifred had purchased a large, sloping oceanside lot in the Point Grey neighbourhood, not far from UBC. Ned Pratt had drawn up a preliminary design, only to find that the Copps didn't like his proposed butterfly-roof scheme.[1] Already overburdened with the firm's larger projects, he handed the commission to his star intern. Ron Thom was twenty-seven years old, and although he had worked on dozens of houses already, the Copp House would be the first to bear his actual signature on the plans.[2]

At first glance, the Copp House plan seems simple: a ground-level shoebox volume running east-west, with another shoebox set perpendicularly over the first, creating a basic L shape. From there, the complex interplay of light and form and land begins. He designed a huge brick chimney as the nucleus, from which the two main wings of the house radiate. He harnessed the slope to rest the upper wing, transforming the slope into a giant strut, creating a tunnel to an outdoor enclave. The plan for the patio off the kitchen is anchored by a deciduous tree, whose leafy crown would poke up through the large

The Copp House, Vancouver, c. 1960, as seen looking west.

rooftop opening above the patio. The site is not merely the land on which the house sits; it is literally *part* of the house.

Ron specified local wood for everything: structural framework, cladding, and built-in furniture. And just as he, Bert Binning, and Ned Pratt had done with their own family homes, Ron left the wood unpainted. Fred Lasserre would do likewise with the design of the 1953 Friedman House near UBC—leaving the wood natural and unpainted soon became another defining trait of the West Coast Modernists. But unlike Ned Pratt and Fred Lasserre, who cited rational and practical grounds for building with wood, Ron expressed a different philosophical motivation. He considered wood to be a primordial material of architecture, something that brings joy to

Living room, Copp House. Ten years after its construction, Ron Thom designed the table, club chair, and sofa as prototype furniture designs for Massey College.

people—and painting over it would be close to sacrilegious. "Probably wood was one of the original materials to be considered as useful in making a structure," he wrote. "Its appeal is universal; its colour and texture and warmth, the flower of grain patterns, all being very close to the human heart." Mainstream architects and builders, he lamented, "insist on endowing it with qualities it does not possess, and overlooking qualities it does possess."[3]

For the plan and form of the Copp House, he employed classic Frank Lloyd Wright principles. The path through the house begins in a dimly lit foyer, followed by steps through a dark, womb-like hallway with a low ceiling, and then segues into a blast of light from its wall of windows in the higher-ceilinged living area. If you look up, you see joists and beams resting upon one another at perpendicular angles, illuminated by high clerestory windows. A singular small square window in a high, isolated corner brings in an uncanny trickle of light.

Adjacent to the main living area, Ron created an underlit zone large enough to accommodate a piano—which, he told the Copps, is one of a home's most important elements. He took care to ascertain the geometry of the incoming daylight to determine the piano's position within the plan. The oddity is that the Copps had told Ron that they didn't need space for a piano; they didn't even *own* a piano. Ron urged them to acquire one. The Copps then dutifully acquired a grand piano, in effect completing his architecture.[4]

Once Ron completed the Copp House, a stream of significant house commissions followed: in Victoria, for the Mayhew family; in Vancouver, custom houses for the Moult, Ames, Cohen, Jarvis, and Rogers families. Each one would project a unique plan, appearance, and character, yet be consistent with Ron's own essential design characteristics. Natural, unpainted materials. A huge masonry fireplace to anchor the plan. Otherworldly light streaming in from discreet sources. Walls that are not flat and smooth but textured and three-dimensional, like a bas-relief sculpture.

Ron's distinctive houses soon punctuated the streets on both sides of Burrard Inlet, becoming a calling card for new clients—and also for future employees. One morning in 1954, a high-school kid named Paul Merrick left his West Vancouver home to walk to school as always. But on this day, he stopped mid-journey—transfixed by the unusual form of a house rising before him on Duchess Avenue. Even under construction, it projected a unique shape, with its deep eaves and continuous strip of windows.

As construction progressed, its design intrigued Paul. All the houses he knew had identical-looking ceilings and walls, all flat and white and plastered. When he climbed up the sloped lot and peered through the row of windows, he beheld a vaulted ceiling sheathed in wood and punctured with triangular skylights that scattered shards of light onto the walls and floor.

Paul decided then and there that if architecture could be like this, then he would become an architect. He didn't know it at the time, but he was looking at the house that Ron Thom had designed for his art school friends Bruce and Joan Boyd. Paul also didn't yet know that he would one day become Ron's disciple, designing fantastical houses and buildings of his own.

IN 1954, Bob Berwick recruited another neck-downer: a recent architectural graduate named Barry Downs. Bob had met him at a local Lions Club meeting and, keen to inject some young energy into the firm, invited him to come aboard. Barry would work under Roy Jessiman, complementing Roy's rationalist approach with artistry and intuition.

From his education at the University of Washington, Barry brought with him the influence of minimalist architect Ludwig Mies van der Rohe. And yet Barry also appreciated Frank Lloyd Wright, Mies's ideological counterpoint. While Wright famously embedded his work with stained glass and complex millwork, Mies favoured minimalism: wide-open interior spaces, no ornamentation, transparency achieved through plate glass framed in slender posts of steel, and precise detailing.

Barry could draw up a paradigmatic Miesian glass box in short order and, even better, had the knack for adding the material features that could make that box look and feel like home.

AS THE 1950s progressed, a strongly collaborative spirit took hold among architects, artists, and academics. At the School of Architecture, Lasserre had recruited sessional lecturers who were also practitioners, including Ron Thom, Arthur Erickson, and Wolfgang Gerson.[5] Bert Binning headed the visual arts faculty, and both he and his fellow artist-instructors, such as the painter Lionel Thomas, taught at the architecture school as well. Gatherings at the Binning House forged new friendships among cultural practitioners of all kinds: artists, designers, writers, poets, dancers, and musicians.

At the office and at the Binning House, Ron came to know Geoff Massey and Arthur Erickson, the two young architects who lived in the West End and worked at TBP. Geoff and Arthur desperately

Dick Sai-Chew's photo of Thompson Berwick Pratt colleagues on coffee break, 1960, with Barry Downs sitting to the left of Ned Pratt (centre, wearing suit jacket).

craved a more creative working environment. They both strongly admired and envied Ron's ability to design creatively in a workplace that Geoff and Arthur found stifling.[6]

Arthur and Ron seemed to have much in common. Both men had grown up in Vancouver with culturally ambitious mothers who influenced them deeply; both first planned to be artists and then switched to architecture; both thought of architecture as an art more than a business. Unlike Ron, Arthur had left Vancouver to attend architecture school at McGill University and had travelled extensively. But like Ron, he aspired to create much more interesting and beautiful architecture than the city seemed able or willing to produce.

Geoff's own prowess lay not in design itself but in helping forge the conditions in which design culture could thrive. And now he had come to Vancouver to make use of all he had learned. In addition to

Back row, left to right: Ron Thom, Ian Davidson, Geoff Massey, Ruth Killam, unidentified bridesmaid, Arthur Erickson at the Royal Vancouver Yacht Club.

befriending Ron and Arthur, he socialized with Ian Davidson, a creative local architect who was making a name with distinctive post and beam houses on the North Shore.

Geoff enlisted Arthur, Ian, and Ron as his groomsmen for his small, private wedding to Ruth Killam in 1955. After their September nuptials in a small church near Lighthouse Park, the wedding party motorboated across the water to the reception at the Royal Vancouver Yacht Club. Boys from modest families with huge artistic ambitions, Ron and Arthur were now connected to a higher social echelon.

Geoff and Arthur soon became regulars at the Tudor-style mansion of Lawren Harris, who invited the cream of Vancouver society to mingle with promising emerging artists. Every weekend, Lawren and his wife Bess hosted an evening soiree that brought together, among others, Earle and Esther Birney, Harold Mortimer-Lamb, Gordon Smith, Geoff Massey, and Arthur Erickson.

Ron Thom did not belong to the lofty group that gathered at the Harris residence. He was more at home hanging out with his long-time friends who were talented but more raggedly bohemian: Don Jarvis, Peter Aspell, Bruce and Joan Boyd, Rudy Kovach. While Arthur Erickson began a useful ascent into Vancouver's moneyed society, Ron's heart remained with a more humble crowd.[7]

IN 1958, Paul Merrick applied to the UBC School of Architecture and soon found himself in the military-hut office of the dean, Fred Lasserre, for his admission interview. When it was his turn to ask questions, Paul asked the dean if he thought it was important for architects to be able to draw. Lasserre responded, "No, drawing is not that important. Mathematics and physics are more important for architects to learn."

I think you're wrong, thought Paul. But he didn't say it out loud during the interview.

The irony is that Fred Lasserre considered art itself to be of supreme importance. Lasserre believed in the Bauhaus endorse-ment of an alliance of the arts and sciences. He supported the intel-lectual and aesthetic underpinnings of art, and hired artists to teach design theory and art history to his students. He was actively lobby-ing for a new modernist school building to be in the university's arts precinct and shared with the visual arts faculty. But Lasserre did not see the physical *act* of drawing as integral to the architect's imagina-tion and subsequent creation.

In Lasserre's mind, an architect should understand art, and he should infuse his creative work with art. But he could delegate the renderings to a draftsman.

In Paul's view, the very act of freehand drawing—the biomechani-cal event that sends a pulse from the brain through the arm and fingers to the pencil and paper—would be part of the essence of artistic creation.

Sixty years later, Paul Merrick would remember that interview, and that question, and Lasserre's disappointing answer, and say: "I *still* think he's wrong."[8]

Ron Thom, heavily immersed in projects at TBP, continued to drop in for critiques of student work, known as "crit" sessions, and the occasional semester as an adjunct instructor. Ron approached his studio lectures in a much different way from Lasserre and other instructors at the university. He treated architecture studio as though it were art studio, prioritizing freehand drawing and encouraging the students to draw with abandon. He ordered his students to buy at least twenty sheets of sketching paper, and preferably a hundred sheets or more. He told them to draw on every single one—and then to burn most of them afterward. "You shouldn't be afraid to throw it all out," he explained.[9]

Ron taught in a different way from the other instructors, and he also dressed differently. Most of the faculty projected an urbane sophistication in well-cut grey suits. Ron's clothing matched his work; he favoured nubby earth-toned tweeds, as though he were attempting to meld into the earth around him.

Ron did not design any buildings for the steadily expanding campus of the University of British Columbia, even though TBP continued to be its main design firm. He had loads of other work on his plate, and his organic ethos would not have been well-suited to the current expansion's high-modernist character. When UBC greenlighted Lasserre's proposal for a proper new architecture school building, TBP named Roy Jessiman to lead Barry Downs and others on the team, designing the four-storey building in the clean, rectilinear International Style. Bert Binning specified a Bauhaus-red hue for the future building's elevator banks, and Lasserre designed a distinctive high-modern flat roof with an inset clerestory between the roof plane and the main building.[10] The school, housed since its inception in decommissioned army huts, would finally move into a structure integrated with the fine arts faculty, not only sheltering the students but also aligning with Lasserre's Bauhaus values.

As construction got under way on the building, Fred Lasserre prepared for an extended period abroad. Canada's Central Mortgage and Housing Corporation had offered him a fellowship to study modern developments in England, with a view to bringing his research and insights back to the architecture school.

The year ahead promised to be transformative. Although approaching fifty, Lasserre looked as fit, lean, and dashing as a younger man. He planned a vigorous year of housing research and family adventure. Lasserre travelled across the water in the spring of 1961 and settled with his family in a London flat.

Soon afterward, he embarked on a mountain hike in the country's Lake District with his sixteen-year-old son. The path evolved into a "scramble," more of a climb than a walk, and they inadvertently veered off the established route. Noticing the precipitous cliff edge beside them, his son implored him to attach a safety rope. Lasserre replied that he didn't need one.

When the path ahead narrowed to a sliver of ledge, Lasserre lost his foothold and fell two hundred feet to his death.[11]

The following year, the University of British Columbia opened its new building for architecture and visual arts students—named the Frederic Lasserre Building, in his honour.

8

ELECTRIFYING
THE WEST

AS NED PRATT'S ambition grew, he cultivated powerful friends in politics and business. His friends became his clients, or conduits to clients. His relationship with Albert Edward "Dal" Grauer, the chief executive of the B.C. Electric Company, turned out to be one of the most valuable. This friendship, nurtured with persuasive conversations over lunches and drinks at the Vancouver Club, helped win Thompson Berwick Pratt the commission to design one of the country's most important new buildings of the decade.

As the head of the province's main utility company, Dal Grauer was de facto one of the region's most powerful men. His personal attributes burnished his persona even further—he had been a Rhodes scholar and, like Ned Pratt, a one-time Olympic athlete, in the demonstration sport of lacrosse in 1928. Both men had grown up in Vancouver, did their undergraduate studies at UBC, spent a few formative years in Toronto, and then returned to the West Coast. Dal had taken the extra step of procuring a PhD, but in general his upward trajectory aligned with Ned's.

B.C. Electric Company, which had begun life as British Columbia Electric Railway, had operated the interurban rail and streetcar lines of Victoria and Vancouver, and the coal-fired steam plants that powered them. Now, in the mid-twentieth century, Dal Grauer was masterminding the most significant industrial transition in the province's history. The company developed an epic plan to shift its core business away from railway operations to hydroelectric power, which promised a lucrative and literally bright future. In the pre-war decades, firewood, and then coal, and then gas heated and illuminated the region's homes and workplaces. The main use of electricity was to power the railways and streetcar lines. Now, the corporation's future growth and power lay in the expansion of electricity in every facet of everyday life.[1]

The province's swelling urban populations had welcomed the electrification of the cities. It brought them endless light, heat, and modern appliances. Electric power would reshape everyday living—and provide the wealth to pay for all that reshaping.

By the early 1950s, Dal Grauer needed a new head-office building to accommodate the corporation's expanding workforce and reflect its new role. He would soon get one.

Ned and Dal worked in perfect symbiosis. Dal bestowed Ned with commissions and connections. In turn, Ned showed Dal how architecture could publicly showcase B.C. Electric's changing function. That would mean a large downtown substation, a new office building in Victoria, and a larger Vancouver head office. The original B.C. Electric Building's low-rise Romanesque architecture suggested an old-fashioned railway company, which was, until recently, exactly what it had been.

In 1953, Ron Thom helped design the electric company's new Victoria office building. Meanwhile, Ned designed the new substation on Burrard Street, south of Vancouver's downtown core. It would process and distribute hydroelectric power for the burgeoning West End community as well as downtown—as it still does today. Ned saw an opportunity for a public art breakthrough: most substations hide their function. Why not showcase and celebrate that function? In collaboration with Bert Binning, Ned designed a three-storey rectilinear building with a transparent glass-walled front that unabashedly showcased much of its industrial guts. Upon its completion in 1954, its illuminated facade enlivened the drab Burrard Street thoroughfare.

Next came the corporation's new headquarters. If B.C. Electric wanted to present itself as a modern company, it had to shed its fusty nineteenth-century image. The building should be tall, Ned argued, using the new construction and engineering technology, and with an appropriately modern architectural expression. The critical and popular acclaim of the new substation had proven that the city was ready for such a bold new building.[2]

Once Ned secured the deal, he orchestrated the entire multi-year project like a maestro. The firm partnered with Otto Safir as the building's chief engineer—a crucial and daunting responsibility, given the building's exceptional twenty-one-storey height and innovative building methodology. Pratt assigned Ted Watkins as project architect, coordinating the various key players. Dick Sai-Chew, a UBC architecture-school grad who had joined the firm in 1953, would serve as job captain. Dick would manage the torrent of plans, sections, technical features, and revisions.

For the role of lead designer—the person most responsible for its main shape, facade, and detailing; for its overall look, feel, and function—Ned chose Ron Thom. Dozens of draftsmen would join forces to produce the cascades of drawings. But as the designated head of the design team, Ron would determine the elements that would turn it into a masterpiece.[3]

The B.C. Electric Building required so much additional staff that the firm's Robson Street office literally didn't have the space to work on it; the firm leased an adjunct studio a few blocks away from the main TBP headquarters. The next task was to renovate this newly leased space. Before TBP took it over, it had been an elaborately designed brothel, containing a section of rooms with doors on either side, for worker-client transactions. The TBP staff did not fail to notice the irony: Western Canada's most powerful resource corporation, designing its new head office in a whorehouse. The repurposing prompted many in-house jokes and double entendres.[4]

Ron worked alongside Dick and Ted, as well as a squadron of other architects, technologists, and draftsmen.[5] Sometimes, the entire group would break for dinner and head to Chinatown, a fifteen-minute walk east of the Robson Street office. Dick had grown up in the area and still convened with relatives there, and he knew the best places to eat and which ones to avoid. No matter that few restaurants had liquor licences; they survived by smuggling in a flask of Scotch in a brown paper bag.[6]

After back-and-forth conversations and through a group consensus, the TBP team elected to place the elevator banks at the building's concrete core, which generated the lozenge shape of its floor plan. That geometry would continue as a leitmotif throughout the entire building, from the diamond patterns in Binning's glass-tiled walls at street level, to the diamond-shaped openings in the concrete cornice that would top the building.

Ron devoted most of his time to the project, directing the firm's other architects and draftsmen in the final design and conferring with Bert Binning on the embedded art. For the facade at street level, Binning created geometrically patterned turquoise-and-green hued walls of small glass tiles. Ron topped its slender steel columns with artfully sculpted finials.[7]

UPON ITS COMPLETION in 1957, the new B.C. Electric tower created waves of excitement across the country and abroad. *The Times* of London showcased it in its editorial pages.[8] Britain's preeminent design journal, *Architectural Review*, described it as "the most gracefully handsome office building erected anywhere."[9] Its slender, articulated form complemented the adjacent substation like a bell tower of a church. Low cantilevered wings flanked the main entrance and served the tower like the rim of a hat. It rose higher than any other building in Vancouver, except for the 1939 Château-Style Hotel Vancouver a few blocks away.[10] But the tower's slender form made it seem even higher than the bulky hotel. Adding to its grandeur was the dearth of any other tall buildings around

The newly constructed B.C. Electric Building on Burrard Street, Vancouver, 1957.

its location several blocks south of downtown. It soared above the rotting wooden houses and dilapidated storefronts around it, like a phoenix rising from ashes.

The reputation of its engineer, Otto Safir, also soared. The tower's reinforced concrete core, cantilevered floor plates, and thin metal piers on the exterior were highly innovative structural elements for its time. Motley suppliers, including the producers of the tower's concrete and its glass "curtain wall" sheathing, showcased and bragged about the building in local newspapers and the national design press. After this transformative shift, West Coast living would never be the same. Nor would life at Thompson Berwick Pratt.

Its creation marked a high point in the integration of art, engineering, and architecture—a true example of the allied arts.

The massive acclaim for the B.C. Electric Building then brought on an absurd—though perhaps inevitable—fight over credits. Beyond the walls of TBP, envious colleagues whispered that the building was a knockoff of the Pirelli Tower, which was then in the final stage of construction in Milan. The office subscribed to the Italian design journal *Domus*, one of the key conduits of European architectural news for North America.[11] The plans and renderings of that as-yet-unbuilt tower dominated the March 1956 issue of *Domus*, with its similar lozenge-shaped floor plan illustrating the cover.

Although the two towers would rise as distinctly different entities, quite likely the early images of the yet-to-be-built Pirelli influenced the design team, consciously or not. This is how architectural schemes logically form and gestate, and why architects read design journals: to absorb ideas and inspiration. That didn't stop a few rivals from grumbling that the Thompson Berwick Pratt team "copied" the Pirelli building.[12] It was a baseless accusation; architects work in their zeitgeist and are alternately influencing others and being influenced by others. The B.C. Electric Building and the Pirelli Tower had in common their elevator-bank location and lozenge shape, but not much else.

Upon its completion, most newspapers and other media properly credited the building as the design of the firm: Thompson, Berwick, Pratt, and Partners. When they credited or named a single design authority, most reports named either Ned Pratt or Ron Thom—much to the irritation of whichever man was not named. The emerging rift between Ned and Ron, which had been widening as Ron's fame grew, now turned into a chasm. Ron returned from an out-of-town conference and, shocked and crestfallen, lamented to

Dick Sai-Chew that Ned was claiming credit for the entire building and not even mentioning Ron.

The notion of a singular "author" was absurd in any case, for the massive project required the coordinated efforts of hundreds of people. Ned and Ron each had the two most important architectural roles, and each man's work brilliantly complemented the other's.

Ron had configured its basic contours; drawn up its slender window mullions; orchestrated the interplay of steel and glass; devised the rhythm of columns and the diamond motif coursing through the structure; decided on the size, shape, and positioning of finials, canopies, and cornices; created its decorative finials; rendered the final drawings and elevations; and was responsible for its overall aesthetic.

The entire design team included many of the firm's top talents and fielded opinions and suggestions from the client as well. Against Ron's own wishes, he deferred to Dal Grauer's request for a row of triangles resembling cartoonish dragons' teeth, running vertically along the side of the building. But the final shaping, detailing, and proportions clearly showed Ron's artful hand, and he drew up the final elevations and perspective drawings—the prime indicator that he was the designer-in-charge.[13]

By the same professional criteria, Ned *was* the chief architect: the one who procured the commission, who argued for a modern high-rise, who coordinated the massive team to make it happen, and who named Ron Thom as its lead designer. A couple of times a week, Ned would drop in on the satellite office to review and approve the ongoing work; he signed off on all the drawings and the final project—which meant, in principle, that he would be responsible for the building's safety and structural integrity in perpetuity.

The project also owed much to its many other co-creators: Bert Binning, Dick Sai-Chew, Ted Watkins, Otto Safir, and dozens of draftsmen and technicians. All of them coordinated their talents to create a building that would be hailed by many as a masterpiece. The textbook answer remains: Thompson Berwick Pratt—the entire firm—authored the B.C. Electric Building. But the two men's dispute over credit permanently strained their relationship and eroded their mutual trust.

AFTER A DECADE as an illustrator, apprentice, draftsman, and designer, Ron completed his exams for professional registration in 1957. He belonged to the last cohort of Canadian designers to obtain the professional title by an apprenticeship rather than a university's school of architecture.

Shortly afterward, he became a full partner at TBP. He could now spearhead more projects of his choosing, with or without Ned's tacit approval.

He could now call himself Ron Thom, Architect.

IN THE SPRING of 1958, Toronto-based *Maclean's* magazine dispatched its marquee writer, Pierre Berton, to British Columbia to gather material for a special edition marking the centennial anniversary of British Columbia. Having lived on the West Coast himself through his teens and early twenties, Berton was keen to opine about his former home turf. Of Thompson Berwick Pratt's architecture, he found much to laud—but much to deride as well. He visited the firm's newly built town of Kitimat and subsequently reported:

> Kitimat is a town of almost frightening serenity. Everything has been foreseen, everything provided for. The financing of a home has been made so unburdensome that all can afford to own one. The design is controlled with such care that, although each house is contrived to appear different from its neighbor, the dissimilarity is so studied that all look oddly alike.

In the decade to come, Berton's observations of Kitimat would be echoed by others in critiques of modernist buildings in general.

For lunch, Ned took Berton to his natural habitat, the Vancouver Club. There, he relayed to the visiting writer how forestry,

From the *Maclean's* magazine article: Dal Grauer, president of B.C. Electric Company, in his office in the firm's new headquarters.

construction, and architecture—the triumvirate of industries that had put the West Coast on the map—stood on the cusp of a new era. There would be winners and losers. "I've got my radar out full scope, these days," he told Berton. "Things are happening. The day is coming when they'll have a machine that can chew up an entire tree, bark and all, and squeeze it out like toothpaste into molds, so that you can shape it to the exact fraction of an inch."

The writer spent a day with Ned, who at the wheel of his Austin-Healey drove the writer around Vancouver and then across the Lions Gate Bridge. When they arrived at the peak of the British Properties, Berton observed the city a thousand feet below them. "Spread out like a carpet," he wrote, "with the forested noses of Stanley Park and Point Grey showing dark against the hard glitter of the sea. Around us new and even more radical homes were rising out of the butchered forest."

Berton also gave prominent coverage to the head of the B.C. Electric Company. The *Maclean's* photography of Dal Grauer shows him in his new TBP-designed head office looking like a man of the future, surrounded by modern teak furniture and framed by the slender steel mullions that Ron Thom designed. The caption summed him up: "The Prophet: Dal Grauer represents Power in B.C.: his mind, like his office, is uncluttered, contemporary and forward-looking."[14]

Ned Pratt was also forward-looking, and more inclined to express his caveats publicly. That same year, in the Toronto-based *Star Weekly*, he critiqued the federal government's shortsighted housing policy.[15] "If we're ever to get a better environment, we have to have town planning in much greater measures," he told the magazine. Ottawa had launched a new entity called Central Mortgage and Housing to insure bank mortgages for single-family homes, but it didn't apply to improvements of existing homes. The result: vacant suburban lots sprouted hastily built homes, banal or ugly or both, while the inner-city neighbourhoods of older homes collapsed into blight. Most presciently, Ned lambasted the low density of the new housing. He bemoaned a political policy that encouraged stand-alone, single-family homes rather than row houses, which would conserve space and costs. He could see the future, that a city hemmed in by ocean, forest, and mountains would soon be incapable of accommodating its growing population.

"A good community is one in which all levels of wealth and position are represented," he declared in the article. "Our suburbs, where all the people earn about the same salary and live in similar houses, are cultural deserts." Moreover, he decried the growing power that real estate owners had over the wider community. "Take advertising signs," he said. "Do the owners of a property really have the right to erect signs that are eyesores for miles?"[16]

Ned Pratt proved that he could see over mountains and around corners and decades into the future, citing issues that would become the focus of intense discussion fifty years later. He excelled as a thinker, planner, business whiz, facilitator, leader, and visionary. He was not an artist—but that didn't matter, because he intuitively recognized and appreciated the value of art. He knew that the way to become a great architect is by forging a diverse team with efficient job captains, hard-headed money minders, reliable technologists, eloquent presenters, high-society connections, and artists.

A YEAR AFTER the B.C. Electric Building opened, British Columbia celebrated its one-hundredth birthday. Ron had already been keen on embedding the allied arts approach to address Charles Scott's decades-old City Beautiful ideas, and the province's upcoming birthday party gave him a timely occasion. In collaboration with his art school pal Rudy Kovach and architect Bill Leithead of McCarter & Nairne, Ron proposed a series of street banners and flags, to be illustrated by British Columbia artists and uniting art, design, and the newly modernized urban infrastructure. In their pitch to the city, the three designers invoked the natural cycle of plant growth: "An annual program of downtown decorations becomes a habit, like the daffodils in the causeway every spring."[17]

The vehicle for the "downtown decorations" would be the city's matrix of modern streetlights, which Ron and his team saw as physical vehicles for carrying public art. They proposed to the city an annual array of banners adorning the streetlights of the main thoroughfares. Rudy would design the template, and local artists would supply the camera-ready artwork. The banners would fly from spring through fall, and then the city could sell them to residents and tourists at the end of their annual run.

Their street banner proposal came to fruition, bringing into the public realm the works of top West Coast artists for the next half century.[18] Festooned on streetlights, the works of Gordon Smith, Jack Shadbolt, Sylvia Tait, Takao Tanabe, and many other artists bloomed from May to October every year.

Ron still fumed at Ned's credit grab for the B.C. Electric Building.[19] But now that the high-rise was done and built, he could return his full attention to designing at a scale that better suited him. Public art, small chapels, and single-family homes allowed him to work with much more creative focus and freedom. And creativity is where

he excelled. Ned Pratt designed handsome but straightforward rectilinear volumes; Ron Thom created structures of distinctive form
and astonishing beauty. Ned thought macro, as in federal housing policy and a contract to design a hundred schools; Ron thought
micro, as in artist-designed street banners and a single-family home
in a glade. Public speaking, negotiating, befriending the big shots to
get the big jobs: Ned Pratt excelled at all of these. Ron Thom did not.

That didn't matter for now, because together they created masterpieces. Ned needed Ron, and Ron needed Ned, and they both
knew it.

They also needed Dal Grauer, the rare kind of man who had both
the power and the judgement to engage the city's best architects. He
appreciated design on a private level as well, commissioning Arthur
Erickson to design a striking cabana pavilion for his family home.

Grauer's days were numbered, though, in more than one sense.
The premier of British Columbia, W.A.C. Bennett, aimed to expro-
priate B.C. Electric, to ensure complete government control of the
massive hydroelectric dams being built in the province. Dal Grauer
vigorously opposed the takeover, vowing to fight it until the end of
his days.

That day came shockingly soon. Simultaneously battling leuke-
mia as well as the government, Dal Grauer died on July 28, 1961, at
age fifty-five. Premier Bennett announced the expropriation of B.C.
Electric a few days later, the same day as Dal's funeral.[20]

Now publicly owned and soon to be renamed BC Hydro, the utili-
ties giant would still need architects for its future buildings. The B.C.
premier, though, would eventually show himself to be a very different kind of client.

9

THE ALLURE
OF THE WOODS

RON THOM SPENT his formative years surrounded and inspired by nature—specifically, by ocean and trees. While growing up in Vancouver, he enjoyed family vacations on the verdant Gulf Islands and Sunshine Coast just a short ferry ride from the city. At the Vancouver School of Art, he and his classmates spent the warmer afternoons sketching in Stanley Park, the forested peninsula at the edge of downtown. The weekend brought opportunities for hiking on the city's North Shore, a zone of Indigenous reserves abutting swaths of settler-occupied land dotted with trees and cottages. By the time he reached full adulthood, ocean and trees seemed inextricably linked in his mind with happiness.

Among all the building materials at his disposal, Ron loved wood most of all. Wood fit into his design edicts—local, organic, transformable into art—and British Columbia was loaded with it. He despised the widespread custom of architects and builders to paint or otherwise disguise wood. But he praised plywood, a material in which the colour and grain of wood remain evident, as "a legitimate heir of the board, as will countless other forms of wood not yet imagined which will resemble the growing tree even less. It is not a superficial resemblance to the tree that makes valid any form of wood

The Plywood Research Laboratory in North Vancouver.

product, but rather an obedience to the nature of the tree." He recognized that industrialization would transform its role in architecture and construction, to the benefit of the creative-minded architect:

> In the future, no discussion of wood will be able to avoid being a discussion of the machine—and that discussion will be unable to avoid becoming a discussion involving the human imagination.
>
> Wood is always wood. It remains for man to see what he can [do with] it.[1]

He designed a structure that paid full tribute to these words: the Plywood Research Laboratory building, built in North Vancouver in 1962. Bankrolled by the Plywood Manufacturers Association of British Columbia, the building served both as research venue and advertisement for the new architectural possibilities of plywood. Designed in collaboration with a multidisciplinary group assembled by Thompson Berwick Pratt, the project was one of many team projects that sharpened Ron's understanding of new materials and technologies. He topped the structure with a stressed-skin plywood roof whose origami-like shape displayed the ability of plywood to make all kinds of interesting forms. The structure had no conventional posts or beams; a skeleton of glued laminated timber (glulam) worked like umbrella spokes to hold it up. And it looked as beautiful as a giant sculpture.

And this lay at the heart of his architectural values. Ordinary wood, so widely thought of as a homely and humble material, can become extraordinary. Wood should not be covered by

Fred Hollingsworth blowtorching industrial pipes into lanterns.

paint but coaxed into forms that respect its essential character—just as human beings should not contort their behaviour and appearance to the point beyond recognition of their personalities.

A kindred spirit in this regard was Fred Hollingsworth. Like Ron, Fred never went to architecture school or any kind of university. His pre-architectural training was drawn from the unlikely combination of music, model-making, and welding. After dropping out of high school, he secured a job at the Boeing factory near Vancouver, designing fuselages for airplanes during World War II.

As a perk of the Boeing job, Fred took home some of the factory's metal pipe offcuts and blowtorched them into cylindrical lanterns with complex cutout patterns. He realized that a career in design would be more fun than working in a factory, and he began his own apprenticeship at Thompson Berwick Pratt.

Freddy and Ronny, as they called each other, had been acquaintances at Magee Secondary School, where Hollingsworth had been a few years ahead of Ron. But they never plotted or planned to be in the same profession. When he saw Ron bent over a drafting table during his first day at TBP, he bellowed happily, "What the hell are *you* doing here?"[2]

From that point on, Fred considered Ron his best friend: creative, down-to-earth, and fun to be around. They prowled through Duthie Books together. They both revered Frank Lloyd Wright, and the American architect's influence manifested itself in most of their work.

In 1951, Fred wrote to Wright's Taliesin headquarters near Spring Green, Wisconsin, to ask about employment opportunities. Delighted to receive a positive reply, he packed up his car and spent a week driving the two thousand miles to Taliesin.

When Fred arrived, he discovered that like any new recruit he would have to pay $2,000—an astronomical sum at the time—for the privilege of working there. If he proved good enough to be taken on as an apprentice in due course, he would be rewarded with permission to work there at no cost to him—although with no salary either.

Shocked and disillusioned, Fred drove back to Vancouver with no job. He couldn't *afford* to work there. It turned out that Wright's business model required the exploitation of his staff. Even Taliesin's top architects like Wes Peters, who was married to Wright's stepdaughter, worked for free.[3] Fred returned from Wisconsin with slide photographs and disillusionment, and shared both with Ron.[4] They felt aghast at Wright's draconian treatment of architects, though they still loved his architecture. Ron made a slideshow of Wright's architecture for clients and friends, and he later talked about Taliesin with some of his children.[5] But there is no hard evidence that Ron ever visited Taliesin or its winter studio, Taliesin West, in Arizona. Ron would have to experience Frank Lloyd Wright by proxy.[6]

Ron would have been hard-pressed to make the week-long trip in any case. Aside from his workload at TBP, his family was expanding.

Taliesin East, the headquarters of Frank Lloyd Wright, photographed by Fred Hollingsworth during his 1951 visit.

He and Chris had a third child in 1954—a son, Aaron. By 1957, Chris was again pregnant, and the plywood walls of their Experimental House were closing in on them. From Ron's TBP colleague Bob Boal, Ron bought their third property: a wood-shingled farmhouse on a huge lot, on Lynn Valley Road in North Vancouver—almost literally right around the corner from their first house on Peters Road.

The move back to the Lynn Valley area seemed like a homecoming. The house itself was ordinary, but it sat on a scenic half-acre of land. The kitchen opened onto a lush garden and a sprawling backyard that stretched all the way up the slope to the edge of a small forest. The Thom family reconnected with the family of Graham Warrington and other neighbours from their earlier years.[7]

In the intervening four years, the neighbourhood had grown, attracting more people of all kinds. The verdant setting presented the illusion of safety, though not the assurance of it. Children still played in the streets and gleefully explored the abandoned wooden shacks that had sheltered miners, lumberjacks, and millwrights a half century earlier. Carloads of hoodlums from god-knows-where cruised the streets some evenings, occasionally vandalizing property, menacing local girls, or shouting at passersby. Exhausted commuters on their way home to their families sometimes drove heedlessly. One day, a car racing down the road smashed into Taffy, shearing off the golden lab's front leg.[8]

As he neared his preteen years, Robin felt bold enough to head off with Peter Warrington and other boys to prowl around the rock-walled gorge of Lynn Canyon Park. The park promised every kind of adventure, from gentle strolls to precipitous scrambles. Once in a while, the kids would glimpse a police and ambulance crew descending the gorge. Compelled by natural curiosity, they would watch with morbid fascination as the paramedics hauled a corpse out of Lynn Creek. Sometimes it would be a hiker whose scramble had ended badly. Other times, an unhappy soul who had leapt from the suspension bridge into the rushing waters below.

CHAINED TO THEIR respective workloads, Ron and Chris remained mostly oblivious to this mortal aspect of the valley. The pastoral surroundings offered the perfect setting for Ron to design a new and permanent family home. That was the plan, at any rate. First, they had yet another birth to focus on. In the spring of 1958, the Thom family welcomed into the world a girl they named Bronwen.

Chris now had to deal with four active offspring and a largely absent husband. Her consolation was the conversion of the pantry room into a compact art studio, complete with a pottery wheel. By now, she was almost wholly cut off from their former art-world crowd, and she desperately needed a way to keep making art. Ceramic pieces, she figured, would be one of the few art forms that she could do piecemeal, between diaper changes. From her tiny makeshift studio sprouted an array of beads, bowls, vases, and jars.[9]

Ron, by contrast, had no shortage of workspaces or human company. He drove to the office every morning and moonlighted in the makeshift studio off the kitchen, where he could experiment on his own at night. Around this time, he designed a series of distinctively shaped houses in West Vancouver. He started with a house on Rose Crescent for a former art school classmate named John Southworth and his wife Sheila. Although John had left the Vancouver School of Art after just one year, he had come to know Ron well enough that he trusted him completely, and Sheila did in turn.[10] Ron thus felt emboldened to start an architectural exploration of the so-called "honeycomb grid."

Most buildings in the world are designed and built on an orthogonal grid—the squared pattern that you see on ordinary graph paper. This conventional grid of right angles generates simple-to-build 90-degree corners and a predictable, if boring, house plan. A hexagonal grid changes the very nature of the spatial experience. The diagonal trajectory creates a dynamic circulation pattern, as though the angled walls themselves are simultaneously moving in tandem with your own motion through a room. The angularity creates a distinctively profound concept of ornamentation: not a surface treatment or add-on but a phenomenon intrinsic to the structure.

This unconventional grid was not Ron's invention. It was his hero, Frank Lloyd Wright, who devised it and showcased it most effectively in the 1936 Hanna House in Palo Alto, California. Wright called it the "30-60-90 grid," in reference to the degrees of its triangular subunits' three angles. Ron called it a "30-60" grid in rhetorical shorthand and harnessed it in his own distinctive way. Because this alternative grid allows the architect to cleave off underused corner space, the hex grid makes a house seem much larger than its nominal square footage. And with the elimination of inert, remote, and often-vacant right-angle corners, a room feels more intimate.

The Southworth House became a prototype for several of Ron's future projects. He used the hex grid again in other house designs and eventually incorporated it within portions of certain larger projects. Eventually, he came to treat the hex grid not so much as an all-or-nothing alternative to the conventional square grid but as a way to enrich parts of buildings with dynamic form.

Right next door to the Southworths, a drafting instructor named Bob Dawson had purchased a lot with a similar irregular topography and couldn't figure out how to build on it. Like the Southworths' lot, the ground was solid granite. The Southworths recommended Ron to their future next-door neighbour; Bob already knew Ron from occasionally sharing the blueprint machine at his workplace, Vancouver Vocational Institute, which stood a block away from the Vancouver School of Art. John Southworth was a professional cartographer and could do the complicated survey that Ron's plan would need.[11]

Ron worked with Bob Dawson to finalize the complex details of his house design, inviting him over to his new Lynn Valley house around ten at night, after all four children were asleep. Their kitchen-table meeting stretched for hours into the night, with Ron exclaiming, "We gotta keep at it!"[12]

At one point during the evening, Ron stepped outside for a smoke break. Minutes later, he called out, "Come on, Bob, get out here!" As Bob followed him into the darkness, Ron lay down on the ground and beckoned him to lie beside him while Ron's image of his own future house took shape in his mind. Ron pointed at the star-studded sky above them as though it were a giant sheet of drafting paper, and described to Bob an imaginary layout: *This is where the house will sit, and that's where the skylight will go, and this will be the view, opening up to the sky and all those beautiful trees . . .*

They lay there a while longer under the night sky, while Ron swirled his fingers in the air, drawing up his dream home between the stars.

AS BOB FINISHED constructing his house on Rose Crescent, that street transformed into something of a three-dimensional advertisement for Ron Thom's inventive brand of architecture. Ron did warn his clients with the caveat that the hex grid was "not for budget propositions."[13] It was architecture whose cost was front-end loaded: a bigger capital expenditure up front, paying off generously in the years to come in the sense of secure, homey enclosure. Building on the triangular grid required the precise mitring of all the window frames and butt-joint glass, trapezoidal built-in furniture, wall sections, and ceilings.

THE HEX-GRID houses caught the attention of many people in Vancouver, including Morton and Irene Dodek. Morton, a young medical doctor, had purchased a lot in Vancouver's Oakridge neighbourhood in 1957 for $7,125 directly from the Canadian Pacific Railway. The 60′×145′ property was part of a great swath of land given by the federal government to the CPR in the late nineteenth century in exchange for building the cross-country railroad.

When Morton mentioned their plans to an electrician he knew, the electrician offered to give them access to five Ron Thom houses under construction that he was in the process of wiring up. The Dodeks drove around the twisting maze of West Vancouver roads and then walked through a series of Ron's most recent creations, including the Southworth, Dawson, and Carmichael houses.[14]

Every house they wandered through astounded Morton and Irene—particularly the Carmichael House, already completed on a cul-de-sac in the east end of West Vancouver. With hardly a right angle in sight, each of its features—the interlocking brickwork, the pillars supporting the deep front-entrance canopy, the ziggurat wall bracketing the house—visually references the hex grid. Its gargantuan fireplace aligns with the home's canted walls.

The centrifugal plan and interconnecting pinwheel of rooms suggests a tightly knit family home. The house *is* the furniture, with built-in counters, banquettes, and desks—all shaped like trapezoids as they follow the dynamic geometry of the walls. The six-sided study revolves around a trapezoidal built-in desk of mahogany, oak, and rosewood. Its wooden ceiling is composed of concentrically arranged cedar boards, making the space read like an oversize jewel-box.

As they drove back across the Lions Gate Bridge, Morton and Irene both felt their hearts pounding and their adrenaline racing. The day launched a decades-long professional relationship, as well as what turned out to be a lifelong friendship.

Ron first designed the Dodek House as a small L-shaped home, anchored by a massive hearth, able to expand into a larger U-shaped structure as their finances and family grew. He used a conventional orthogonal grid, but with his characteristic inventive arrangement of space. The ceiling in the upper-floor master bedroom is vaulted and girded around its perimeter with wooden planks to create a version of Wright's "tray ceiling." The triangular prism of space created by a tray ceiling serves to visually break up the inert feeling of an ordinary rectangular room.

Ron's ideas for creating a sense of energy and expansiveness came at a practical cost, as Irene found out. She asked Ron how she would be able to clean a high-up tray ceiling. Ron's straightforward answer: "You don't." And then, when she worried that the open stairway to the second-floor bedrooms posed a danger for their small children, Ron shrugged and replied, "Irene, your children aren't going to be small forever."

Morton, too, took Ron's exhortations in stride. As with many of his other custom homes, Ron incorporated Wright's "cavern and cave" concept, beginning with the unusually low ceiling in the entrance hallway, which segued into the adjacent over-height living room. This shift in ceiling height makes the initial entrance warm and reassuring, and then generates a sense of vitality to the house and to the inhabitant moving through the higher spaces.

The bureaucrats at Vancouver City Hall didn't much care for design theory, though. In December, the house neared completion, a city inspector brought over a stop-work order, because the foyer's ceiling height was lower than the building code allowed. On Ron's advice, Morton headed to City Hall and argued for an exception, on the grounds that the *high* ceiling in the adjacent living room more than compensated for the foyer's *low* ceiling. The Dodeks applied for the variance, and in an astute follow-up, Morton also sent the inspector a bottle of good Scotch. Not a bribe, he emphasized, just a Christmas present. "You can give *us* a good Christmas

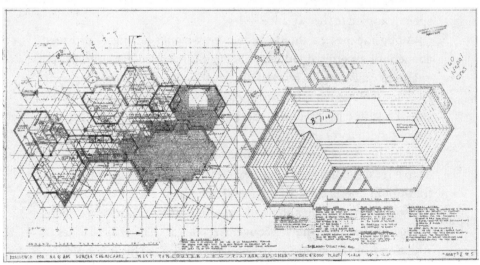

The Carmichael House, West Vancouver.
TOP LEFT North facade and main entrance area. TOP RIGHT Front door.
BOTTOM Floor and roof plan.

The jogged tiles that rim the Dodek House courtyard evoke the variegations of nature.

present by just taking off that [stop-work] sign," he suggested. The inspector agreed to the variance.

Alongside the hearth, Ron employed Wright's Japanese-informed concept of an embedded niche: a cushion-topped concrete bench, enclosed on two sides by wall and the third side by hearth. As the Dodeks evolved from clients to close friends, that fireplace niche would become his favourite seating place, a tiny haven within the larger sanctuary of their home.

With its steeply pitched roofline, off-white plaster cladding, and deep eaves, the finished house evokes an exotic fusion of Japanese traditional and European medieval. The house went on to earn a Massey Medal for Ron and was featured prominently in a 1961 exhibition of his work at the Vancouver Art Gallery. The critical mass of attention from these late-1950s houses entrenched his reputation as the best architect in town, and therefore one of the best architects in the country.

10

THE HOME FRONT

EVERY THOMPSON BERWICK PRATT employee with ambition spent long days that stretched into evenings, or weekends, or both. They worked over whiskey and gin with clients, partners, and associates; or on all-night work marathons preparing competition entries or client presentations. Friday afternoons ended with more whiskey, cigarettes, and craps games, which often extended late into the evening.[1]

For Ron Thom, the long hours were both a requirement and a personal obsession with the work itself. On paper, he and his peers presented everything a young family could wish for: backyards that bordered on a subdued wilderness, temperate weather, healthy children, a spouse that would be there at the end of the day—whenever that day happened to end.

The competitive battles among architects for projects intensified. So did the domestic battles between Ron and Chris. Their marriage buckled under the strain of Ron's long workdays and off-hours meetings with clients, which—in a vicious circle—also served as his escape from the volatile home front.

RON EXTENDED his workday into evening work sessions, or trips to clients' homes: architectural house calls. He especially loved

Dodek House living room, with Ron's favourite seating nook to the left of the hearth.

visiting Irene and Morton Dodek, offering whatever refinements, repairs, or additions they wanted for the 1958 home he had designed for them. The Dodeks own happy household presented a stark contrast to Ron's fractious domestic scene.

He adopted their home as a kind of satellite home of his own; adjacent to the home's giant hearth, he had designed a nook with a built-in banquette which he proclaimed as his own custom seating spot for his frequent visits. He would sometimes stay late into the evening, while Chris was trapped up on the North Shore with the children. As the night wore on, Irene would gently ask him if he had let Chris know where he was, if she knew that Ron would be late coming home. He usually just shook his head. Irene and Morton worried, hoping that Chris would be all right.

Ceramic beads crafted by Chris Thom.

Chris was not all right. For so long, she had trudged around on the concrete floors of their North Vancouver house, lonely and livid and very far from downtown. Her life had been much different just a few years earlier, during the war—and, in certain ways, better. "There was no masculine-feminine crap then; that happened *after* the war," recalled Chris. "The women were all doing a man's job. *I* was doing a man's job, selling automobile parts."[2]

Once the war ended, most women—by choice or by social compunction—retreated from the workplace and back into the home. Any work they might do—childcare, pottery, art—was not likely to be assigned a quantifiable value. Chris strung some of her intricate ceramic beads into necklaces for clients' wives. And she felt proud when Fred Hollingsworth thought them beautiful, and he told her so. He then asked her if she could fashion a curtain of beads for his own family home in North Vancouver. She spent weeks stealing more moments of time, stringing it together for Fred. She brought the elaborate beaded curtain to him at his home on Ridgewood Drive and laid it out carefully on the living room floor. Fred thanked her. She waited for him to say something more, to gasp at the work she had put into designing and firing and glazing and perforating and stringing hundreds of uniquely designed beads—maybe even to open his wallet—but he didn't.

Chris grew quietly furious. *Did her work have no value at all, beyond a simple thank-you?* She waited some more and then stormed out of his house. Fred sensed her anger but couldn't figure out its origin, and Chris did not tell him. Fred had thought she'd offered it as

Ron Thom's architecture exhibition at the Vancouver Art Gallery, 1961.

a gift. Chris had assumed that if he valued her art, he would offer to pay for it, the way everyone paid men for *their* work.

For the rest of their lives, Fred remained perplexed at Chris's anger that day, and Chris remained infuriated at Fred's indifference to her professional value. Neither of them ever thought to ask the other what was the matter with them that day.[3]

IN 1961, the Vancouver Art Gallery (VAG) mounted one of the first solo architectural exhibitions in its thirty-year history, formally titled *Ronald J. Thom Architecture*. The VAG had featured Ron's paintings in past exhibitions, including a double billing with Don

Jarvis in 1946, but this affirmed his public identity as an architect.[4]
In correspondence and conversation, his community shortened
the official title to "Ron Thom, Architect." The contents would be
straightforward enough: a selection of architectural photographs,
plans, and models. To make it visually and spatially interesting—to
transform the exhibition itself into architecture—Ron designed
a series of angled plywood wall sections, creating a jagged path
through part of the gallery. He enlisted Bob Dawson, Fred Hollingsworth, and a few other loyal buddies to help him move and install
the plywood sections. In the gallery, they also laid out a paving stone
pathway lined with plants for visitors to walk along.[5]

When the VAG show was wrapping up six weeks later, Ron summoned Bob to the Thompson Berwick Pratt office to pick up a set of
plans for the Rose Crescent house that Ron had designed. Ron had
wanted the TBP structural engineer to review Bob's plans to see how
he had used the flitch plates to keep Ron's famously deep eaves aloft.
When Bob arrived at 1553 Robson Street, Ron seemed itchy to leave
the office. They gathered up the rolls of drawings and then Ron proclaimed, "Let's go for a drink!"

Once they had downed a few glasses, Ron shared the news with
Bob: he had just received his divorce papers from Chris's lawyer earlier that day.[6] Years after his affair with Marya, Ron had indulged in
a brief but highly public dalliance with another woman. For Chris,
that was that.[7]

Her terms called for custody of their four children, alimony,
medical and dental expenses, and a big enough cash settlement to
allow her to buy a house in Victoria. As the facts and language contained in the letter show, their breakup transpired well before the
era of no-fault divorce passed into law. The divorce petition reads
like a lawsuit—which it essentially is: Chris had to sue for divorce on
the grounds of adultery. Her petition named "the first Defendant"
Ronald James Thom, and "the second Defendant" the partner in his
latest indiscretion.[8]

Bob listened as Ron hashed out the gruesome details. More drinks followed, along with conversation that grew louder and more robust, before they were ejected for their boisterousness, recalled Bob.[9] "It was the only night in my life that I ever got kicked out of a bar."

RON MOVED OUT of their Lynn Valley Road home and into an apartment at 2001 Beach Avenue in Vancouver's West End, a few steps from the beach and not far from the TBP office. The scenic location couldn't quite make up for the dispiriting blandness of its interior. Although it was a rental, Ron still felt compelled to transform its pallid white walls.

He enlisted Bob Dawson and Fred Hollingsworth to help him move the plywood panels installed at his Vancouver Art Gallery retrospective, now wrapping up, so that he could repurpose them for his newly rented apartment. They nailed the plywood panels over the blank white walls and over parts of window openings that Ron felt were wrongly proportioned. And they zigzagged some panels along the hallway to dramatize the entrance into the living room.

At one point, his new landlord knocked on the door, bothered by the incessant hammering. As the landlord eyeballed the utterly transformed apartment, he shrugged and said, "Well, at least it looks like you're here to stay."

A week later, Ron invited Bob over to the finished interior. When Bob entered, he saw a large sheet of brown paper, kidney-shaped but with one straight edge, in the centre of the room—a placeholder for a special piece of furniture yet to arrive. Ron turned to Bob: "What do you think of that, Bob?"

"What's going there, a fancy-shaped coffee table?" asked Bob.

"Grand piano," replied Ron.

A baby grand, to be precise. Shortly afterward, a crane hoisted it up through the window into his post-separation bachelor pad, where it dominated the space. He would launch the next phase of his life by reclaiming his musical skills, playing the piano in private, just for himself, with never a soul around to hear him.[10]

While Ron grappled with the painful logistics of his impending divorce, he took solace in reconnecting with Marya, who was now pursuing a master's degree in poetry under Earle Birney. Several years had passed since their earlier affair—but her eyes were clear this time. "Once in a while, when rather drunk, he tells me he still loves me," she wrote to Molly Bobak. "I'm thinking wryly of the moment that those whom the gods wish to destroy, they first have fall in love with the god-damned intransigent Calvinist Scots! Thank god I have my own life now and I am no longer vulnerable the way I was years ago. And I must do what I can to help him. I cannot endure hearing he was drinking himself into insensibility and behaving stupidly—I'd rather hold his hand and talk about Mies van der Rohe."[11]

Marya signed off her letter to Molly Bobak with happy anticipation for the two women's plans to meet again in the summer. And then she added a postscript in black ink: "Don't let Ron know how much I've told you. He lives under the illusion that he doesn't wander from apron-string to apron-string. Well, what's one illusion more."

On the other side of the country, Robertson Davies was thinking much the same thing, albeit in a more misogynist tone. "Ron is one of Nature's *victims*, and I suspect women are Nature's means of bamboozling him," the incoming master of Massey College wrote in his diary (italics his). "A man of genius, without self-knowledge or self-protection, naked, bruised, and wandering."[12]

AS TIME PASSED, several other of Ron's friendships with his youthful cohort faded, but a select few deepened into lifelong collegial and personal bonds. Rudy Kovach became a professional illustrator and visual communications specialist; he and Ron would collaborate on projects throughout their careers.

Ron also remained deeply attached to Molly and Bruno Bobak, even after they had moved across the country to Fredericton. Bruno had assumed a position at the Art Centre of the University of New Brunswick, and Molly devoted more time to painting. Their local acclaim grew into national renown. Although they sometimes missed the noisy excitement of their past lives in Vancouver and London, they savoured the rich character of Fredericton's red-brick nineteenth-century downtown and the Saint John River that meandered around it.

The Bobaks corresponded frequently with Ron by mail, with Bruno sending invitations to lecture or exhibit at the Art Centre, and Molly sharing more personal stories. She sometimes vented to Ron about her grief and frustration with married life, and half-joked with him that the two of them should have married each other and avoided all this grief. "Ron was a giver. Ron was a genius. I loved him dearly," recalled Molly. Still, their friendship remained platonic. She saw the obsessions, architectural and otherwise, that dominated his life, and concluded, "You'd have to be a saint to live with Ron."

11

DIGNITY, GRACE, BEAUTY, AND WARMTH

IN FEBRUARY OF 1960, Ron received a letter that would change his life forever. It came from Batterwood House, Port Hope, Ontario, the family home of Vincent Massey, who had just retired as governor general of Canada.

The letter invited Ron to submit a preliminary design for a building to be erected on the grounds of the University of Toronto, a residence for graduate students. Not a run-of-the-mill student dormitory, this would be a legacy project for the Massey family, an exemplar of the kind of living and dining quarters to nourish hale young minds. Larger than its immediate practical use, this building would be both a symbol and an attestation of the values that the family sought to express. "It should, in its form, reflect the life that will go on inside it," read the memorandum, "and should possess certain qualities: dignity, grace, beauty and warmth."

He would be competing with three other Canadian architects—Arthur Erickson and two Ontarians, John C. Parkin and Carmen Corneil. The family's trust—the Massey Foundation—would pay the costs of the project, which would include a $3,000 stipend plus expenses for each of the four competing architects for the preliminary design. The letter did not mention a construction budget.

The invitation was signed by Vincent Massey, but it was the two architects in the family—Vincent's son Hart in Ottawa, and his nephew Geoff in Vancouver—who compelled the older man to make the building a landmark. Vincent had wanted to hire a neoclassical firm, but Hart and Geoff both argued for a modernist scheme.

Dignity, grace, beauty, warmth—could the era's high modernism, so often accused of coldness and austerity, embody those qualities? The rapidly churning economy seemed to deprioritize them. Maybe that is why those four words seemed to resonate so deeply with Ron. He read the letter and circled each of the four words in pencil, and he underlined the word "warmth."

Then on 8.5″ × 11″ scrap paper, he pencilled what can be perceived as a four-line project thesis:

Dining room is for conversation and for its special function as a room should be introverted
[therefore] it should be lit by high windows
[therefore] there is no view as such
[therefore] the amenity the room could enjoy is sunlight[1]

Then he set about scribbling forms, shapes, details on a hundred pieces of paper—some merely a few hastily scribbled lines, others a series of highly complex, multicoloured renderings. The stack of sketches, which survives to this day, starts with the simplest possible floor plan: a square. Then a square fused with a rectangle. Then some ideas for walls: columns, arches, brickwork. An arcade. Then the innards: zigzagging stairway forms, mirroring and scissoring each other. Fragments of curves and corbeils. Niches. Floor plans with softly rounded walls. Then grandly detailed drawings flecked with colour. The sketch fragments, though rough and half-finished, are unabashedly ornate. Some sketches appear

FACING Preliminary sketches by Ron Thom for the Massey College design competition.

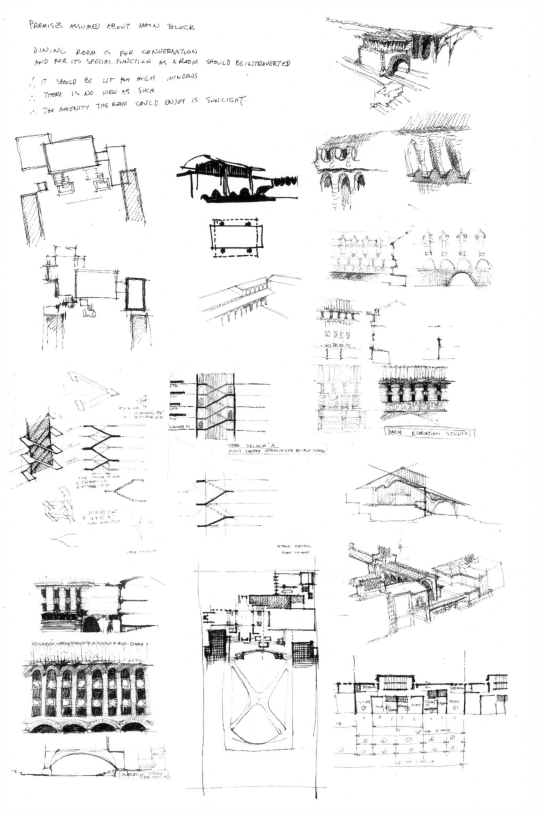

PREMISES ASSUMED ABOUT MAIN BLOCK

DINING ROOM IS FOR CONVERSATION
AND FOR ITS SPECIAL FUNCTION AS A ROOM SHOULD BE INTROVERTED

1. IT SHOULD BE LIT BY HIGH WINDOWS
2. THERE IS NO VIEW AS SUCH
3. THE AMENITY THE ROOM COULD ENJOY IS SUNLIGHT.

Renaissance-like, even rococo. Doodles expand from single arches into arcades.

He scribbled up hundreds of images to accompany his initial forty-two-word design concept. He wrote few words but unpacked his thought process in pictographic language over 120 pages of sketches. One could read the stack of sketches like an animated flip-book filled with characters in a story, whose contents move and morph from one page to the next, as though you are reading his mind and he imagines one fragment of shape after another.[2]

In preparation for the first-round presentation for the Masseys, Ron plunged into a phantasmagoria of design possibilities. He penned a more elaborate gestural plan with rooms designed as ovoid cells, like the egg-crate windows he created for the Pratt and Dodek houses.

He drew up a conceptual main floor plan with a wing jutting prominently into the interior courtyard. In this wing, he denoted two spacious rooms dedicated solely to music: one labelled "music practice" and the other "music listening." The Masseys' design mandate did not require or even mention any sort of music room; he might well have been drawing up his own fantastical idea of "the perfect house." At any rate, the music rooms would not survive to final design.

Music did pervade the design process, though. Ron worked on the Massey College competition with a tight-knit team at Thompson Berwick Pratt, including Barry Downs.[3] Barry had the drawing skill for the intricate kind of rendering Ron wanted, and the skill to pastel in the rich colours of the secondary detail boards. They worked on it largely in the evenings, forgoing dinners with their families for weeks on end. The architects made do with food delivered to the TBP headquarters. Ron supplied recorded music to accompany these nocturnal sessions: mostly Beethoven, Bach, and Japanese koto music. Barry ached to hear some jazz, but the late-night soundtrack was not his call to make.[4]

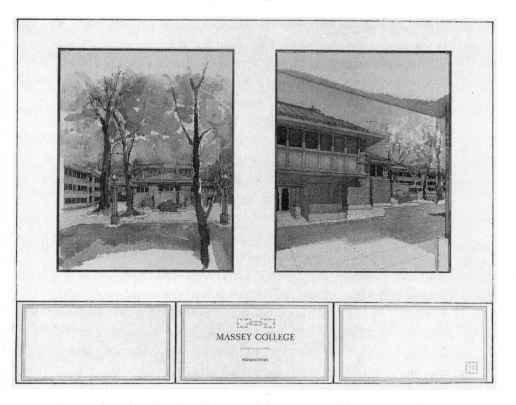

Watercolours from Ron Thom's first-round design proposal for Massey College.

AFTER THE FIRST ROUND of presentations, the four Massey family jurors—Vincent, Lionel, Hart, and Geoff—saw no clear winner. They did agree to drop the Parkin scheme from consideration. Parkin's wide-open minimalism negated the sense of refuge that the Masseys wanted. Plus, it was boring. They also deemed the Corneil and Erickson schemes to project austerity rather than intimacy, and with their wide openings to the street, both of those schemes looked outward rather than inward.

Then they examined Ron Thom's scheme: a dozen hand-drawn and hand-painted images on framed presentation boards with gilded lettering. The jury sat flummoxed. They beheld a series of exquisite renderings that heeded their request for an enclosed space. But with its ornate brickwork and pitched rooflines, it looked disturbingly like a reworking of Frank Lloyd Wright's Imperial Hotel in Tokyo.[5]

The jury did not want Wright redux—but they wanted beauty, and they wanted what they saw as Thom's understanding of a sanctuary. They issued this directive to Thom: Proceed to the next round—but let go of this slavish imitation of Frank Lloyd Wright. Design something original.[6]

Back to late nights, catered dinners, Bach and Beethoven and koto music. For round two, Ron let go of his Wright mimicry and created something wholly his own. He flattened the roofline and streamlined the massing into a more modernist image. Yet the new proposal evoked warmth and intimacy with its materials and forms. Brick walls with rhythmic setbacks and slot windows allowing slivers of light to seep inside. An expansive common room on the main floor and a grand dining hall on the second floor, each of them anchored by a gigantic concrete hearth. A giant clerestory—a crown of coloured-glass windows in a hexagonal grid—projecting above the dining hall. Windows in the main floor common room, looking onto greenery in the narrow space between the college and the building next door. Small "zones" of sunken floor within the common room, to encourage smaller and more intimate conversational groupings. Streamlined built-in furniture for every room, including the students' residences. And every dorm-room window looking onto a leafy courtyard.

All three remaining schemes appeared as modernist. Ron's also nodded to historic tradition—not by copying it literally, but conceptually, through artisanship: the decorative wrought iron of the entrance door, the intricate woodwork, carved stone, calligraphy, and handmade ceramics throughout the building.

Ron's scheme offered a completely closed-off structure—a secular monastery, architecture as sanctuary. He described his ambition: "This building should be capable of unfolding itself by

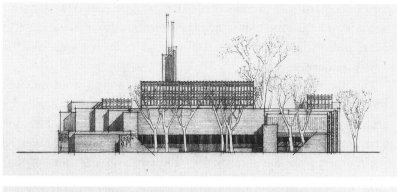

MASSEY COLLEGE
UNIVERSITY OF TORONTO

Ron Thom's south and east elevations for round two of the Massey College competition.

degrees—probably never completely. It represents to the student within, a condensed piece of the world that must accommodate all his changing moods and attitudes."[7]

This building would serve not just the successive cohorts of graduate students who would reside there, but also the wider intellectual community that would convene there. The college presented not only enclosure but also eternity with conceptually medieval elements: the ornamental wrought-iron entrance gate, huge sculptural fireplace hearths, high-backed leather dining chairs along heavy wooden communal tables, dark but cozy rooms looking out onto a leafy courtyard, like monks' cells. He designed an operatic staircase whose limestone balustrade is patterned with alternating horizontal and vertical apertures, an effect that seems both age-old and overtly modern.

The four-man jury considered Ron's second-round scheme alongside those of the two remaining competitors. Those still featured large openings to the street: extroverted buildings, designed to be open to the world. But Massey College required introverted architecture, to create a haven for its inhabitants. *He's the only one who really gets it*, thought Geoff.[8] They unanimously selected Ron Thom as the winner.

His real-life introversion may have helped him understand this at a more personal level than his extroverted competitors. Even as his house commissions became progressively grander, they looked inward, to the back garden or courtyard; they almost always included a giant hearth alongside a nook, niche, or sunken conversation pit to hide in, and zones of dark that morph into light.

A conceptual homage to Wright's "cavern and cave"—wherein a dark zone abruptly expands into light, Ron's approach was more painterly, with ethereal light seeping into wells of darkness like a Caravaggio canvas.

THE MASSEY COLLEGE commission allowed Ron to oversee and collaborate on every element of the project. For the signage, printed matter, logos, and wall calligraphy, Ron worked with one of the country's top graphics firms—Cooper & Beatty Ltd.—and its top designer, Allan Fleming. As the firm's creative heart, Fleming designed logos and graphics for several of North America's major corporations. Shortly before taking on Massey College, he'd designed the instantly iconic logo of CN, the national railway. Fleming's graphics and logos defined the contemporary as well as the eternal, making him a natural choice to work with Ron. It also marked the beginning of their close friendship.

To ensure the college had a homey feel, Ron chose leather, oak, and brick to sheathe, line, and clad it. And finally, he needed ceramics to complete it. For the ceramics, he turned to John Reeve, a fellow Vancouver School of Art graduate and Hornby Island denizen. Reeve would create the dozens of lamp bases and hundreds of ashtrays that would furnish the rooms and tabletops of the college. Each ceramic piece would be a unique work of art, with Reeve's distinctive expressionistic glaze designs and colours.

IN TORONTO, the Massey College team grew frustrated with the pace of the design process and Ron's tardiness in responding to their mailed queries. Long-distance telephone calls, which at the time cost an astronomical sum per minute, were not a practical option.

Outside of the Massey clan, the team included the incoming master of Massey College, Robertson Davies, the only other man who could haggle with Ron about the design scheme. A senator's son, Upper Canada College alumnus, literary editor, professor, playwright, novelist, newspaper editor, and publisher, Davies steeped himself in tradition and protocol. To this finely tailored, pipe-smoking man of letters, Ron's casual dress and demeanour bemused him.

But what really annoyed the incoming master were the communication blackouts. Between Ron's trips to Toronto, Davies mailed letters to Ron expressing ongoing design concerns, but he often received no response. Such was the case when Davies and Hart Massey were squabbling over the college chapel in June of 1961. "It can be dignified, not too expensive, and confined to prayer only," he told Hart. Davies suggested a simple plan, gathered around a single religious icon. But as he wrote, "Hart wants a crypt-chapel under the Examination Room—not a cellar, oh, no, no! but a crypt. I ask him to urge Ron Thom to answer my letters. What difficult chaps architects can be!"[9]

In the late stages of the project, when it came time to finalize the graphics and silverware, the Cooper & Beatty office grew just as frustrated; in the summer of 1962, both Allan Fleming and his professional assistant, Molly Golby, sent multiple letters and made follow-up phone calls to Ron with requests for comments and decisions. Ron, by now grappling with divorce negotiations as well as a swelling workload, was more elusive than ever.

Allan wired Ron a message begging him for a final decision on which silversmith to commission for the dining hall's custom sterling silver tableware. Ron wrote back immediately, apologizing for the delay but assuring him he had just finished studying the various options and had a recommendation.[10]

The list of silversmith candidates was overwhelmingly British. His own country's lack of design talent and consumer taste in silverware seemed to chagrin Ron. "Why are Canadians so bad?" he wrote to Allan. "They range from really atrocious in the best tradition of Birks, to just dull Canadians who could not be excited by silver if they were boiling in it."

In collaboration with Allan and the Masseys, Ron chose the British silversmith Eric Clements, who had "a kind of potter's sense of form," he wrote. "The various parts of an object are beautifully related to one another."

Ron concluded the letter with a request to "please thank Molly for her vain efforts in keeping me going on this matter." Fleming told his assistant that the architect owed her a dinner the next time he came to town, to make up for his laggard communications.

At Fleming's behest, Ron did arrange a dinner with Molly during his next trip, their first in-person meeting. They dined at a restaurant in Yorkville, near the Massey College construction site. The conversation flowed easily: Molly spoke of her student years as an English major at the University of Toronto, and of her work for a community theatre company. Far from being intimidated by his dining companion's university education, Ron loved that she had been a member of Victoria College at U of T, just as his mother had been.

Ron spoke of his own work and life, sharing that he had separated from his wife. And naturally, the two of them spoke about the project that had brought them together. Molly, who had done so much administrative work on Massey College, had never toured the actual building site.

As their dinner concluded, Ron hatched an impulsive plan: he would lead her on an impromptu tour. They drove the short distance to the college, which was still under construction and sheathed in hoardings. Ron pried away enough of the hoarding to let them both in, and off they went—stepping through the unfinished interior by moonlight. Molly then walked him through her own project under construction a few blocks away, the Coach House Theatre.

By the end of the night, Ron had grown enraptured by this petite, delicately attractive woman. He asked Molly if she could take him to Caledon, about an hour's drive from Toronto. He had never been there and wanted to view the autumn foliage. Molly drove him there the next day. The maple, oak, and dogwood trees had erupted in shades of amber and scarlet, and Ron broke off several branches. They returned to Molly's Leaside apartment, where she lived with her mother, Betty Golby. Ron spent that evening filling every vase and urn with fragments of the Caledon landscape, until the entire apartment shimmered with autumn colours while Molly watched in awe.[11]

Molly left for a planned trip to England the next day, and Ron returned to his temporary home at the Park Plaza Hotel. He still conducted most of his design work—of Massey College and a mother lode of other projects as well—from TBP's Robson Street office. But his kind of architecture demanded frequent on-site visits to confer and collaborate with builders, artisans, artists, and landscapers.

As well as filling the courtyard and edges of Massey College with "real" nature—shrubs and trees—Ron designed the building as an abstraction of nature. The walls and courtyard pond are not streamlined like a conventional modern building; they are jogged and asymmetric, evoking the irregularity of a wooded landscape. But the jogs serve a functional purpose as well, providing enhanced views and an extra measure of privacy for the occupants. To this day, a visitor or resident glancing out of any window at the college will confront an image of greenery.

AS THE DEMANDS of Massey College piled on top of a new stream of incoming commissions, Ron knew that he couldn't carry on commuting from west to east every few weeks. Aside from his architectural responsibilities, the long-distance relationship with Molly was growing even more important. For months, Ron wrote a letter to Molly almost every single day between his periodic visits to Toronto. His beloved West Coast became something of a burden in his changing life. "Back to the land of instant coffee and torrents of rain—and low spirits—albeit the sound of the ocean's quiet roar in the background,"[12] he wrote to Molly on one such re-entry.

He had to decide which part of the country would be his home. The Park Plaza Hotel, his de facto Toronto home, offered high-end accommodation and a rooftop bar thrumming with prominent writers, musicians, and other cultural workers. But as soon as he would touch down at the Vancouver airport, his attention would have to pivot from the endless details to untangle at Massey College to the endless commission requests at TBP. He had more than twenty projects under his direction. "What is the earthly use of me attempting to be efficient about architecture," he wrote Molly. "This is why I have to live and work in one place. Even the lovely houses follow this faltering progress. Or maybe I wrongly blame architecture."[13]

Ron Thom and Ned Pratt now locked horns at regular intervals. Ned had evolved from being Ron's mentor to his rival, and to some office staff, it seemed he resented the meteoric rise of his one-time protégé. Ron grew less soft-spoken and more self-confident—cocky, in Ned's eyes—as his fame outgrew that of his one-time boss.[14]

The office tensions dissipated at the firm's year-end Christmas party, held on a boat that had been transformed into a floating restaurant. Ramping up the bacchanalian spirit, the staff and partners bellowed out songs with their own spoof lyrics, sung to the tune of "St. James Infirmary Blues."[15] Corny or not, the parody lyrics were memorable enough for Ron to transcribe and send some of them to Molly in a letter. "Ouff! My apologies all over the place," he wrote, "but you have to find out sooner or later what a pack of literary hods we are . . .":[16]

> *We went down to the back of the office*
> *To see if anyone was there,*
> *Found the usual people around,*
> *Stretched out or propped up in their chairs.*

Ned sang out a stanza that conflated jibes about moonlighting with his modernist preference for precast concrete over the more traditional poured-in-place method:

> *I went down to the back of the office,*
> *Heard Kiss[17] give a mighty groan,*
> *Designing my pre-cast museum*
> *With a scheme on the side of his own.*
> *Now there ain't room for nothing but pre-cast*
> *'Cept maybe there's one little case,*
> *And that's for my pre-dinner cocktails,*
> *I don't mind if they're poured in place.*[18]

AS THE HOLIDAYS approached, Bruno and Molly Bobak invited Ron to spend Christmas with them in Fredericton. By now, however, the other Molly had become the most important presence in Ron's life. The Golbys had extended an invitation to their Leacrest Road apartment in Toronto for the holidays. He accepted, and enjoyed a three-week respite from the turmoil on Robson Street.

On January 9, Ron typed up a letter to Betty Golby,[19] thanking her for her hospitality during the holidays. He looked forward to an upcoming visit from his sons Robin and Aaron, who had spent

Christmas in Victoria with their mother. And then he spoke of the possibility of starting a new life in Toronto. During his very first day back in Vancouver, he wrote, the TBP partners launched into lively discussions with him about the prospect of a Toronto satellite practice:

...I hope this is so, for many reasons, some of which would be obvious to you and some not so.

Firstly, I think it would be good for the children to have me removed distantly for a few years at least. This wouldn't mean that I wouldn't see them, but it would be on a different basis than it now is where I am removed but not quite.

Secondly, it would force me to work in a different climate architecturally, one which may be less free in some ways, but altogether more critical. This could be a good thing or a bad thing, depending on me. But it is a chance I feel like taking.

The state of having both one's feet in two worlds is not a good one. It could be all right if I were selling soap, but it doesn't work for producing buildings. I received a letter from Lew Crutcher,[20] of Portland, whom you've heard me speak of, on this subject. I told him of my hopes in this direction, and he had the following to say... "I know how you feel about going East. The intellectual climate is so attractive to us in the provinces. Yet you've made so many rich contributions to your own city, because you were deeply involved. Designing in a new climate is always exciting, but somehow impersonal. I think of Gaudi who never left Barcelona or cared much about what happened outside, and of Belluschi who outgrew Portland, but who is happy to add onto his fine Museum here, and who hopes his son will come here to start his practice. He's been an administrator since he left. You belong in the Eastern league, but it really gets down to where you can do the most good."

Well, this is just one reaction, albeit from a very sensitive man. I will tell you more about him eventually. But in spite of what my good friend says, I would still like to try the East, having enough faith in my ability to at least back out gracefully if I prove to be mistaken.

Apart from all this, I have come to like Toronto very much, no doubt because of all the Golbys.

Anyway, I don't think we are capable of twisting fate too much, so I will just have to have patience and see how this works out. In the meantime, thank you again for your generosity and forbearance... it did more than you realized to restore the spirits.

Kindest regards,

Ron

In Ron's near-daily letters to Molly, he recounted his agonizing divorce proceedings, which mercifully evolved into joyful discussions of their upcoming wedding. He also shared with her his appreciation of the Canadian intelligentsia: the ideas of Northrop Frye, the music of Glenn Gould, the prognostications of Marshall McLuhan. Usually too busy to read their books, he listened to them speak on CBC Radio.[21] He listened to parts of Frye's 1962 Massey Lectures series, "The Educated Imagination," in which the famed University of Toronto literary critic Frye unpacked the nexus of intellect and emotion, using the allegory of shipwrecked humans building a community from scratch:

This human society after a while will transform the island into something of a human shape. What that human shape is, is revealed in the shape of the work you do: the buildings; the paths through the woods; the planted crops, fenced off against whatever animals want to eat them. These rudiments of city, highway,

garden, and farm are the human form of nature. This is the area
of the applied arts and sciences, and it appears in our society as
engineering, and medicine, and agriculture, and architecture.
In this area we can never say clearly where the art stops and the
science begins.[22]

While living on opposite sides of the country, they mailed letters to each other almost every day. "You have become a part of my
thoughts about everything and everybody," he wrote her. "It has
become impossible to consider any kind of action without some kind
of reference to you," he wrote. "Except in the *inner inner* of making
architecture, which is my totally personal realm."[23]

And then he would cite his long list of projects, in addition to the
epic work of completing Massey and Trent. A chapel on the Sunshine
Coast, a museum competition, a resort in Quebec, and—always—
houses. When engulfed in conceptual design, Ron would enter into
that "inner inner" as though it were a portal into another universe.
He designed intuitively, roughing out plans and windows with a soft-
lead pencil and sketching the roofline, doorway, and windows not by
logic but by feeling.

He would leave the hard-pencil details to the draftsmen and the
engineers. The result would almost inevitably be an interior space
whose circulation flowed as naturally as that of a river, and whose
proportions just felt right. For the most part, Ron could not or would
not explain the actual process of his design. That creative sanctum
inside of him had no doors or windows or skylights for others to peer
through.[24]

That was true of Massey College, as elsewhere: Molly could not
enter that sanctum of the creative process, even if the Master of
Massey College suspected otherwise. By early spring of 1963, Ron
began tweaking the final design elements of the college, enriching
some of his earlier drawings with extra details. Robertson Davies
grew concerned. "Ron wants to add ironwork to the tower and gate

to enrich the stone," he wrote in his diary. "Whence this new yearning for ornament? The influence of Molly Golby perhaps?" Later, the incoming master noted, with apprehension, Ron's roller-coaster love life. "He is more cheerful and exuberant than I have seen him and talks of *warm colour* in the College!" wrote Davies in his diary. "I suspect a woman," he grumbled. "I fear that the decoration and colour scheme of the College has suffered dreadfully from Vincent Massey's old age, Hart Massey's affliction, and Ron Thom's divorce—all life-diminishing."[25]

But Molly had never weighed in on the design or ornamentation of the college; that yearning issued from Ron himself.[26] In any case, the design aspects that Robertson Davies bemoaned would soon make Massey College one of the most celebrated buildings in the country. Ron would consider neither the warm colours nor intricate ironwork of Massey College to be "ornament." To his way of thinking, they are part of the architecture. Beauty is integral to the design of the building, he averred, just as Vitruvius had declared two thousand years earlier.

> Massey College as a college for graduate students, will be unique in Canada. There is nothing comparable to it in any Canadian university. It is of great importance that it should, in its form, reflect the life which will go on inside it, and should possess certain qualities, dignity, grace, beauty and warmth. Such a college as we have in mind possesses antecedents in various countries, and whatever their physical forms may be or the date of their erection, they have a character in common. What we wish is a home for a community of scholars whose life will have intimacy but at the same time, academic dignity.

Excerpt from the February 4, 1960, memorandum sent by Vincent Massey to Ron Thom.

Ron Thom, c. 1963, at the drawing board.

12

THE GREAT
TRANSITION

BY EARLY SPRING OF 1963, Ron and Molly had committed themselves to marriage. Their relationship had met the approval of Ron's mother, Elena. "She has really grown the warmest feelings towards you," wrote Ron. "It is easy to tell by her whole attitude, and the questions she asks, and so on. This is really marvelous to see."

Ron bemoaned to Molly the swelling pressures at work. Aside from squabbling with Ned and the other partners, he had to deal with a disgruntled client bringing forth a professional grievance, calling Ron and the entire office "every kind of scoundrel imaginable" before a professional committee. Ron's solution, during a break in proceedings: "I poked him in the arm, and said, 'School's out, let's have a drink.' So we did—and five martinis later have arrived at an amicable working arrangement to finish his miserable remodelling." With that, the formal grievance—which Ron had deemed unfair—was dismissed. "I suppose this all proves something," he wrote Molly, "even if it is only about martinis."[1]

Then, onto a subject much closer to his heart: wood. He was arranging to have all the cabinetry for their future home built in Vancouver and shipped flat-packed to Toronto for reassembly there. He offered Molly her choice of wood—giving himself a chance to show off his encyclopedic knowledge of the material. "You can name any kind of exotica you know of. Birch, teak, walnut, mahogany, cherry, oak, korina, sen, rosewood, myrtlewood or ash or anything... I just remembered some more: sycamore, ramin, poplar, maple, limba, ironbark, paldao, hickory, and jarrah—and beech—and primavera—and butternut—and alder and elm."[2]

He also arranged shipping for his baby grand piano: a sign of a continued determination to get that technique back after all, so it seemed. Ron never played piano in public. Not even at small gatherings in front of family and friends, and certainly not in any larger setting. He had told Molly it would take him too long to get back to the high level of technical proficiency that had once been his standard.

ONE SPRING MORNING, while taking his usual stroll to his job at the University of Toronto, Tom Symons noticed something unusual. It was a man in a suit, at the construction site of Massey College, talking with the men in overalls and hard hats who were building it—talking not as an authority to underlings, but as one peer to another. He saw the man again in the days that followed, and learned that the man in the suit was Ron Thom, the building's architect.

To Symons, who headed Devonshire College across the road, this seemed exceptional for the Toronto of 1962. He could already see the beauty in the rising forms. And he knew that architects of his era didn't usually hobnob with builders—certainly not this intensely. The besuited man seemed to be listening carefully to everything the builders said to him and paying rapt attention to every detail. They looked like a band of craftsmen working together.

This kind of architect was exactly what Symons had in mind for a massive project he was spearheading for Peterborough, Ontario: the future Trent University.[3]

Symons aspired to create a new kind of post-secondary institution, one based on very small group learning, with interactive conversations rather than large classes of students passively listening.

Its name would pay homage to its location in the Trent Valley on the Otonabee River.

One of Peterborough's architects felt assured his own firm, Craig & Zeidler, had the inside track to win the design commission for the new university. Eb Zeidler and his wife Jane counted Robertson Davies among their circle of intimates. Davies published the local daily newspaper, the *Peterborough Examiner*, wrote plays and novels of growing acclaim, and dined with Ontario's highest-flying academics, blue bloods, and corporate titans. And he had just been named the Founding Master of Massey College. As well as a man of letters, he was a man of influence.

Davies had been a longstanding public champion for a local university in Peterborough, in his own newspaper and other publications. In a 1956 edition of *Canadian Architect*, he argued for an architectural as well as pedagogical landmark:

Canadians realize that there has been little distinguished building in our country, and that of the little that has come into being much has been destroyed, or tinkered to death by "improvers." If we are to have fine buildings, we must put them up. The desire to build in earlier styles—or what is more often seen, vulgarizations of earlier styles—is exaggerated; committees and councils like what is traditional because they are afraid of criticism of their taste.

But private persons, who know what they want, and such groups as church congregations, whose taste has not been debauched, often feel an urge for architectural adventure. People who are spending public money are cautious; those who are spending their own money are not.[4]

Eb and Jane regularly met Rob (as friends called him) and Brenda Davies at the York Club in Toronto for dinner. And through the Davieses, the Zeidlers grew closer to the future university's founding board of governors, including Stanley Adamson, vice president of Canadian General Electric (CGE).

At a dinner party with Rob Davies and Adamson, table talk centred on the university's planned location in downtown Peterborough. "What?" said Jane. "You've got that beautiful river; why not put it on the riverbank?" At that point, Jane recalled, Adamson responded that the company owned land on the banks of the Otonabee River that perhaps it could donate.[5] To the Zeidlers, this seemed like a watershed moment.

CGE—at the time the biggest employer in Peterborough—then donated a hundred acres of land along the Otonabee River toward the future university.[6] The embryonic university's board acquired land on both sides of the river to complete the permanent campus site. The Zeidlers felt proud that, in their mind, they'd helped procure the university's magnificent site. They presumed it was only a matter of time before Craig & Zeidler architects would be asked to design its campus.

Rob Davies admired and personally liked Eb Zeidler, but he was not in charge of selecting the new university's architect. That responsibility fell to Tom Symons, whose mind was already set on Ron Thom. Other architects didn't stand a chance.

The choice of Ron Thom over his own firm enraged Zeidler. He had grown accustomed to receiving the plum commissions in Peterborough—churches, schools, community buildings. And yet he had lost the most important commission in the city's history—one he had personally championed—to an outsider from the West Coast, who had never before set foot in Peterborough.

The rejection prompted Zeidler to move his architectural practice and his family to Toronto. He would soon be designing major landmarks like Ontario Place, Toronto's Eaton Centre, and the Ontario Science Centre. His firm, Zeidler Partnership Architects, grew into one of the most important and prolific firms in the country, designing several university buildings in other parts of Ontario, and eventually opening satellite offices in Calgary, Victoria, China, United Arab Emirates, London, and Berlin.

The relocation to Toronto and its many opportunities might well have allowed Zeidler to create a much larger name for himself than if he had won the Trent commission and stayed in Peterborough. But for the rest of his life, he would never understand nor forget being bypassed for the Trent University commission, the biggest snub of his career.[7]

IN MID-JUNE OF 1962, the incoming board of Trent University officially confirmed Ron Thom as its master planner. At the first meeting with Tom Symons following his appointment, Ron asked him for his instructions. Symons found his question absurd. "Here was this man, clearly a genius, asking a duffer like me, 'What are your instructions?' I told him, 'Ron, I have no instructions. Here are my requests.'"[8]

The commission marked a quantum leap in scale and complexity from anything Ron had attempted in his career. He knew how to design stand-alone houses and buildings, but he had no idea of how to go about master-planning a university campus from scratch. And now he faced a cavalry of university board members and trustees demanding meetings, action plans, spending rationales, and receipts—and all to be delivered to them in bureaucratic dialect on reams of paperwork.

Ron detested this part of architecture. He needed to harness the prowess of Thompson Berwick Pratt's senior partners. Bob Berwick and Ned Pratt knew how to manage large projects, and they knew how to delegate. "The partners are beginning to take the Trent business much more seriously now," he wrote Molly Golby. "One of them is preparing me with the mysteries and realities of university planning."[9]

The logistics of designing Massey College from Vancouver had already proven to be a challenge. Designing an entire campus would turn out to be almost insurmountable.

TOM SYMONS had his own preparatory plan for Ron. As founding president of Trent University, he arranged two exploratory trips for his chosen architect. The first would entail two days of driving around the Ontario countryside in the Trent Valley. The second: a trip to the United Kingdom, with university officials, to tour the most significant old and new college campuses.

Ron met and soon befriended Denis and Dawn Smith. Denis, a fast-rising star in Ontario academe, had been tapped to be a political science professor while simultaneously serving as vice president of the new university. Dawn was slated to be a professor of modern languages. In a sea of grey-suited bureaucrats, Ron found an island of easy camaraderie with Dawn and Denis, who valued culture and nature and who appreciated the art of architecture. And Ron loved the Smiths' own house in the Peterborough countryside, built in the mid-nineteenth century from local fieldstone.

Ron embarked on Trip One, the formal excursion around the hills and valleys north of Peterborough with Denis Smith and Dick Sadleir, a key member of Trent's Academic Planning Committee. Denis drove while Ron gazed out the window. The landscape looked so different from the West Coast, and yet it captivated him just the same. He rhapsodized about the wooden barns and stone farmhouses, nestled in the rolling hills as though they had simply taken root and grown there, like the oak, maple, and dogwood trees that surrounded them. The Ontario countryside fascinated Ron, and Ron's running commentary fascinated Denis and Dick. *He's seeing things that I've never noticed before*, thought Dick.[10]

One time, while driving with Dick to Peterborough, they passed fields of corn rippling in the wind, and Ron begged to alight from the car for a rogue harvest. Wading through the yellow-green tassels, he grabbed a husk, took a bite, and then spat it out in disgust. It turned out to be a field of maize earmarked for livestock feed, not human consumption. For Ron, it was an unexpected revelation about the Ontario landscape, and a harbinger of more lessons to come.

Next, Ron began preparing for the expedition to England. Symons had found it incredible that Ron had never been overseas, especially with Ron's intuitive grasp of the Oxbridge-like quad he had designed for Massey College. A tour of the old and new colleges of Britain would further Ron's understanding of campus architecture, and Symons arranged an eight-college itinerary. Denis Smith and Dick Sadleir would accompany him, and Ron secured permission for Molly to join them as well.

AS RON PREPARED for his next trip to Toronto, his letters to Molly burst with anticipation. This wouldn't be just any red-eye journey to the Park Plaza Hotel, but the landmark cross-country trip of his life. It would mark his permanent departure from his West Coast base, his official resettlement in Ontario, and his wedding to Molly a few days later, on July 9. Then they would depart on their grand overseas tour to the universities of England—the client-sponsored architectural research trip that would now double as a honeymoon.

Everything seemed to be falling into place. Ron had arranged shipping for the new plywood built-ins he had designed and had manufactured on the West Coast; they would land in Toronto just in time for his own arrival. They enlisted a United Church minister to conduct the service at the University of Toronto's Hart House chapel with just a handful of guests, including Molly's mother Betty; Allan Fleming, the best man; and Molly's friend Anne Tait, the matron of honour.

Ron's own parents had already planned a road trip to visit friends in Manitoba that month, and so they wouldn't be attending. But they knew it would be a small affair, and their son was very much a grown man, now on his second trip to the altar. Their long drive through the Prairies would be their celebration of the marriage. Elena wrote Molly to let her know that their wedding present of cash and CorningWare was on its way. "We shall be thinking of you on the 9th & hoping to meet you in the sweet by & by," she wrote, referencing a popular Christian hymn. In the nineteenth-century song and its twentieth-century gospel reiterations, "meeting in the sweet by and by" refers to eventually joining loved ones in heaven. She penned her final words: "I wish you could have gone by boat. Sincerely yours, Elena M. Thom."[11]

AFTER A FRANTICALLY intense period of wrapping up projects at Thompson Berwick Pratt, and an equally frantic round of visiting friends for "last evenings out," Ron finally made it to Toronto—literally the day before his wedding.

The minister met them at Hart House the next day and conducted the brief, quiet ceremony. They celebrated afterward at their Washington Avenue apartment with a larger group of friends and colleagues. Molly radiated beauty and happiness, while Ron fired up a celebratory cigarette with Allan. The overseas honeymoon-plus-research trip awaited them.

Setting foot in England in 1963, Ron beheld a country in the process of modernizing, like his own, but with a vastly greater existing stock of architectural history. Even Canada House—headquarters of the Canadian High Commission, where the team registered their travels—was built in Greek Revival style.

First, launching their tour: two of the country's oldest universities, Oxford and Cambridge. Oxford's buildings spanned the millennium, from 1040 (the Saxon Tower) to 1962 (St. Catherine's College, by Danish architect Arne Jacobsen). The team spent a day at St. Catherine's. Ron found the building itself—a long, three-storey glass facade overlooking an open courtyard—cold and unremarkable.[12] But he was impressed by how Jacobsen designed or commissioned everything in St. Catherine's: furniture, cutlery, ashtrays—much as Ron had done at Massey College, and what he would soon do for Trent.

Ron also strolled around the centuries-old town. He headed to Broad Street and stepped into Blackwell's, a book and music

Left to right: Allan Fleming, Ron Thom, Molly Thom, and Anne Tait at the Thoms' wedding reception.

emporium housed in a gable-roofed Jacobean building. There, he purchased three thick sets of sheet music: two volumes of Johann Sebastian Bach's preludes and fugues, and a collection of Beethoven's sonatas.

They trekked on to Cambridge University. Within that campus, Ron marveled at Trinity College, particularly the seventeenth-century library designed by Sir Christopher Wren, with its courtyard space, shadowed cloisters, and intricate detailing.

This man who had never been overseas nonetheless brought revelations to the well-travelled men around him. "We walked through courtyards and colleges that I had been through many times before," recalled Sadleir, "but I felt I was seeing it all fresh—from an artist's point of view. He would often stop as we entered one, look around and make comments about the features of the building and its location, the way it fitted into the landscape; the sky, the colour—amazing."[13]

The team then toured the six contemporary campuses of Sussex, Kent, Warwick, East Anglia, Lancaster, and York.

Most of the newer universities failed to impress Ron. What he could see of the University of Kent at Canterbury, which was then still under construction, seemed charmless and clunky. And he actively despised the concrete brutalism of the University of Sussex, built in 1961.[14] An in-person meeting with its architect, Sir Basil Spence, didn't help matters. Ron and Molly both found Sir Basil to be pompous and elitist, prompting Ron to refer to him thereafter as "Sir Basil Stench."[15]

Both Ron Thom and Tom Symons preferred the basic, age-old "Oxbridge quadrangle"—smallish buildings that surround and sequester the occupants.[16] As their college-viewing itinerary concluded, it turned out that the two oldest universities in the British Empire—Oxford and Cambridge—were the ones that this modernist Canadian architect loved the best.

After the university site visits, Ron stayed on in England with Molly. His first overseas sojourn had progressed perfectly so far: practical, insightful, and paid-for. He and Molly rented a car to explore the North York Moors and attend the theatre in Chichester. Then they settled into London to celebrate their belated holiday together. They met up with Bruno and Molly Bobak, who were spending a sabbatical year there, and took in Bruno's show at a South London gallery. The rest of their days were spent sightseeing, relaxing, and basking in the early August sunshine.

And then one evening, near the end of their honeymoon week, the telephone rang in their hotel room. A call from Canada House, bringing dreadful news from home. His parents, James and Elena Thom, had been driving across the western edge of Ontario on their vacation road trip. As they neared the Manitoba border, his father had apparently fallen asleep at the wheel and crashed the car.[17]

His father was in hospital, seriously injured. His mother was dead.

Ron unleashed a terrible howl and then wept inconsolably.

They adjusted their flights to return earlier to Canada, with Molly heading to Toronto and Ron to his family in Vancouver. After arriving, he updated his bride by telegram:[18]

CN   Telecommunications

local time · heure locale

```
    VA023                    1963 AUG 9  AM 2 48
V LLG086 43/39 NL= CNT VANCOUVER BC 8=
MRS R J THOM (DELIVER)=
      7 WASHINGTON AVE TOR=

=MOLLY DEAR = EVERYTHING UNDER CONTROL. FATHER IN
HOSPITAL HERE. WILL RECOVER. FUNERAL ON THE 9TH. I AM
NEEDED TILL SUNDAY MORNING. WILL BE ON TCA FLIGHT 850
LEAVING 9:55 A.M. MISS YOU BADLY. HOPE YOU ARE O.K.
ALL LOVE=
      RON==

9TH  850 9:55 AM.
```

J. R. White, general manager · directeur général, Toronto   6122b

Elena Thom's memorial service and cremation took place that Friday. Two days later, Ron climbed aboard a DC-8 airliner and headed to his new home in Toronto.

The West Coast era had come to an end.

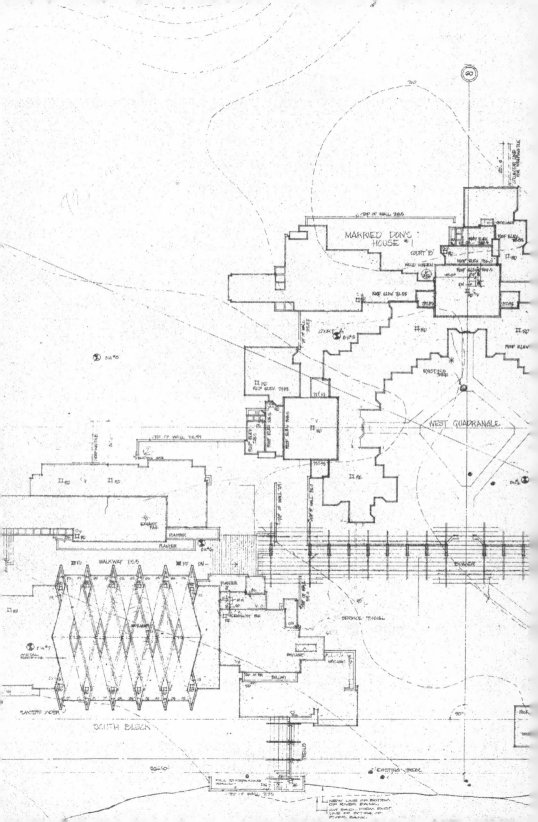

PART TWO

EAST

13

RISING
IN THE EAST

ON AUGUST 11, 1963, Ron Thom arrived in his new home city on a dry and balmy day. Over the past few days, he had bidden farewell to two of his life's touchstones—his mother and the West Coast. His deep anguish at losing Elena was evident to Robertson Davies and others he worked with at Massey College.[1] But Ron had little time to grieve. He and Molly now needed to focus on preparing their new apartment on Washington Avenue for when the built-ins arrived. His practice was about to be immersed in the epic mission of designing Trent University. But he didn't even have an office upon his arrival. He needed to find one, fast.

The lead to his Toronto workplace turned out to be architect John Andrews. The tall and stocky Australian émigré chaired the school of architecture at the University of Toronto and rented a workspace in a renovated nineteenth-century warehouse near the downtown core. Within days of Ron's arrival in Toronto, he and Molly went for dinner with him, and by the end of the night, Andrews had convinced Ron to rent the space available on the floor above his own office.[2]

Ron checked out the premises at 47 Colborne Street and liked what he saw. The Milburn Building, as it was originally called, had been designed by Edward James Lennox and served as a storehouse

Drawing of 47 Colborne Street by Bob Montgomery.

for patent medicines. Among the most prolific architects of his time, Lennox had helped define Toronto in neo-traditionalism, including its 1889 City Hall. In the case of the Milburn, that meant a facade of rough-hewn stone and arched windows in good Romanesque style— and an interior of craggy exposed brick and overheight windows.

In the nineteenth century, the neighbourhood served as the mercantile heart of the city. Some years later, Ron would note that among these surviving buildings, "few of them lay claim to great architecture, but all express most eloquently the history of the city, its people, their attitudes, postures, and ethics."[3]

He hired an architectural technician, Bob McIntyre, and an architect named Don Nichol,[4] but his staff remained skeletal while he struggled to settle into his new professional locale. John Andrews also had a tiny staff consisting of just one other architect: a young South African immigrant named Jack Diamond. Jack would eventually become one of the country's greatest architects and make his own mark on Toronto and other parts of the world. For now, he was an employee of John Andrews Architects, hoping for a partnership.[5]

To make their staff seem more impressively large, Ron Thom and John Andrews extended a professional courtesy to one another: John's two or three employees would move to Ron's studio when an

R.J. Thom client visited. In turn, Ron's small staff would dutifully shift over to the office of John Andrews Architects before his pre-scheduled client meetings.[6] Appearances mattered, especially in Toronto.

Ron carted in pots full of greenery to complete the interior. He loved his new space, with its sandblasted brick walls, oversize industrial metal gratings, huge century-old beams, and raw cedar. And the floors: industrial "mill floors," heavy-duty warehouse flooring built of timber so thick that it served as joists. The small gaps between each timber beam of the flooring brought in dust, so the draftsmen had to cover their drafting tables in protective canvas every night.[7] But it was worth it.

The formal name of this new TBP satellite office was Ronald J. Thom, Thompson Berwick Pratt Architects. Colleagues and clients simply called it "R.J. Thom." Rough-hewn and strewn with greenery, the workplace at 47 Colborne had an entirely different character from the Vancouver head office.

IN THE EARLY DAYS, the smell of raw onions haunted the air around 47 Colborne, and even permeated the brick walls. The pungent scent derived from the adjoining building's recent function as a vegetable warehouse. One by one, the warehouses transitioned into a microcosm of the new Toronto. At 47 Colborne, lawyer George Miller—who would soon become Ron's personal and professional lawyer—set up his storefront office. Sculptor Gerald Gladstone installed his studio, more architects and urban designers moved in, and a basement printshop serviced them all. Even long after the entire block had been repurposed from produce to professions, the vegetal aroma seemed to linger in the air.[8]

The Milburn Building's nineteenth-century facade embodied all the features that twentieth-century architecture was now jettisoning. By this time, Toronto's leading architects practised high modernism and celebrated its adherents. The design community was still reeling from the loss of one of its most ardent young champions, Peter Dickinson. Born and trained in London, Dickinson had immigrated to Toronto and brought the minimalist International Style with him. He designed a handful of sleek and superlative buildings, including the 1955 Benvenuto Place Apartments off of Avenue Road[9] and the O'Keefe Centre on Front Street, completed in 1960. The following year, at just thirty-five years of age, he died of stomach cancer. Though tragically brief, Dickinson's career nonetheless left an important legacy, proving that minimalism could produce masterpieces in the hands of the right architect.

Ron soon became acquainted himself with another minimalist firm, John B. Parkin Associates, whose chief designer—John C. Parkin—had lost to Ron in the Massey College competition. Despite having nearly identical names, the two principals—John Burnett Parkin and John Cresswell Parkin—bore no biological relationship with one another. To reduce the inevitable confusion, they would usually be differentiated by their middle initials: John C. and John B.[10] Their firm, a powerhouse of high modernism, would soon be the largest architectural firm in Canada.

That firm's size and clout hadn't been enough for John Andrews, who had logged three years with the Parkins. Andrews had grown up and done his undergraduate studies in Sydney, and then headed to the other side of the world to study architecture at Harvard. He moved to Toronto in 1959 at the behest of John C. Parkin to enter the Toronto City Hall competition together. Their team made the shortlist but lost to Finnish architect Viljo Revell. In the interim, Andrews established himself well enough in his new city that he would make it his home for the next decade. But he didn't like the Parkins' sleek, finely detailed, minimalist aesthetic—or the Parkins themselves. When John C. first made a cold call to Andrews at his home in New England, as Andrews recalled it, "he wore bloody *nail polish!*"[11] Parkin's nails might simply have been buffed to a shine from a manicure, in dapper Torontonian style. But this burly Australian still found his manner too precious to tolerate. John Andrews projected a kind of swaggering machismo, just like his big, muscular, concrete architecture. And he thought John C. Parkin was effete, just like his spare, white, refined architecture.

Ron still worked with the TBP team in Vancouver, via long-distance telephone and mail, but had to keep expanding his Toronto team as well. He poached a young architect named Bill Lett from another firm,[12] and, six months later, a British newcomer named Peter Smith. To both of them, recalled Bill, "Ron was like a breath of fresh air." Bill had found his work and the environment at his previous firm, Shore & Moffat, to be tedious and free of much creative spark. Ron, by contrast, enlivened everything—even his Washington Avenue apartment, which he invited his associates to see. At a time when almost every contemporary office had white walls and full-height glass windows, Ron took an entirely different approach, carpeting the floors with sisal and sheathing the walls with burlap, unpainted plywood, and, for good measure, a dartboard. His office environment wasn't cutting-edge cool; it was warm and intimate.

Staffers periodically unwound with dart games and Friday evening beer sessions. Ron invited neighbouring architects from other firms to join these sessions at a time when nobody else did.[13] "Architecture firms at that time were all very insular and tight-lipped about their work, so this was all very liberating," recalled Bill.

IN TORONTO, both the retail and the social infrastructure were far more organized and refined than what Ron had known in Vancouver, and he wasted no time in plunging in. He found himself in high demand for dinner parties, lectures, and high-powered meetings. For the entire first year of their marriage, he and Molly rarely managed an evening alone together.

A half-block from the office, Ron established an unofficial secondary office at the "King Eddy"—the restaurant and lounge at the King Edward Hotel down the road, where he spent most lunch hours.

He befriended many of the nation's cultural leaders, including legendary National Gallery of Canada director Alan Jarvis, who shared Ron's devotion to the alliance of art and architecture, and Alan's successor, Jean Boggs.[14]

Ron and Molly became regulars at architect Irving Grossman's parties on his studio rooftop.[15] There, the city's elite painters, artists, and architects would gather at open-air soirees anchored by a jazz quartet, much like Lawren Harris's Sunday night gatherings back west—with the added bonus for Ron that he was explicitly invited.

Ron and Molly also became fixtures at Karelia, the Scandinavian design emporium launched by architect Janis Kravis in 1960. Here in this retail showroom, Ron found physical examples of all the topflight European chairs and other design objects that he had previously viewed mostly as photos in *Dansk Form* and other rarified European publications in the TBP library. He brewed the most audacious idea: for Trent, a public university that would be geared specifically to the progeny of the Peterborough working class, he would specify contemporary high-end furniture.

Though nominally a commercial sales showroom, Karelia also served throughout the 1960s as a contemporary design gallery and a gathering spot for Ron and others, especially after it moved to Front Street. Kravis also designed the space that would captivate Ron by night: a restaurant called Three Small Rooms, in the bowels of the Windsor Arms Hotel. Before this point, Toronto's fine dining options offered little beyond raucous and smoky steak houses. The typical decor centred on ostentatious dark millwork, brass hardware, and red velvet. Three Small Rooms presented an entirely different atmosphere: modern *and* cozy.

Ron loved that combination. He passed many languid evenings at Three Small Rooms with his good friend Leslie Rebanks, a British émigré and architect who had moved to Canada in 1965. Leslie had married Wendy Weston, a scion of the high-society Weston family that controlled a food and retail emporium, and designed the

Weston Centre head-office tower at St. Clair and Yonge Street along with other Weston company projects and stores. Although both his background and his architecture stood in sharp contrast to Ron's, the two men shared a ribald sense of humour and could regale each other for hours.

Three Small Rooms offered Ron and his friends an acoustical as well as an architectural haven. Even the largest of the three dining rooms had sound-absorbing textiles, bulkheads, slatted wood, and upholstered banquettes. "This is how a restaurant should be—a place where you can sit quietly and listen to your wife talk," he told Leslie.[16] They would hear little else but the clink of glasses, the sear on the open grill, and the *whuumpf* of a tableside flambé.

Its kitchen staff included a seventeen-year-old aspiring chef named Jamie Kennedy, who would later become known for modernizing the city's cuisine, just as Kravis had modernized its restaurant design. Urbane Torontonians could now order fondue and bask in the fragrance of kirsch-splashed Gruyère, in a warmly designed and comforting room.[17]

And then Ron would return home, where he had reconfigured their small apartment to have a mezzanine studio for after-hours work. At night, Molly lapsed into sleep to the staccato rhythm of Ron's pencil as he painstakingly dotted the foliage for his presentation drawings.

AS RON EMBRACED the cosmopolitan life of Toronto, he grew more rooted in his adopted city. Week by week, he became less of a satellite architect and more of his own man. The Vancouver partners at TBP still made the big decisions and mailed the paycheques to the Toronto staff. In a reversal of the norm, Vancouver was head office and Toronto was, effectively, its branch plant, even if the Toronto office nameplate and stationery was called R.J. Thom & Associates. Most Ontario clients had never heard of Thompson Berwick Pratt. They wanted Ron Thom.

The Forrest House, West Vancouver.

For a while, the West Coast partners didn't complain. They knew the Ron Thom name would bring in business. And Ron continued to work on house designs on the West Coast.

While preparing for his move to Toronto in the early 1960s, Ron had started work on one of his most significant house designs: the family home of Terry Forrest, a young philosophy professor at UBC. The lot he had purchased at 1143 Eyremount Drive, near the summit of the British Properties in West Vancouver, offered a stunning panoramic view of the plateau of the city and the region beyond it.

Working with TBP associate Dick Mann, Ron devised the house to read like a taut geometric abstraction of the rocky outcropping on which it stood. From the street below, the house itself is barely visible: the rhythmically pitched roofline seems to hover just above its rocky plinth. With floor-to-ceiling walls of glass crowned by a roof with absurdly deep eaves, it evokes a giant bird on the bedrock, poised for flight.

Its overlapping peaked rooflines actually continue into the
interior of the house, with two of
the "wings" visibly intersecting
in the hallway, in an oddly literal
importation of the outside roof
into the house.

A side room off the main living area generates the Wrightian cavern-and-cave. The ceiling
starts off low above the niche
and then soars into the main
living area, curving just enough
to seem as though it's somehow
alive. Then the "cave": a step
down into the sunken zone off
the main living area, with a low
ceiling and daylight seeping in
through a hidden slot skylight.

The Forrest House interior and
gently sloping ceiling.

The Forrest House turned out to be one of his most imaginative and visually dramatic houses on the West Coast, destined
to join many of Ron's other houses in earning the coveted Massey
Medal. The shelter magazines extolled its ingenuity, its uniqueness, its brilliance. The house very quickly became a "name" that
attracted other creatively ambitious clients to Ron.

With their magnificent new home and panoramic view of the city
below, the Forrests seemed destined for a beautiful life together. A
few months after its completion in 1963, however, Terry Forrest suddenly fell dead of a heart attack, at age thirty-four. As for his new
home, he hadn't even had the chance to move in.

The Forrest House hit the market at $30,000, putting it far out
of reach for most home buyers in 1963. A young couple named Dennis and Adele Case, impressed by this house but unable to afford it,

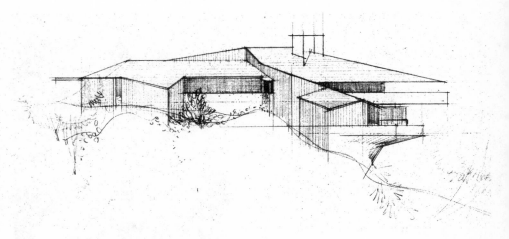

Case House, perspective drawing by Paul Merrick.

contacted Ron and asked him to design something equally imaginative. Dennis was a naval architect and the couple were avid sailors; they had a mutual friend in Bob Dawson, whose house they admired. The Cases had bought a cliffside lot near Horseshoe Bay in West Vancouver and wanted a house that reflected their love of boats—a house that *felt* like a boat.

In purely practical terms, the project didn't make financial sense for either the clients or the architect. Ron was living in Toronto, buried in the design of Trent University, and had no need of additional work. Dennis and Adele weren't wealthy, but they figured they could afford a complex Ron Thom design if they did most of the construction job themselves. They wanted drama and mystery in their home, they told Ron, and encouraged Ron to continue experimenting with Wright's honeycomb grid. "Angles supply the most mystery," said Adele.

Paul Merrick, who as a teenager fell in love with Ron's Boyd House in West Vancouver, had now joined Thompson Berwick Pratt and helped draw up the details. When it came time to break ground, the Cases enlisted help from friends and neighbours, including Bob Dawson, who had already built his own hex-grid house. Still,

Dennis Case (left), Bob Dawson, and Ron Thom discuss plans at the Case House construction site.

nothing could quite make up the extra time and money involved in crafting all those angles. Building on the hex grid meant cutting and assembling interesting but complicated new shapes. Their front door would be not a conventional rectangle but a trapezoid—and so would the floors, walls, interior stairs, countertops, and furniture.

Even something as basic as a window detail became a convoluted thing to construct. Its jambs, stiles, and casing all had to be carefully angled with a mitre saw. The rendering of them was arduous enough; their construction was even more daunting. "Nobody but a naval architect would do all the window mullions on a 30-60 grid," laughed Paul.

THE COUPLE eventually realized the risk and the cost of a genius artist like Ron: he worked at a level far above the ordinary cognitive skills of the average human. Even if they hauled and placed the lumber themselves, the Cases later acknowledged, Ron's plans required a lot more "thinking time" of the contractor. As construction progressed, their bank balances evaporated while an incredible house took shape, its angular framework nestling into the slopes like foliage.

Ron travelled out to West Vancouver and the Case House site in 1965, to help sort out the complications and clarify the design instructions. Molly gamely followed, even though she was now heavily pregnant with their first child together. Life would only get busier from there. The challenge of designing custom homes while overseeing the design of an entire university would be harsh enough. The geographic distance between client and architect in the pre-internet age made it nearly impossible at times.

Despite its complexity—or because of it—Ron continued to experiment with the honeycomb grid on more projects throughout the 1960s. For Ottawa clients Earl and June Lacharity, he drew up an exuberant combination of honeycomb and orthogonal grid, in which the floor plan evoked angular shards of wrapping paper bursting out of a gift box.[18] And for Phil and Mairi Narod, a husband-and-wife team of physicians living in the Vancouver suburb of White Rock, he designed a sprawling angular home on the shores of Boundary Bay.

As with the Cases, the honeycomb-grid clients inundated him with letters of concern about details, rising costs, and contractors' befuddlement. Often the best he could do was to promise an in-person site visit on his next trip to Vancouver. "Designing is such a struggle at the best of times," he wrote, "let alone when it's to do with something that exists three thousand miles away."[19]

The in-person visits remained crucial not only for client concerns but also to maintain his relationship with the TBP head office. Normally, he would fly out as early in the day as he could manage, and then take the overnight "red-eye" flight back to Toronto. Efficient for the schedule; exhausting for the body and mind.

Yet he continued to accept Vancouver commissions of all sizes, even small additions to previous house designs—and always for his coterie of treasured friends, for whom he charged little or nothing for his services.[20] And whenever possible, he agreed to be a guest speaker, visiting critic, design juror, or anything else—as long as it offered the opportunity to return to the West Coast.

As an artist-architect, Ron struggled continually with the norms of Toronto's intensely capitalist culture, as did the artisans he commissioned. In Vancouver of the 1950s, he worked directly with artists, metalworkers, woodworkers, and potters. In Toronto of the 1960s, he encountered a world of officiousness, in which paperwork and middlemen began encroaching upon the architect's domain.

The finishing details of Massey College created additional headaches. As the college neared completion, Vincent and Hart Massey harangued Ron frequently, and not always fairly, for delays and rising costs. The ceramic artist, John Reeve, haggled with Eaton's department store, which was contracted as the retail supplier and wanted its middleman's cut on everything—including Reeve's one-off lamps and ashtrays. "I do not consider myself a manufacturer or supplier of goods to the T. Eaton Company or any other department store," Reeve huffed to the Eaton's agent. "Presumably, if the architect had wanted factory-made pottery for Massey College, he would have ordered it from a factory."[21] As their correspondence grew more heated, Ron intervened to smooth things over.

"Vincent Massey," wrote Davies in his diary, "inveighs constantly against Ron, and I fear for Ron. He is dreadfully incompetent, dilatory and ill-organized, but he is an artist of capacity and should not be bullyragged."[22] In one of several irritating quibbles over money, Hart Massey sent a letter to Ron questioning the propriety of his invoice of $150 "in long-distance telephone calls, printing etc." that Ron had incurred while consulting with another firm about the project. "I am curious to know why the Foundation is being asked to pay for this," wrote Hart in the letter.

Ron responded by scrawling—in pen and across Hart's entire typewritten letter—a single word: *Bastard.*[23]

AFTER SOME DELIBERATION, the Massey family selected the motto for their new college. They had rejected a few proposals from incoming master Robertson Davies. Among others, Davies had proposed the spiritually pragmatic *Dilige, et quod vis fac* ("Love God, and you may do as you please") and the more cryptic *Tamquam scintillae in harundineto* ("As sparks in the reed bed"). The Masseys rejected both, no doubt to the relief of many, and settled on *Sapere aude*—"Dare to be wise."

Their concise Latin motto would expand into philosopher George Santayana's philosophy of happiness, to be embedded somehow in the dining hall. Allan Fleming worked with Ron to affix Santayana's entire seventy-two-word maxim into the wraparound frieze of the dining hall.

Fleming designed an original, gently curving font specifically for the adage, one that resembled his own personal handwriting very closely. His voluptuous calligraphy is positioned high, in a limestone frieze that runs the perimeter around three walls of the room, between the brickwork and the gridded clerestory lantern that would crown the entire space. On the two flanking walls, the quotation pauses at regular intervals where the room's columns soar up through the frieze and form part of the clerestory. The column-induced pauses give the quotation a sense of rhythm and actually make it more legible, like the bar lines in a musical score.

Its wraparound positioning requires not only tilting one's head to the heavens, but also rotating it a full 180 degrees in order to read to the end. This way, Santayana's directive is both literally and psycho-logically elevated:

> Happiness is impossible, and even inconceivable, to a mind with-out scope and without pause, a mind driven by craving, pleasure, or fear. To be happy, you must be reasonable, or you must be tamed. You must have taken the measure of your powers, tasted the fruits of your passion, and learned your place in the world and what things in it can really serve you. To be happy, you must be wise.

Of course, easier said than done.

Massey College courtyard, with Founding Master Robertson Davies and unidentified man.

TOP Massey College common room, the "living room" of the college.
BOTTOM Massey College Round Room, designed for thesis defences,
wherein a student would be surrounded by a semicircle of examiners.

14

THE
BIG TIME

AS RON SETTLED into his new life in Toronto, his relationship with the other TBP partners in Vancouver began to fray even more. He bristled at the paternal authority exerted by head office in Vancouver, and head office grew exasperated with the lax communication and disorganization of the Toronto satellite. Like an estranged couple who live apart but stay legally married out of duty and pragmatics, R.J. Thom & Associates and Thompson Berwick Pratt maintained a legal union during Ron's early years in Toronto, but each side knew the relationship had to end sooner or later.

He began his slow disentanglement from the mother firm. Ron Thom the Artist had to transform into Ron Thom the Entrepreneur—seeking out his own projects, managing a growing staff, and much else. He had to learn new rules: which clubs to join, what people to meet, what protocol to follow. The way of doing business was much more officious than what he had been used to. In Vancouver, he had been a big fish in a small pond. Now, in Toronto, it seemed he was a big fish in an ocean.

R.J. Thom & Associates soon expanded again, so that it comprised the two upper floors of 47 Colborne Street, while John Andrews spread his practice more fully over the floor below. John

Andrews had entrenched his celebrity among architects with the 1966 completion of Scarborough College. And John C. Parkin's pristine, white, orthogonal architecture proliferated in and around Toronto, a visual and ideological contrast to both Ron Thom and John Andrews.

In a 1956 professional journal, John C. asserted that "the architect's role in the future will require the closest collaboration with all the other specialists participating in the building process—engineers, builders, and economists."[1] As for artists, John C. didn't even find them worthy of mention, while Ron considered them essential collaborators. Ron laid out his own counterpoint in a 1962 essay in *Canadian Architect*, "The architect, in proposing a building, makes a choice—an imaginative choice which outstrips the facts."[2] This would not be a credo that any sharp-pencilled economist or engineer would care to embrace.

John C.'s artfulness manifested itself not through enlisting artists but in taking care to create his unadorned architecture with beautiful proportions and precise detailing. His sleek, spare minimalism—exemplified in the Don Valley headquarters of Bata Ltd. and the white cubic volumes of the Art Gallery of Ontario—contrasted dramatically with Ron's organic approach. John C. embraced rectilinearity; Ron favoured the oblique and idiosyncratic. John C. restricted his palette to black and white; Ron excelled at using colour in architecture and specifically informed his staff to avoid black and white.

Even on a personal level, John C. Parkin and Ron Thom projected a study in contrasts. Ron favoured nubby, earth-toned tweed jackets and ties; Parkin unfailingly wore black pants, white shirt, and black tie. Ron arranged his retreating hairline into a straggly combover; Parkin pomaded his thatch of black hair into a neat whorl. Ron festooned both his home and his office with hanging plants and raw cedar; Parkin's home and office both resembled elegant white-and-black machines, with careful placement of each of their small number of interior objects.[3] And in both cases, the architecture reflected the man.

Despite their starkly opposite design aesthetic, the two men periodically met up with each other at the King Eddy, for conversations that sometimes lingered well into the afternoon and beyond.[4] Every year around Christmastime, the two architects convened for a long round of martinis. Though not overtly a competition, the unspoken challenge was to outdrink and outlast the other, although by the time they staggered out into the street, victory would be moot.

Among engineering firms, the city's most prominent team in the eyes of most architects was the Yolles Partnership. Ron would get to know Morden Yolles and his partner Roland Bergmann through their position as the main civil engineers of the Trent University campus. That, in turn, led to Morden inviting Ron to his home for dinners and commissioning him to renovate part of his Beaux-Arts mansion in Rosedale. It was a ridiculously small job for an architect of Ron's stature, and Ron himself made it even smaller by refusing Morden's request to remove the home's original crown mouldings and cornices. Morden had wanted a more contemporary look, but Ron explained that they spoke to their time and formed part of the mansion's original character.

When Morden tried to praise Ron's penchant for artistry, it backfired. "I said to Ron, 'I really like the way you embellish your work,'" he recalled. "At that, he got so furious, I thought he was going to punch me! I probably should have said 'articulated.' But I said 'embellished.'"[5]

Ron had long struggled with clarifying the crucial difference between the two concepts. He ascribed to Frank Lloyd Wright's concept of ornament as an integral element of the architecture, embedded within it like a pattern or texture—not tacked on, hence his aversion to the word "embellish." Deep overhangs, fine millwork, interlocking wood members, craggy stone fireplaces, centrifugal plans, a sense of rootedness in the earth: these are the features that Wright employed to create beauty, and which Ron embraced in turn.

Wright himself described ornament as "an element so hard to understand that modern architects themselves seem to understand it least well of all and most of them have turned against it with such fury as is born only of impotence."[6] Architects bereft of artistic talent could copy an International Style building much more easily than a Frank Lloyd Wright building. And it would be the same for Ron's work. For better and worse, a Ron Thom structure would always be one of a kind.

Ron's associates at 47 Colborne were struck by his distinctive approach—how he could feel his way around a project, "coming at it from a direction none of us would have thought of," recalled Peter Smith, who revered Ron's mode of thinking. In one of his characteristically impromptu analyses, Ron summed up a window's shortcomings by wiggling two fingers above his brow and declaring, "Needs an eyebrow."[7] He rarely offered a strictly rational explanation for his decisions; usually, he decided by way of gut feeling.

His new home base seemed both exciting and terrifying. More architects to bond with, and more to compete with. Bigger projects, bigger overhead. High society, high social expectations. Young idealists loved Ron's informal West Coast spirit, but the more highly polished Toronto establishment tended to look askance at his casual demeanour and his rumpled wool ties.[8]

WHILE STILL WRESTLING with post-occupancy fixes at Massey College, Ron plunged into the epic job of designing the new standalone campus of Trent University on the outskirts of Peterborough. In mid-October, Ron secured funding from the university for a scouting trip to New England to view some new campus architecture. One building truly stood out in his mind: Ezra Stiles College at Yale University. Designed by Eero Saarinen, the building exuded all the geometric elegance that characterized the Finnish-American architect's work. What struck Ron the most, however, was its cladding: it looked something like the stonework of the old farm buildings he had seen in the hills of the Trent Valley. And yet this Saarinen building projected a sense of the contemporary. The cladding was, and is, in fact, concrete—the same material that many had come to loathe for its austerity and ubiquity. Saarinen had embedded the concrete surface with pebbles and stones, to create a mixture called rubble aggregate. The huge expanses of wall would continue to evoke warmth and craftwork and eternity, as though they had been built a thousand years ago and would still be standing a thousand years from now.

Ron had found his defining material for Trent University.

Now he needed a stellar group of architects to help him realize his vision.

BY 1967, it had become clear to all that the complexity and enormous scale of the Trent project required a satellite office near the campus site. To lead the new Peterborough operation, Ron sought out his stalwart former associate Dick Sai-Chew. After leaving Thompson Berwick Pratt in 1960, Dick had moved to Montreal to work as a staff architect at CBC. Ron beseeched Dick to join him at R.J. Thom & Associates, and, after a few months of hesitation, he agreed to join Ron's team.[9]

Ron had also given a standing job offer to Paul Merrick, although Paul had just begun a year of travel with his then-wife. But the opportunity to work with the designer of that West Vancouver house that had lured Paul into architecture in the first place? Irresistible. After negotiating a delayed arrival with Ron, Paul finally joined the team and plunged into the work of creating Trent University.

RON DREW UP the basic master plan of the campus with the most primordial geometry: three overlapping circles on one side of the river, with a segment crossing the water to connect them to a fourth circle on the other side. Each circle corresponded to a zone for one of the main campus colleges; the segment connecting them would be a pedestrian bridge.

The initial work, however, involved transforming several existing buildings in downtown Peterborough. These would be the interim university buildings, which could open in time to serve the university's first students in the fall of 1964. The rest of the campus would take the better part of a decade to design and build. The renovations created Rubidge Hall, the interim university's main building; Catharine Parr Traill College, for women; and Peter Robinson College, for men. While the firm swiftly refurbished and retrofitted these, Ron Thom began conjuring up the future campus layout north of town, and the flagship university building: Champlain College.

He kept Tom Symons involved with his ideas as he went along. As soon as Ron picked up a pencil and started drawing, Symons felt that he was watching a certain kind of genius at work, one who expressed his thoughts in images rather than words. "He would draw freehand, and with just a few strokes of a pen, he would precisely conceptualize something I couldn't even imagine," recalled Symons. "It was breathtaking."[10]

Following Thom's schematic design, architect Paul Barnard laid out the rooms of the master's residence and the dorm rooms of Champlain College. Ron's critique: "We've got to have a better view for them."[11] He urged Barnard to try to get as many views toward the river as possible—for the students, an end-user group that Ron prioritized as much or more than the university's top brass.

Molly Thom also came on board to work alongside her husband. The skills and sensibilities she had honed through working with Allan Fleming made her a natural fit to help select and oversee the interior design and furniture logistics.

Ron assigned architect Paul Martel the responsibility for wood furniture built-in or designed in-house. Martel drew up basic dining tables, chairs, counters, and side tables. Drawing up a typical

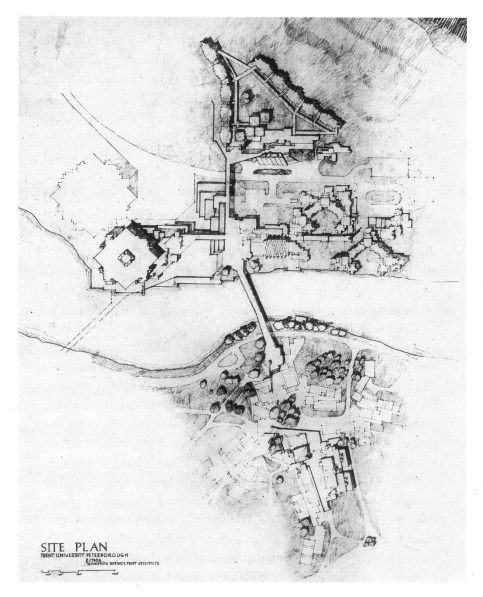

SITE PLAN
TRENT UNIVERSITY PETERBOROUGH
R.J.THOM
THOMPSON BERWICK PRATT ARCHITECTS

Pencil rendering of the master plan for Trent University's main campus.
Clockwise from top: Lady Eaton College, Champlain College, Science Complex
(across the river), and Bata Library (centre left).

table design, Martel would fashion a straightforward 90-degree-angle corner. And then Ron would come by Martel's drafting table and instruct him where to apply strips of wood veneer, and to cut a small square out of each tabletop corner. "Makes a shadow," Ron explained, with a click of his tongue for emphasis.[12]

Alastair Grant was named project architect for Lady Eaton College, and also helped draw up the Thomas J. Bata Library with architects Paul Barnard and Bill Lett. Yolles Partnership came on board as the project's main engineer.

For the university's main complex—Champlain College—Ron designated himself as the principal designer. This would be the most important part of the campus: the main dormitory wings, the dining hall, the administrative and seminar rooms, the conference room, and the master's residence. The look and feel of Trent would be defined more by this series of buildings than any other part of the campus.

Even with the nominal "principal designers" allotted for each building, authorship remained hybrid and fluid from early conception to completion—with one architect conjuring up an early scheme, and then handing it over to another for design development, and then a third architect for design details, and a fourth for working drawings, all under Ron's oversight. This kind of sequential collaboration is typical and appropriate for buildings of this scale. But problematically for all, the entire project began to lag behind schedule.

The delays were inevitable. Ron was simultaneously juggling the massive responsibilities of Trent with many other smaller projects that he couldn't seem to refuse. His ambitious architecture required more time and money than expected, and much more than government and university bureaucrats were willing to offer. And on the home front, he and Molly were in the exultant but exhausting throes of welcoming their first child together, a baby girl they called Emma.

Ron wrote a letter to his father, pouring out his frustrations about his burgeoning workload and other life issues, and letting him know that he'd be coming to Vancouver the next month to visit him. Now retired, James Thom had concluded his working life as a partner of a successful sheet metal manufacturing business. Like his woodworking grandfather John, his stonemason father George, and his architect son Ron, James Thom had earned his living contributing to the built environment. It was a career bereft of the artisanship of his son and forefathers, though. James Thom had devoted his working life to the profitable business of producing cold, hard steel—one of Ron's least favourite materials.

The car crash that had killed Elena still weighed heavily on James Thom's body and mind. In his letter back to Ron, he described his double vision and limited mobility resulting from his collision-related injuries.

> It will be two years next Monday when we had our accident. And it doesn't make me feel good to think about it and I keep asking WHY it should have happened.

Ron's sister Heather was now married and living in California, but his father managed with the full-time help of his other daughter, Mavis, who cooked and cleaned for their father.

About his illustrious son's growing prestige and the correlated stress and overwork, James Thom had just this to say:

> As I sit by idly watching the human race I wonder what it is all about and I doubt the prize is worth the effort. Are matters of more importance being passed up en route? Life is short at best and I doubt if material gain measures up to what I consider a full life.

If Ron had written to his father in the hopes of getting back a word of sympathy, praise, or affection like his late mother used to offer, he must have been disappointed. His father's densely typed three-page letter largely detailed his own minor grievances. Among other complaints, he griped about the frequent haggling with Mavis, who expected more pay for the daily housework she did for him.

And then he signed off:

> Well we will be looking forward to seeing you soon and hope you will be able to find a solution for the work overload.
>
> Fawcett's T.V. repairman has just arrived. The picture blanked out last night. That is after my having paid him $93.40 to have it repaired just over a month ago. You can't win.
>
> Best wishes from Dad.[13]

Back in Ontario, the toil of Trent continued, with Ron's architects struggling to get their projects back on schedule while producing thousands of meticulously rendered hand-drawings and details. The working atmosphere was sometimes chaotic but mostly congenial, with each team member moving in and out of various roles in creating the new university.

By the time Lady Eaton College was drawn up, Alastair was designing the central core while Bill worked almost simultaneously on the working drawings that would go out to tender. "Not normal, and a very difficult and frustrating experience," recalled Bill, "especially since Ron decided at the last minute to change all the windows from metal to wood."[14] Why the expensive last-minute change? Ron didn't offer a reason.

AT TRENT, Denis Smith and Tom Symons did their best to help Ron, defending his work to the bureaucrats and the accounting departments, and monitoring things to ensure nothing went off the rails for long. Apprehension grew among Ron's colleagues as to whether he could carry out such a huge and complex undertaking, especially as the months passed without any sign of the design for the signature building, Champlain College.

When the presentation drawings for Champlain were unveiled, their fears dissolved into awe. A huge and highly detailed hand-coloured drawing projected its monumental beauty. The massive 8′×20′ axonometric rendering, done with the assistance of Paul Barnard and his team, still adorns one of the common rooms at Trent.[15]

LIKE MASSEY COLLEGE, Champlain College defies categorization. The dining hall has turrets, buttressed walls, and slot windows, like a medieval castle. The interconnected dormitory buildings display a series of vertical and horizontal planes that look like a cubist painting, anchored by a bell tower at its centre. And along the riverside south wall, Ron had designed an arcade, for students to walk in shelter, with the college's stone wall on one side and the Otonabee River on the other—inside and outside at the same time.

Neither the stone-stippled planks of the bell tower nor the inverted-peak turrets look like anything built in history, or modernity. It was as though the architect had appreciated all that is logical and loved about turrets, buttresses, arcades, and bell towers—and interpreted those elements with a thoroughly modern sensibility.

Champlain College would be the sole campus building for which Ron Thom served as principal designer. His design was so beautiful that it set a near-impossible standard. Meanwhile, the campus library's initial design disappointed Ron. His design team had made a preliminary design of a rather generic, three-storey square building, its central core stuffed with service rooms and mechanicals, and its stacks lining the perimeter. It would be built on a section of riverbank that jutted out like a small peninsula, and Ron knew it would be one of the most visually prominent structures of the entire campus.

Barnard then left the firm and Ron asked Paul Merrick to take over work on the library. Merrick, studying the blocky and inefficient form of the initial conceptual design, saw a way to bring more volume onto the compact site—he imagined one cube inscribed within a second cube, and then rotated one of the squares to create a block with triangular masses jutting out of each of its four facades, creating unique architectural interfaces. Essentially, he pulled all

Drawing of Trent University campus architecture by Bob Montgomery, showing Faryon Bridge and Bata Library.

the library spaces which had been initially located at the centre of the solid cube and placed them around the perimeter of the building, creating an open atrium-courtyard in the process. These projections would make the rear facade of the library appear to float over the water.

Paul then worked with engineer Roland Bergmann of the Yolles Partnership on one of most defining forms of the campus: the Reginald Faryon Bridge. The bridge was to arc across the river, uniting the two halves of the campus. Ron knew how important its visual presence would be. He told Morden Yolles his most important criterion: to ensure that it doesn't look like it was designed by an engineer.

Paul and Roland worked collaboratively to devise a support system that would work with the curve of the Otonabee River. They designed the abutments as parabolic curves, which would look dramatic and also make structural sense. Architect Barry Griblin, whom Paul had recently recruited from Vancouver, then designed

Paul Merrick's rendering of his Chemistry Building design for Trent.

the upper zone of the bridge, echoing the parabolic forms below with a balustrade whose gentle curvilinearity would evoke a contemporary *art nouveau*.[16]

The more prosaic task of walking across the bridge from one class to the next would later prove challenging in winter months, when ice sheathed its convex surface. Ron, a seasoned veteran of mild West Coast winters, didn't foresee the extra time that students and faculty would require to travel from one campus building to another on icy pathways. "The reality of climate in central Canada is something that he had to live and learn about," acknowledged Symons.[17]

In the end, and to this day, the Faryon Bridge does indeed follow Symons's directive—"a bridge that students could write songs about, sing songs about, and make love on for a thousand years"—in addition to its workaday function of getting students across the river. Even though the bridge came to fruition by Paul Merrick and Roland Bergmann applying structural logic, it's also a thing of beauty, following Ron's directive.

As much as Ron instructed and inspired others, he had his own educational touchstones. One evening during the design of Trent,

The master's residence (now Alumni House), part of Trent University's Champlain College, clad in aggregate concrete.

he invited Paul over to his Washington Avenue apartment to unwind on the rooftop deck. Over a bottle of Rémy Martin, he spoke with Paul for hours about their personal evolutions as architects. Ron's animosity with Ned Pratt had festered for several years after the B.C. Electric credit tussle. But now he had come to appreciate that he had learned a lot from his onetime boss and mentor, more than he had realized. Ron had always recognized Jack Shadbolt and Bert Binning as his early teachers. Ned had an impact of a different sort, he told Paul. "He's the kind who leads you to an understanding, teaching you in such a way that you're not even aware of being taught."[18]

The next day, rather bleary-eyed, they headed back to 47 Colborne for the morass of work still to be done on Trent University. The biggest—and most expensive—challenge turned out to be the application of the rubble aggregate—that cladding he had seen when he visited Ezra Stiles College at Yale. This kind of job needed more than intuition; it required science and patience. The design and construction team spent weeks learning to perfect the technique of applying the semisolid cladding in a way that would ensure its proper drying and curing.

They had to figure out the precise ratios of rubble to cement to lime for strength and endurance, and then had to quickly scrape off the top layer of concrete to expose the rubble aggregate—while the concrete was partly set but not yet hardened. It turned out to be a process that was time-consuming, exhausting, and expensive—with shockingly beautiful results.[19]

A modern version of a medieval stone village, the rubble aggregate did not look or behave like the concrete now commonplace in construction everywhere. "I hate concrete!" Ron would tell colleagues.[20] "When it rains, the buildings look like they're crying." But Trent's rubble aggregate doesn't "cry" in the rain; the drops wick off the rubble naturally.

The decade-long Trent project made for a much more complicated and headache-inducing project than Ron had ever taken on.

Champlain College, Trent University.

Although Tom Symons had championed Ron from the start and thereinafter, his authority was not as singular as that wielded by Vincent Massey or Dal Grauer on their respective building projects. Ron had to answer to a series of committees. He wasn't used to so much intrusion in his design process, and he hated it.

As construction of Champlain College and the adjoining master's residence neared completion, Trent's cost consultants sounded the alarm on the skyrocketing construction bills. Champlain College *alone* cost seven million dollars to build—close to fifty million today—and was the most expensive public building in Ontario history up to that point.[21] The heavy timber beams, handcrafted cedar lanterns, ubiquitous fireplaces, and especially the rubble-aggregate all devoured the budget.

Ron Thom had planned for every building to be clad in that same textured concrete. As the provincial government money stream dried up, the Trent brass vetoed the rubble aggregate for the remaining buildings, prompting the team to replace it with conventional concrete cladding. The university brass also cut back the original plan for twelve residential colleges, an on-campus art gallery, and a museum. More budget-slashing followed, halting Merrick's sciences complex in mid-construction. Only the Chemistry Building would be completed.

The cuts and compromises infuriated Ron, as did the endless red tape and second-guessing of so many design decisions. He poured out his frustrations to friends and colleagues.[22] Denis Smith shared some of Ron's frustrations. He had known Trent's construction would be expensive, but they had considered it an investment for the future. *Damn it, Canada is a rich country*, thought Smith. *And we should be building for the ages, not just for the next ten years.*[23]

Thus far, Trent has endured over fifty years and seems like it has been there for a millennium. Walking now through the dormitory sections to the master's residence at Trent,[24] one gets the same sensation Ron had intended for Massey College: of unveiling itself a little at a time, and never completely. The planes of grey seem to move as you walk through and past them. Thick stone-and-concrete walls, buttresses outside the dining hall, diamond-shaped skylights poking above the roofline, the bell tower—all evocative of a medieval hamlet, abstracted into a contemporary form.

Inside each of the common rooms and many of the residential rooms are hearths—built to be real, working fireplaces. Their inclusion completes the idea of Champlain College as "homey," though they quickly proved too difficult to operate and maintain properly. They have been sealed up ever since, and yet their physical presence still evokes a sense of home.

Champlain College, dining hall ceiling.

In a final touch, Ron specified artist-designed ceramic ashtrays for the students' quarters and common rooms at Trent, commissioning Calgary potter Ed Drahanchuk. Just like the handcrafted ashtrays at Massey College, the handmade Trent ashtrays vanished from the dorms and common rooms within a couple of years. They were beautiful while they lasted.

A hundred metres away, the serpentine design of Lady Eaton College came to fruition, with bare concrete walls which have their own rustic, authentic charm.

Despite the restrictions and compromises and functional glitches, Trent opened to a flurry of laudatory reviews and adoration from both local and international publications. As well as copious covers in the national shelter magazines, *Time* magazine gushed over it. And in a rare accolade for a Canadian project, Trent graced the cover and a twelve-page editorial in the September 1969 edition of New York–based *Architectural Record*. From the journal's critique:

> There is a reminder of Frank Lloyd Wright in this architecture which cannot be overlooked. The reminders come in the material of large aggregate selected from the region and placed and exposed in the concrete; in the insistent horizontal bandings which carry consistently through the vertical elements, becoming broad cantilevered overhangs in places, which hug the ground. There is the pinwheeling of groups of rooms in plan about some dominant vertical stair tower or chimney; or the careful, studied tiers of similar forms in elevation, composed to reach a peak, a crescendo, and subside again in preparation for the next ascent.[25]

Back in his own country, Ron's admirers and even his rivals enthused about the new university. In *Canadian Interiors*, Arthur Erickson praised Trent's collection of buildings as having "everything going for it to become a landmark." The brilliance of the Trent plan lay in its siting, noted Erickson:

Thom removed the university from the banks of the river and rather put the river back into the heart of the university, so that banks would not dilute the direct contrast of the buildings with the river. The river becomes the core of the university—the counterpart of the dialogue to which the university responds joyfully with bridges, terraces, rising steps and walks, and the marvelous play of reflections.

Erickson noted ominously in conclusion, "One hopes that other architects that may be commissioned to design other colleges on the periphery of the campus will have sufficient sensitivity to the quality already established. But Thom himself is the only one who can see and make real his special vision."[26]

FOR TRENT'S future expansions, the four-bubble master plan offered wide flexibility rather than codified rules, to allow subsequent architects their creative freedom. Their primary directive would be to follow Ron Thom's approach of deferring to the river valley site. This didn't always happen.

By the time Ron and his team had finished the original campus, public and corporate patronage of architecture across the country had transitioned to a more businesslike model, with every design decision now subject to scrutiny by a board of directors.

The devaluing of the kind of intuitive architecture practised by Ron would later prompt even Ned Pratt to defend him, despite their longstanding feud. Years later, Pratt told the *Globe and Mail* that "Thom and Merrick are the only two architects Canada has ever spawned who design from the neck down. They have an Elizabethan mix of heart and mind. I'm sick to death of architecture from the neck up."[27]

15

HIGH FLYING

UPON THE 1952 provincial election, and for the next twenty years, British Columbia fell under the rule of the Social Credit government of W.A.C. Bennett—"Wacky" Bennett, as he was called by admirers and detractors alike. Bennett promised to ramp up the B.C. economy by constructing massive hydroelectric dams, long highways, and big buildings. To this end, he installed a fiery pro-development Minister of Public Works named Philip Gaglardi, later nicknamed "Flying Phil" both for the speeding tickets he amassed while zooming down those new highways, and for his hard-core habit of buying and using government aircraft.[1] (Gaglardi often boasted that when pulled over on the highway for speeding, he would flash his pilot's licence to traffic police, asserting that he wasn't driving too fast; he was flying too low.)

Ron Thom and his entire architectural cohort benefited from the pro-development charge of this new government, their client base fired up by the burgeoning resource economy and the slopes of newly cleared and wired lots throughout British Columbia. Trees, mountains, and rivers made the province beautiful—but clear-cutting, mining, and damming made the people rich enough to create architecture with splendid views of the remaining trees, mountains, and rivers.

Like Ontario, B.C. directed a chunk of its growing wealth to university buildings. In 1962, the University of British Columbia's architectural school finally moved out of its military huts and into the newly completed Frederic Lasserre Building, designed by TBP and named after the school's founding director, who had died the year before.

While the UBC campus continued to fill in with new buildings, almost all designed by TBP, the biggest event in university architecture transpired atop a mountain in the Vancouver suburb of Burnaby. Arthur Erickson and Geoff Massey had suddenly catapulted to fame, winning the competition to design Simon Fraser University.

Their scheme exemplified the primordial difference between the design ethos of Arthur Erickson and Ron Thom. On Burnaby Mountain, Arthur followed the conceptual model of Cairo's thousand-year-old Al-Azhar University, where the street life thrums noisily under the latticed windows of the dormitories, and passersby can stroll in and out of the campus, intermingling with the students.[2] Although there are few such *flâneurs* atop of Burnaby Mountain, it does imbue a visitor with a sense of external connection. If you stand in the courtyard of Erickson's Convocation Mall, the columned walls are placed to frame in a window-like fashion a jaw-dropping cinematic view of the snow-capped North Shore mountains. The mountains are over fifteen miles away, but you almost feel as though you can reach out over three entire municipalities and touch them with your bare hands.

At Massey College, Ron had taken the opposite approach, celebrating the sense of being inside and *protected* from the world. He cocooned the students in small rooms and divided larger common rooms into smaller intimate zones. And at Trent University, at which he was now immersed, he would do the same. He believed that this would be more conducive to contemplation and human connection.

In the most reductive terms, Arthur favoured openness, and Ron craved enclosure. It was an approach that both men seemed predetermined to take, always. Arthur, an extrovert in his personal life, designed houses, buildings, and university campuses the same way: as porous structures that would make great gathering places for dozens or hundreds of people. Ron, an introvert, designed the same kind of structures with a similar level of artistry but an overtly inward approach, for much smaller gatherings—or solitude. Arthur created piazzas and party places; Ron created havens.

Still, the two architects did share some primordial values, above all a strong appreciation of nature and its integration with architecture. Ron praised this aspect in his review of Simon Fraser University in *Canadian Forum*. "The natural environment of the mountainside develops into a man-made one most subtly," wrote Ron. "Emerging though a cleft in the trees, one first sees the edges of the playing-field terraces and then, upon sweeping around these gigantic earth forms, the first glimpse of the buildings appearing as a delicate crown, inseparable from the top of the mountain... The whole composition does not just sit on the mountain top, but becomes a part of it, extending quite naturally and easily down the slopes on either side."[3]

THE DESIGN and construction of the Trent campus had sprawled over a decade, with the flagship buildings under construction throughout the latter half of the 1960s. By 1970, Ron Thom had become an eminent speaker on university design. He presented a paper at the International College and University Conference and Exposition in Atlantic City with a surprisingly candid update. As everyone in the audience would have known or suspected, governments were losing their appetite for bankrolling the high construction costs of universities. The present rethink of free spending was "long overdue," Ron conceded. As the presentation pointed out, "lower income groups pay a disproportionate share of the cost of public higher education, while middle and higher-income groups derive a disproportionate share of the benefits."[4]

The Atlantic City conference paper unpacked a thoroughly candid assessment. For instance, the use of aggregate concrete at Yale and Trent had been expected to serve as a paradigm of a beautiful and economically feasible building method. That didn't happen. Pouring crushed stone into the formwork of partially set concrete walls turned out to be much too expensive, much too time-consuming, and much too difficult to get right. So did a number of the planning assumptions that were made at the outset. Modifications to the original designs would be required in several areas as the campuses developed.

"When looked at honestly, though," concluded Ron, "North American campuses on the whole are a pretty dreary lot, even if most were built in the good old ivy-covered days of academic and architectural affluence."

While Ron grappled with the epic Trent project throughout the 1960s, other demands on his talent and time surged in. The staff was often in flux as a slew of young designers streamed on and off the payroll. Sometimes a new graduate would just show up at the office entrance, and Ron would often take him in. Some architects and draftsmen would stay a few years before leaving for more financially reliable opportunities in conventional firms, or for a more tranquil boss. Others turned out not to have the skill that architecture of Ron's standards required. But despite his legendary temper, Ron had no appetite for firing people, so he usually delegated that task to others.[5]

As the office staff grew, Ron floundered at the overwhelming task of running the firm. He exemplified the so-called Peter Principle: a person of brilliance who is continually promoted until he rises to a level beyond his competence. Ron was an excellent designer, and a lousy manager.

Ron had convinced TBP to let one of their top managers, Bob Mutrie, relocate to Toronto in 1967 and help him sort out the office structure and growth plan. The actual corporate structure of the Vancouver and Toronto offices remained ambiguous; despite the

firm name emblazoned on their
stationery and business cards—
R.J. Thom & Associates—the
staff at 47 Colborne Street in
Toronto still received their paycheques from 1553 Robson Street
in Vancouver.

The years leading up to Canada's one-hundredth birthday
proved exciting and lucrative to
many in the building industry,
including architects. Expo 67,
the World's Fair slated to take
place on Notre Dame Island built
just off downtown Montreal,
would coincide with the centennial year. The federal government

Paul Merrick, c. 1972.

saw the publicity value of architecture and shared in the party spirit,
opening its wallet for creative—if temporary—architecture across
the sprawling Expo site.

R.J. Thom & Associates won commissions to design five zones of
shops, restaurants, displays, and bandstands. Unfortunately, as Ron
wrote to clients-turned-friends Dennis and Adele Case, "We have
absolutely inhuman deadlines. Expo is a mad, mad place—an 'Alice
in Wonderland' world that is quite unrealistic and which gives no
quarter to anyone involved in it."[6]

For the display pavilion of the Polymer Corporation, a federal-
government-owned manufacturer of synthetic rubber, Ron tapped
Paul Merrick as the design lead. His pavilion design turned out to be
extraordinary: a sculptural, free-form shape that presaged the kind
of amorphous architecture of the late 1990s, when architects had
access to computers and the new CAD (computer-aided design) soft-
·ware that could help them achieve such ethereal shapes. Merrick
had no computer and no CAD software. He had his pencil, his reams

of drawing paper, and his imagination. He designed a free-form pavilion that at certain angles evoked a seashell or, at other angles, the wings of an insect—and, of course, the concept of elasticity, rubber's main attribute.

Peter Smith, who was one of Ron's most reliable architects, worked with engineer Roland Bergmann of the Yolles Partnership to devise reinforcing rods to support this magical form that was more sculpture than structure. "Ron didn't have a lot of confidence in other people designing anything, but once Paul came over from B.C., you realized there was a connection there," recalled Smith.[7] Paul Merrick's designs looked different from Ron's—more curvilinear and fantastical. But like Ron, Paul designed by intuition, moving his pencil wherever it wanted to go, until the sketch felt right to him.

Later in 1967, a University of Toronto math professor named Don Fraser hired Ron to design a home for himself and his wife Judith, on a spectacular site on the slopes of Rosedale Valley. Don Fraser was just twenty-nine and already wealthy, in part from textbook royalties, and offered him a construction budget of $85,000—an astronomical sum at the time.

Ron began the project in his usual way, with a gestural sketch. Drowning in other obligations, Ron transferred the project to Paul Merrick. "Ron just handed me a scribble one day and said, 'I haven't got time to do this; do you want to do it?'" recalled Paul.

Paul took the scribble and played around with it in his mind. The initial scheme required just a house and garage, rather tightly wound up. "I pulled it apart like a piece of toffee and created this walkway along the edge of the green. Pushed it out over the edge of the cliff, over the ravine." Inside, he designed a sinuous central stairway that would be the nucleus, from which the rooms and walls of the house would radiate.[8] The scribble morphed into a sculpture whose coiled heart leads into an arcaded linear artery.

Midway through the design, Don Fraser separated from his wife, and the design brief suddenly transformed into a bachelor's house. The kitchen and bathrooms changed three times, but the essential

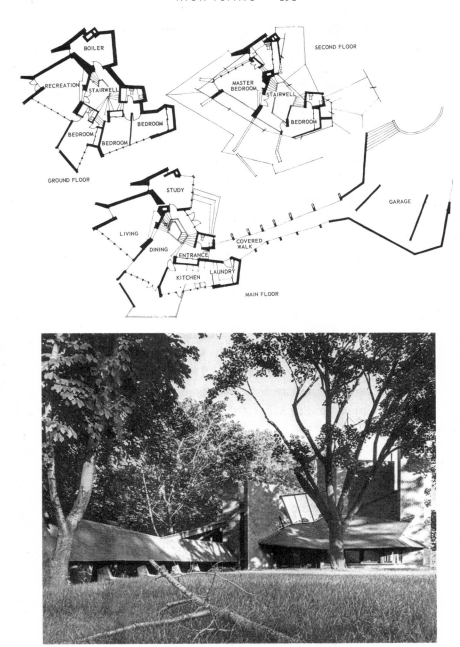

BOILER

RECREATION STAIRWELL

BEDROOM BEDROOM BEDROOM

GROUND FLOOR

SECOND FLOOR

MASTER BEDROOM STAIRWELL

BEDROOM

STUDY

LIVING

DINING

ENTRANCE

KITCHEN LAUNDRY

COVERED WALK

GARAGE

MAIN FLOOR

The Fraser Residence, Toronto.

scheme of a home that radiated outward like a kind of web-legged starfish—that stayed intact. The house became an instant landmark upon its completion, a destination for design students and aficionados then and now.

It's usually described as a "Ron Thom" design, with little or no mention of Merrick's key role. But unlike Ron's squabble with Ned over the B.C. Electric Building, this time neither architect cared much who received credit for it, according to Paul: "Ron said to me once, 'You know, when I started out in architecture, it seemed like the guys above me always got the credit for work that I'd done. And now it seems that I'm getting all the credit for work that others have done.' I've got to say, that's turned out to be the case in my life too."[9]

That same year, Fraser published *The Structure of Inference*, an important textbook for the field. By this time, the mathematician had befriended Ron and Brian Kilpatrick, the other Thom Partnership architect who had assisted with the design. When Ron and Brian[10] saw the book jacket's initial conservative blue cover, they suggested a visual overhaul; the book launched with Ron's Wrightian colours: earthen burgundy and Hopi white—a striking departure in the conservative, mostly monochromatic world of statistics textbooks. In a more obscure sense, the allied-arts ethos persisted.

IN 1970, after years of haggling over money and power and protocol, R.J. Thom & Associates and Thompson Berwick Pratt finally made their separation legally official. Several of Ron's Toronto associates bought into the satellite-turned-independent office, and it became officially known as the Thom Partnership. And like many collapsed marriages, the breakup sparked a firestorm of confusion and divided loyalties. One of the biggest complications would be how to carry forward what many expected to be the firm's next landmark: the future British Columbia Government Centre in Vancouver.

Conceived in 1968 by Bennett's Social Credit government, this massive new complex would transform the entire city. The site: three blocks in the heart of downtown Vancouver. On the northernmost block stood the existing 1911 neoclassical Vancouver Courthouse, designed by Sir Francis Rattenbury. The Government Centre would reconfigure the site to accommodate a new larger and modern provincial courthouse, an office tower for government services, and a large civic square.

The need for a new provincial courthouse and government centre had become imperative several years earlier. Both had outgrown their respective compact buildings on Georgia Street. That, combined with the city's need to densify, compelled the Community Arts Council to commission a conceptual study of downtown Vancouver, including the Courthouse area. They enlisted Arthur Erickson, Geoff Massey, and their associate Bruno Freschi to study ways of adding density and modernity. Tall buildings promised both, but Vancouverites remained wary of them, in many cases worried—quite reasonably—that a proliferation of towers would occlude their beloved mountain views. The architects devised a scheme that played to both sides: at the core of the two-block Courthouse site, a sixty-five-foot tower—which, Bruno argued, could also be turned on its side, for low-rise density. A horizontal tower, in effect.

Bennett wasn't interested in any horizontal schemes. A decade earlier, in his first term as premier, he had seen how the B.C. Electric Building had become an urban landmark and entrenched Dal Grauer's legacy. Now Bennett wanted to erect a building of unprecedented height. And what better choice of architects than the authors of that other landmark high-rise?

The B.C. government then anointed an architectural joint venture team of Thompson Berwick Pratt and McCarter & Nairne, another major Vancouver firm. The lead designer, the government stipulated, would be Ron Thom.

They aimed to break ground in time for the 1972 provincial election, a vote that was expected to extend the Socreds' twenty-year-long reign even further. They ordered the architects to make it tall—fifty-five storeys, to be precise. That directive would make it taller than any building in the city: more than twice as tall as the seventeen-storey Hotel Vancouver and twenty-two-storey B.C. Electric Building. It would be the second-tallest building in the country, after the fifty-six-storey TD Centre in Toronto.

Behind the scenes, the split of Ron from the mother firm created problems. McCarter & Nairne and TBP could see the project through on their own—Ned Pratt would make sure of that, and insisted that TBP remain the joint venture partner, as per their contract. Paul Merrick, who had moved back to the TBP headquarters in Vancouver, would serve as the creative mind on its team. But the government wanted Ron Thom on the job somehow—as its chief architect, George Giles, made clear.

Giles rejigged the job into a three-firm joint venture, giving Ron Thom the title of Design Coordinator. Ron flew to Vancouver at semi-regular intervals, but the demands of running the Toronto office engulfed him. He couldn't make it to many key meetings—nor was he always in a clear frame of mind for the ones he did attend.

Meanwhile, the rest of the team drew up plans for a fifty-five-storey tower with a huge twenty-thousand-square-foot footprint. Following W.A.C. Bennett's directives, it would be so tall and slick that it would lord over the city like a giant rectilinear finger, a starkly modern obelisk.

Absolutely the bloody wrong building in the wrong place with the wrong personality for its purpose, thought Merrick. The law courts didn't need that much space, and it made no sense to concentrate retail government services like driver's licence renewals in the most expensive downtown real estate. The construction costs would spike enormously after twenty-some storeys, so there was no financial justification. The B.C. premier, concluded Paul, just wanted to build a *shtoinker*—Paul's term for any ego-driven, illogically tall, phallic tower.

This monolithic tower would send a terrible message, looming aggressively over what would be the city's main civic space, argued Paul. "It feels like a Prussian soldier standing over the public square," he told the three-firm design team.

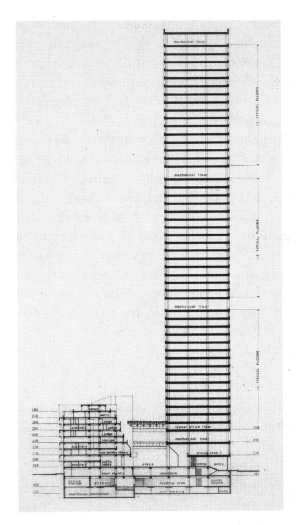

Erectile dysfunction:
section drawing
of the quashed
B.C. Government
Centre proposal for
downtown Vancouver.

Paul sketched up two of his own alternative proposals and showed them to the team. One—the most politically viable option—would be a fifty-five-storey tower reshaped into a triangular building, with a canted roof, which would look less forbidding. The triangular massing would open up more views for pedestrians around it, defy the ubiquitous shoebox form that people were tired of, and be less costly because of the reduced facade area.

The second alternative scheme reimagined the two blocks as a much less intimidating development: a long rectangular civic square flanked by multiple five-storey buildings. Even as he drew it up, Paul himself considered the horizontal mid-rise scheme to be a "hair-balled hippie fantasy." He knew the height-obsessed premier wouldn't accept a design so close to the ground.

The McCarter & Nairne architects could not see their government clients accepting either of Paul's alternatives to their tower. That, Paul expected—they had all worked for months on the design and had staked their reputations on it. But if Paul Merrick—the lead designer from the TBP side—could get Ron Thom on board, together they could prevent this giant Prussian soldier from rising up over the city.

In December of 1971, during one of Ron's stays in Vancouver, Paul invited him to his home for supper. Over tumblers of Scotch, he presented his case against the mega-tower. He urged Ron, as the Design Coordinator, to back him in fighting for his more discreet alternative to the fifty-five-storey "Prussian soldier."

"Nyaah... I'm ambivalent," replied Ron.

"Does that mean you don't give a shit?"

"I guess so."

He *guessed* so? Outright rejection might have been tolerable. But— *ambivalent*? That word signalled to Paul that his mentor, one of the greatest architects in the country, had lost something invaluable: his artistic conviction.

For a long time afterward, that word "ambivalent" would grate on Paul Merrick's ears. The famous Ron Thom, who obsessed about everything, right down to the border design of the napkins that graced the tables in his buildings—now he seemed to care about nothing. Maybe he just didn't care about this one behemoth of a building. Or maybe he just didn't care during this one Scotch-soaked evening. Or maybe he no longer cared to design anything, other than a house.

Ron still thought of the human domicile as the most noble kind of structure in the world. A house seemed to be the only kind of commission that interested him now. He knew he couldn't control the design of large buildings. Neither could his peers. And the premier's insistence on an austere black skyscraper reminded them both that architecture was not always determined by architects.

Paul resigned from the project, but grudgingly came back on board a week later at the behest of the government. Eventually, the design and engineering teams completed a full set of working drawings for the massive project—a long, expensive, labour-intensive feat. By late summer of 1972, the B.C. Government Centre project team stood poised to break ground and transform the city.

Riding high in the polls and with a new landmark tower in the works, Bennett had called an election for the end of August. He and Phil Gaglardi, whom Bennett had appointed Minister of Highways, seemed confident of victory. But then, one week before the election, "Flying Phil" gave a jaw-dropping interview to a Toronto newspaper, calling Bennett "an old man who doesn't understand the young people of this province." He then suggested to the newspaper that he—Gaglardi—would likely take over as premier shortly after the election. And with that, Wacky Bennett's approval ratings instantly plunged.

A few days later, the desperate-sounding premier—on the brink of giving Vancouver a huge new civic square—warned the public that "the socialist hordes are at the gate of British Columbia!"[11] His plea didn't work; on August 30, B.C. voters threw Bennett's Social Credit regime out of power.

The new NDP government quickly annihilated its predecessor's legacy project, in the tradition of newly elected politicians everywhere. They scrapped the entire B.C. Government Centre—courthouse, skyscraper, civic square. Everything that the entire joint venture team had worked for over the past three years dissolved into nothing, into reams of paper for future archives. Paul Merrick didn't get to build his triangular courthouse, but he felt relief at the cancellation of the skyscraper. W.A.C. Bennett wouldn't get his legacy *shtoinker* after all.

The NDP government relaunched the project from scratch. They still needed to fill those two city blocks, and they still needed a new and larger courthouse. But the new administration did not continue with the existing joint venture team led by Ron Thom; instead, they appointed Arthur Erickson to design everything—courthouse, offices, public space.

At learning his archrival would design the replacement project, Ron's apathy crystallized into anger. But he shouldn't have been surprised. Erickson and the new premier, Dave Barrett, were friendly with one another. Erickson had presciently supported Barrett prior to the election. The tall tower ordained by one premier and its cancellation by the next—that was just one example of how deeply political a nation's public architecture tends to be.

After the B.C. Government Centre saga, Paul stayed on at Thompson Berwick Pratt. He had been made a partner and had some important new projects in the works, including Vancouver's striking CBC headquarters on Hamilton and Georgia Streets, nicknamed "the bunker" both derisively and affectionately, after the building type it resembled. And in 1972 he completed a landmark house in West Vancouver for his own family, a phantasmagoric treehouse-like structure of reclaimed wood and glass. For its front door, Paul repurposed the huge wooden drawing board from Ron's now-retired TBP drafting table—an enduring architectural homage to his early mentor.

Dejected at losing the Government Centre to Erickson, Ron bemoaned what he saw as the unfairness of it all. The profession had once beckoned and tantalized him with its huge menagerie of opportunities. Now it menaced him. Neither raw talent nor past glory held the same currency for getting work. Architects had to seek out clients in their habitats, prowl around the dinner-party circuit, and lure them with fine manners; they had to court politicians and corporate presidents and pray that their chosen benefactors could hold onto power.

16

ROILING FAME

IN THE 1960s, Ron Thom's new fame drew a wealth of plum commissions, including Sir Sandford Fleming College in Peterborough and the library at Queen's University in Kingston. By the end of the decade, his senior associates were assuming more design authority, always careful to ensure that every project remained characteristically Ron Thom. As well as organic colours and materials, "Ron Thom" traits include chamfered corners, angular stairways, and "shadow-form" massing, wherein cutouts and slots in the building's main form create dark shadows that define and lend mystery to the buildings.

Universities and community colleges had become the de facto kingmakers for Canadian architects and a keeper of their ongoing reputation. After Simon Fraser University vaulted Arthur Erickson to Ron's level of acclaim in the mid-1960s, the two West Coasters recognized each other as peers in a rarified league. Arthur, speaking to a *Maclean's* reporter in 1970, said, "This business of using the site properly is one area where I'm probably one of the two best in the country. The other is Ron Thom in Toronto."

Out for dinner one night with Thom Partnership associates Frank Hamilton and Boris Theohar, Arthur and Ron kept their heads together, talking so low that neither of the other two men could be privy to their conversation. Sporadically, Ron would swivel his head and shout, "Frank! Shut up!" Frank shrugged off these and other outbursts as rhetorical licence that Ron had earned. "He liked to treat me with disdain and I didn't take offence," Frank recalled. To him, Arthur and Ron were the *authentic* architects. "Others, even the well-known ones, weren't authentic," said Frank. "They weren't interested in architecture. They're businesspeople and they just talk about it."[1]

Ron and Arthur were hardly alone in protesting the economically driven architectural banality. The demolition juggernaut had galvanized the preservationists and prompted a renewed appreciation of historic Beaux-Arts architecture.[2] Societal upheaval had energized calls for architects to pay more heed to the broader urban context and social purpose of their work.[3]

For Ron, the "art" component of the Vitruvian triad remained the essence of architecture. He viscerally understood how this core element, the *venustas*, exerts subliminal power to inflect the way we think and feel and act within a space, beyond rational explanation.

Ron struggled to transfer his design intuition to others, to teach the unteachable. At one point, he distributed an excerpt from *Confessions of an Advertising Man* to his staff, describing the text as "powerful" reading. The 1963 bestseller, by British ad mogul David Ogilvy, had become a staple textbook of marketing courses. Its many aphorisms include the basic criteria for success at R.J. Thom & Associates:

> To be successful you must, of necessity, accumulate a group of creative people. This probably means a fairly high percentage of high strung, brilliant, eccentric nonconformists.
>
> Most original thought isn't even verbal. It requires a groping experimentation with ideas, governed by intuitive hunches and inspired by the unconscious.[4]

An ad man's memoir might have seemed like an unlikely text for an architect like Ron to expound upon, but it came close to expressing his way of thinking. He shared this perspective at architecture schools and in public talks, speaking in simple terms and tangible concepts, or making analogies to painting or music. Like the titular Advertising Man, Ron appreciated outsiders, oddballs, individualists; he distrusted mellifluous or polysyllabic prose, which wasn't his strong suit in any case. He actively hated the abstruse vocabulary beloved by certain architects. "There goes bullshit-baffles-brains," he would sneer, in frequent reference to the worst offenders.[5]

Ron's friends sensed that he struggled with a chronic sense of insecurity. Some of them presumed it was his regret or self-consciousness about not having gone through university. Many years earlier, the University of British Columbia arts and science department had mailed him a letter of acceptance. By then, he had already begun training at the Vancouver School of Art, which was not yet a degree-granting institution.[6] Architecture school hadn't been a practical option at that time, since British Columbia didn't have one yet. But art school had instilled the kind of visual thinking and artistic skill that distinguished him from the herd of ambitious architects around him.

Ron also retained a lingering envy of Ned Pratt—not of his architecture or his press coverage, but of his aviation experience. Ron's own thwarted ambition to get his wings in World War II still bothered him. Ned's pilot licence earned him so much extra professional respect—or so it seemed to Ron.[7]

In the early 1970s, he took a series of lunch-hour flying lessons at Toronto Island Airport. Shanna Fromson, recently hired as the Thom Partnership's interior designer, took lessons along with Ron. They would each climb into a Cessna 150 two-seater and, backed up by their trainers, fly high above Lake Ontario and then circle back toward the city again.

Shanna reliably attended each flying lesson, motivated partly by her own strong will to fly, and partly by falling in love with her trainer-pilot, whom she later married. As for Ron, his unpredictable workload at 47 Colborne overwhelmed him, and Ron started missing his scheduled lessons. Eventually, after losing his driver's licence permanently for multiple impaired driving convictions, he was forced to drop his flying ambition forever. Grounded once again—by the demands for his architectural services, along with other burdens.

AS THE WORLD around him became more officious, Ron retained a sense of relaxed and spontaneous creativity at the Thom Partnership. For better and worse, he refused to change his primordial design values to align with the new corporate reality.

Thom's organic aesthetic fit the 1970s countercultural spirit embraced by much of his staff. The Friday afternoon drink of choice transitioned from hard liquor to beer. Smoke-wise, Ron stuck to his daily pack of Craven A cigarettes, although many of the younger crew favoured cannabis. Back-alley dealers sold bags of it over the transom of the downstairs print shop at 47 Colborne. A few of the staff would then repurpose the supply room's cardboard drawing tubes into makeshift bongs.[8] Productivity may have been unpredictable, but creativity—or at least the *perception* of creativity—soared.

Jamie Smallwood, a tech-savvy draftsman, was typical of the young blood that found a creative utopia at 47 Colborne. He had spent two tedious years designing Toronto subdivisions at a corporate firm before joining Ron's office. Working before the age of office computers, Jamie and his fellow draftsmen wielded compass, protractor, French curve, and T square like artisanal tools, brought to life with trigonometric calculations and subjective artistic discretion. "We didn't have CAD, but we had trig," he recalled.[9] Their direct hand in the creation helped confer a sense of ownership in many of the designers. "You always felt that you were creating—no matter what you were doing."

Throughout the 1970s, technology began its overhaul of creative production. Architects and draftsmen still sketched their rough ideas and drew up their embryonic forms on huge sheets of drawing paper, redoing the process with every change of the design. But now, photomechanical reproduction replaced many of the client presentation drawings. Office archives now began to fill with huge black sheets of film embedded with the negatives of the designs. The technological advance saved time and money; the lines of the photomechanical reproductions were clean and sharp and allowed them to make multiple copies with ease.

One of Ron's early gifts propelling him to the top had been his ability to hand-render presentation drawings that looked as beautiful as a work of art. He could still do this, and such drawings could be especially helpful in presentations to the public. But now the manual drawing for this stage was no longer essential. Some architects and clients began to wonder whether freehand drawing served any real purpose at all. The ghost of Fred Lasserre would likely have replied that it doesn't.

Architecture schools began scaling back their once-imperative drawing courses. Every working architect cognizant of technology's momentum must have sensed the future, with either hopeful anticipation or foreboding. Drawing, watercolour, and visual arts in general—all were destined to become less important to the schools and the profession with each passing year.

Does the physical act of drawing affect the nature of creation, or is it just mere replication? The question became more pertinent as technology began its takeover of the drafting table. Ned Pratt had first hired Ron back in 1948 because of his exceptional skill in visually representing the ideas of others. And then Ron's own ideas turned out to be exceptional. Was that a coincidence, that the man who could craft the most beautiful illustrations could also dream up the most beautiful buildings?

Decades earlier, in *Canadian Art*, Bert Binning had described the dual end-goals of drawing. First, as a study of forms and their relationships to one another, as the artist-architects scrutinize the subject or problem before them. Second, as a key stage in the creative process, as they sense what to add, subtract, emphasize, and move around during that scrutiny. "A vital and important preparatory study toward painting, sculpture and architecture,"[10] concluded Binning—not a mere plan or illustration of the final product, but an embedded part of it.

To Ron, the receding emphasis on drawing and painting threatened the creative heart of architecture. He saw freehand renderings as an essential part of the design process. For each project, he continued to create or delegate a series of intricate drawings or paintings, and he exhorted the younger generation to do the same. Doug Shadbolt, who now headed the architecture school at the Technical University of Nova Scotia, brought Ron to Halifax many times to give instructions on watercolour rendering.

Drawing was its own language to Ron. To explain something to a client, instead of talking it out, he would whip out the silver lining-paper of his pack of cigarettes and scribble a miniature freehand sketch about how a window would fit into a wall.

At the workplace, Ron sometimes treated even the medium of writing as an artwork—literally a collage of text. "He handled even the written texts explaining the project as though they were graphic elements," recalled Alastair Grant. "His associates wrote out their notes in longhand, and then Ron would take a pair of scissors and slice up the text, cutting and pasting the notes on an elongated roll of paper. And then at that point it was typed out by [an assistant], and then it would get cut and pasted again, and other things written in."[11]

Whereas Ron used to be admired for being avant-garde, now he was adored for being old-school—maintaining the priority of drawing and art within architecture. Angela Cadman, an executive assistant who worked for several architects before joining the Thom Partnership in 1976, strongly respected the fact that Ron, unlike any of her past employers, had a drafting table in his own office.

Ron's usual routine—a primary bonding exercise—would be to meet with the clients over Friday afternoon drinks, listen to them talk about their lives, and then grab a cocktail napkin to scribble up a rough sketch of how he imagined their future home. Such is how his design for Pamela Goh's house took shape. "Let's go for a drink!" Ron exhorted Pamela and her husband on a Friday afternoon. Jamie Smallwood accompanied them to the bar at the King Eddy. The conversation wrapped up a couple of hours later, with napkins crumpled on the table amid an orchard of empty glasses.

Jamie stared, ashen-faced, at the now-soggy napkins; they were precious—and highly perishable. The pen lines that were now bleeding into the napkin marked the conception of the Goh residence's future design, and could well be Ron's last hands-on involvement with the project before it was handed on to others at the firm to develop and render.

Jamie knew what he had to do next. As Ron and his clients vacated the table, Jamie carefully removed the sodden napkins from the tabletop, took them home, and pinned them up to dry over the weekend. Then on Monday, Jamie and the rest of the crew at the Thom Partnership began extrapolating and formalizing the ideas embedded within the sodden scribbles. It was a job as delicate and meticulous as a forensic examiner extracting DNA from a fabric sample. Decades later, he would think: *How I wish I had kept them!*[12]

IN 1972, Ron received disturbing news from his friends Bruno and Molly Bobak in Fredericton, where Bruno headed the Art Centre at the University of New Brunswick. A massive "urban renewal" proposed by Montreal-based Marathon Realty[13] was about to steamroll the city's century-old core. It would raze a block of nineteenth-century brick buildings along the main downtown artery and replace it with a huge concrete retail office complex. The proposed development made no practical sense; Fredericton had a population of barely 20,000. But Fredericton's mayor, Bud Bird, backed the project and had convinced his council to approve it; they narrowly approved the massive development in a six-to-five vote.[14]

Like many other residents of Fredericton, the Bobaks felt anguished but helpless. Bereft of the power of the mayor and money of the developer, they knew they had to persuade Fredericton's city council to cancel the deal. They explained the horrible predicament to Ron, who then offered the most valuable contribution he could make: his name and his presence. Bruno sent Ron a plane ticket and an invitation to give a guest lecture at the University of New Brunswick. Ron waived his lecture fee; the main purpose of his trip would be to convince Fredericton's city council to defy their mayor and rescind their approval.

After Ron's talk at the university wrapped up, the three of them returned to the Bobak home for the evening. There, in that haven of friendship and comfort, they talked and drank and laughed until the early hours of the morning—and then prepped the living room couch for Ron to spend the night.

Sometime after Bruno and Molly settled in upstairs to sleep, a jostling abruptly woke them. It turned out to be Ron, who, like a pet or a small child, was trying to climb into their bed. They both recognized his intentions as clearly platonic, "like a child wanting comfort," recalled Bruno. Still, they needed their sleep, and the mattress wasn't big enough for three. They swatted him back to his designated couch.

In the morning, they walked downstairs to find him sleeping on the floor of their living room. He had wrapped himself in their rectangular area rug, cocooning himself. The Bobaks found this gesture strangely endearing. It was so much like Ron—the introvert, averse to open spaces, always seeking enclosure, wanting to be bundled up.[15]

Shortly afterward, Ron Thom roared back to life. The three of them headed to City Hall, where Ron joined the throng of historians and angry citizens, lending his name and his words to argue against the massive new development. And then, the councillors rescinded their approval—on a technicality, officially.[16] But the Bobaks felt Ron's persuasive talk had made the difference.[17]

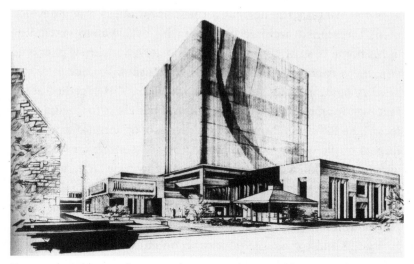

Corporate juggernaut: the 1972 urban renewal proposal for historic Fredericton by Marathon Realty.

When David Mooney, the vice president of development at Marathon, got wind of the proposed development, he was enraged as well. He hadn't been aware of the proposal and he saw that it made no sense. It wasn't just the casual destruction of the city's historic architecture so much as the fact that he saw no business rationale for a large office and retail development in such a small city. It must have come about from pork-barrelling, or old-boy favour exchanging, or simple grandiose vanity, or some combination thereof, he figured. Technically as the Toronto-based head of development, he had the right to stop it, and he did just that, firing the two Montreal-based project managers who had brought it this far. But killing this behemoth of a project would have been much more difficult if Fredericton's council had maintained its approval.[18] Ron's intervention gave the mega-project's cancellation an additional kind of moral authority.

Ron exuded joy in his follow-up letter to Bruno and Molly. "I ran into David Mooney... yesterday and was very happy to discover that they have dropped all plans for their Fredericton development," he wrote. "So congratulations to everybody."[19]

RON FELT THAT the new juggernaut of mindless urban development threatened architectural integrity everywhere—including in his home base of Toronto. "We are involved in a new phenomenon, the very large city," he told *Saturday Night* magazine in 1975.[20] "History has not shown us what to do with that." He seethed at the fact that Toronto farmed out key cultural buildings to foreign architects. The Robarts Library at the University of Toronto, one of the targets of his wrath, was "designed by someone from New York, who I suspect knew Toronto as well as I know New Orleans. I find it hard to believe that any architect from Toronto, knowing the university and the surrounding neighbourhoods, would have been capable of inventing such a gross intrusion."[21]

By the mid-1970s, the political economics of architecture had shifted to the point that they threatened the kind of artistry within architecture that had made Ron famous in the first place. Politicians and business leaders now felt more pressure from voters and shareholders to display the optics of cost-saving.

Ron's apathy about the B.C. Government Centre project from a few years prior shifted into claims of deep concern in a series of public talks he delivered from 1976 through 1977. In Vancouver, Saskatoon, and Toronto, he gave variations of the same message: architecture is losing something critical—namely, the architect.[22]

In these talks, the notes for which he laboriously wrote out by hand, he railed against the reduction of the architect to the position of referee and producer of contract documents.

"The architect's role as artist must none the less continue to be *the* most important *raison d'être* for his existence—and for the existence of his profession—as it has been throughout history."[23] He invoked the seventeeth-century British architect Sir Christopher Wren, who had the comprehensive authority to design St. Paul's Cathedral, and much else, as a thing of beauty as well as function. He might equally have cited many more throughout history—Michelangelo, Bernini, Vitruvius—all of whom surely would have bemoaned the lowered priority of visual harmony and delight.

An architect's wits have always needed to be political, he argued—and by that he meant generically political, as in negotiating with the client to achieve the necessary leverage to make great architecture. "There has always been the house client who wants the living room in the front facing the traffic, instead of in the back facing the garden," he noted, "or the commercial client who *knows* his survival is dependent on huge crass signage."

Conceptually speaking, he continued, "It was very little different for composers like Bach or Vivaldi, for instance, who also had to deal with the vagaries of those who commissioned their works." Yes, it was ever thus—except that the times were changing, and not just in the measure of a government's purse strings. Until now, noted Ron, the architect could see and deal with his client directly. This one-on-one relationship could still happen with house clients and sometimes with a single institutional board, he conceded. But the kind of intimate persuasion an architect could conduct with a client—such as himself with Tom Symons at Trent, or Arthur Erickson with Gordon Shrum at Simon Fraser University—those days were gone. There could be no more "committees of one" for projects of that scale.

So what had changed? Three main characteristics of society, he concluded. First, its densification—especially in cities; second, its economic, legal, technical, cultural, and social forces were now interlocked; third, the surge in technological advances. All three factors served to separate the "artist-architect" from the clients and thus weakened the "precious exchange: request and reaction."

Yet Ron's public laments about the dissolution of art within architecture did not gain much traction. His generation of architects came of age surrounded by cheap building lots, burgeoning economies, and patrons who appreciated the value of beauty within architecture. All of these assets seemed to be diminishing with each passing year.

Meanwhile, the world of visual arts, in which he had once collaborated so intensely, had cleaved off into a more distinct realm. Jack Shadbolt had emerged as one of the country's most important artists, with monographs, solo exhibitions, and dozens of paintings and drawings in the National Gallery's permanent collection as well as other important museums across the country. Jack's wife Doris had escalated into a lofty position of her own, as a curator, critic, and director of the Vancouver Art Gallery. Bruno and Molly Bobak were enjoying continued critical and commercial success as artists in Fredericton. Gordon Smith had left teaching to devote himself to painting, which would soon bring him international acclaim.

As for the alliance of arts that had been so ardently championed in decades past—much of that world had vanished. Even as public art proliferated, artists were no longer brought in at conception, the way Bert Binning had been for the Dal Grauer Substation and B.C. Electric Building, and so art more often became "tacked on" after the fact, rather than embedded within the architecture. And by the end of the 1970s, pottery—once among the most exalted of the arts— had become a marginalized activity, often lumped in with "craft"—a term that was devolving into something vaguely pejorative, no longer at the head table of architecture. The midcentury embrace of the allied arts gave way to a more fragmented, individualist art culture of stars and discrete disciplines.

That shift seemed to affect Ron's alma mater, the Vancouver School of Art, which continued to grow in stature and student size after Ron's late-1940s graduation. By 1978, the provincial government would finally take the art school under its wing and assume its primary funding. Instead of calling it the British Columbia College of Art, as many assumed, the government announced that it would henceforth be named for the West Coast's most iconic artist, Emily Carr.

Ron and much of his art school cohort hated the new name. So did the school's founder, Charles Scott. The problem wasn't the choice of Emily Carr; they simply objected to the concept of honouring an individual painter rather than a collective or a place. Ron expressed his displeasure in a letter to education minister

Pat McGeer: "The name should first and foremost identify with its region." What's more, he added, it would associate the school mostly with painting—effectively marginalizing the sculpture, pottery, commercial art, and typography taught within its walls.[24]

Their protests fizzled out. In 1978, the Vancouver School of Art was officially renamed the Emily Carr College of Art. For many, the gesture marked a belated recognition of one of the West Coast's greatest artists. At the same time, the idea of cultural regionalism lost ground to the larger trend of star-making, for better and worse.[25]

By no coincidence, almost all of Ron's aphorisms referenced the concept of the *site*. "A building has to make love to its site," he often said. In a humanist and slightly ribald way, it conveyed his main design value—that the surrounding landscape should not be a mere backdrop but a careful interplay between two equal entities: humanity and nature.

He also proclaimed its corollary: "The site always wins." To Ron, that was true; he felt the landscape should determine the architecture, that a good building defers to whatever site it's built upon, and that the site—the world not built by human hands—trumps whatever people might want to heap upon it.

The catchy epigrams became less persuasive as the century wore on and humanity repeatedly trumped nature. Thom's deference to the site relied on the presence of the West Coast's verdant, topographically interesting, affordable land. Vancouver's North Shore, which once beckoned architects like an empty green canvas, was filling up. By the 1970s, the region no longer offered the plentiful and inexpensive supply of lots that architects could experiment on as though they were a hundred sheets of drawing paper.

Toronto had almost no such land in the first place, or at least not since Ron's arrival in 1963. "The problem with Toronto is that there are no *sites* here," he griped to colleagues.[26] That assertion was not technically true, except by his own definition. In architecture, every physical location is a site, whether on a forested slope overlooking the ocean or in the middle of a teeming metropolis or next to an acre-wide parking lot. To Ron, though, a "site" should be contiguous with the natural world. He did attract clients whose semirural sites near Toronto had some semblance of nature—in Caledon, and the outskirts of Peterborough. But even here, he missed the gloriously rugged topography of the West Coast. With their expansive flat lawns, many of the sites looked more like golf courses. As for Toronto itself, he couldn't understand how a major city on the edge of a Great Lake offered such an overtly manufactured setting.

RON'S CHARISMA and artistry helped serve as his get-out-of-jail-free card on many occasions, both personally and to the world at large. Much like a few other revered artists, Ron harboured a dual personality. "In the morning, he was the sweetest, most wonderful guy you could imagine," recalled Peter Smith, one of his top architects. "If you were working on something, Ron would come up to you and say in a very soft voice, 'That's really great, I like the way you've done that...uh...Maybe we can push this a little bit over here,' and so on. And you'd be delighted, and then after he left, you'd realize that he'd changed everything you'd drawn." Almost always for the better, noted Peter.

But then, at lunch, when Ron had reached the last sip of a second drink, his kindly Dr. Jekyll persona transformed into Mr. Hyde. "Two drinks and then—*phwoo*! His personality would change in a moment, just like that," recalled Peter, with a snap of his fingers. And then, back in the office, the sweet and gentle man seemed possessed. "*That's the most boring fucking thing I've ever seen!*" he would bellow. For Peter and others, there was only one way around it: if you had anything you had to discuss with Ron, you'd best make it a morning conversation.[27]

Even when "into his cups," as Alastair termed it, Ron's charisma could still keep many people under his spell—as long as they were enraptured by Ron's talent. Some of his buttoned-down corporate clients even loved Ron's hard-drinking persona. In the early 1970s,

Time magazine had featured extensive and laudatory coverage of the Trent University architecture, along with an accompanying sidebar profile on Ron Thom himself. The timing was propitious—this was one week before a high-level meeting with the board of directors of his other Peterborough client, Sir Sandford Fleming College, and *Time*'s seal of approval reconfirmed his star status.

At the board meeting, all went well until Ron finished the last sip of his second drink. And then he grew brutally frank with everybody around the table. When one of the board members made a benign comment, Ron slapped him roughly on the back and growled, "Henry, you're just a fucking farmer. You don't know what the shit you're talking about."

The room fell silent while Ron berated the board member. Peter Smith winced and muttered to himself: *Goodbye, job!* To his surprise, the next day Peter found that same board member fawning over Ron, appearing more enamoured of him than ever. "He thought Ron was the living messiah, that he couldn't do a thing wrong. And I thought: this is a Dylan Thomas moment. It was as though he were proud to be slapped and berated by someone who had been in *Time* magazine."[28]

Many of the country's less-prominent architects also fell deeply under Ron's spell, especially when they could match him cup-for-cup. Such was the case with architect Tim Murray, who received a telephone call from Ron at his Ottawa office in the early 1970s. Although an architect of some renown himself, Tim was enthralled to receive this out-of-the-blue call from Ron Thom—the renowned and illustrious genius of their profession. He was calling to ask if his firm, Murray & Murray Associates, would like to join forces with the Thom Partnership to pitch the design of Carleton University's new building for their school of architecture.

Although Tim only knew him by reputation, the mere possibility of working with Ron Thom filled him with delight. Ron told Tim he'd seen his work in "the glossies"—the slick full-colour shelter magazines that proliferated in the 1970s. Tim had designed the sanctuary-like Campanile church in Ottawa's Alta Vista neighbour-hood. Murray & Murray had also designed two buildings at Carleton University. "I knew that the Carleton connection was likely what interested him—although I'd like to think that we had even just a lit-tle bit of talent to offer him," he recalled. [29]

When Ron asked Tim to travel from Ottawa to his office for a meeting, he did not hesitate—the request itself was an honour: "I'd have had the meeting in a pickup truck, if he wanted." Tim drove to Toronto, arriving first at 47 Colborne—and from there the two archi-tects drove to the Thom family home, stopping en route at Ron's request at the liquor store for a bottle of Beefeater gin.

While Molly prepared a meal for them, Ron and Tim strolled out onto the rooftop deck and cracked open the gin. "I wasn't that aware of his enthusiasm for drinking, nor, perhaps, was he aware of mine," recalled Tim, "but I certainly didn't need any further persuasion." They talked about the Carleton project, about universities in gen-eral, about Ottawa, about architecture, about everything, as they slowly drained the bottle. Tim found himself in a supremely relaxed, pleasant, and friendly conversation. He knew that famous architects tended to be egotists, and yet here in Ron's own home, Tim found himself bantering with a gentle, charismatic, self-effacing man.

Meanwhile, the evening sky darkened, the city lights blinked on, and the woman in the background murmured helplessly. They talked away as the stars brightened and then morphed from twin-kling dots to blurry spirals. As the bottle emptied and the night shut down, they still hadn't made it to the dinner table, let alone come up with an action plan for the Carleton University proposal.

The convivial evening came to nothing, professionally speaking. Carleton awarded the architecture school commission to Carmen and Elin Corneil instead.

"So we didn't get the project," shrugged Tim. "But we *drank* enough to get it."

17

CULTURALLY
DEFINING

AT THE DAWN of the 1970s, with the demands of Trent largely over, the Thom Partnership took on several benchmark cultural projects almost simultaneously. The Shaw Festival Theatre, Pearson College of the Pacific, Metropolitan Toronto Zoo, St. Jude's Cathedral, and the Japanese-owned Prince Hotel. Each in its own way challenged Ron to expand his own cultural horizon.

Ron deeply admired Inuit sculpture,[1] and he relished the opportunity to work on St. Jude's. Completed in 1972, the small Anglican church project offered the challenge of a different regional context. He travelled to Iqaluit—then called Frobisher Bay—for the first time, met local artists and artisans, and returned with a soapstone carving and an enhanced appreciation of the region. He designed St. Jude's as an igloo-like dome, clad in white shingles, with a steeple-topped skylight that shed celestial light throughout its interior demisphere. Local residents did much of the construction work and equipped the interior with Inuit wall hangings, woven baskets, a cross of whale tusk, and a carved soapstone baptismal font.[2] Inside and out, the structure reflected the rich culture of the Inuit rather than the fraught history of the Church.

The commission for the new home of the Shaw Festival Theatre turned out to be more complicated. Theatre lover Brian Doherty

Watercolour rendering of St. Jude's Cathedral.

had launched the first Shaw Festival season in 1962 at Niagara-on-the-Lake's former courthouse. Doherty's dream of celebrating the works and themes of Irish playwright George Bernard Shaw was now half-realized. The other half would involve constructing a purpose-built theatre to house the festival.

The site for its permanent home turned out to be a government-owned army training compound, now decommissioned but still boasting a few wooden huts from World War II. Development coordinator Doug Buck then worked with the board on the next crucial step: prying open the government funding taps to get an architect and a building.

Doug and a few staffers and board members trekked from Niagara-on-the-Lake to Toronto to consult with Walter Gordon, widely seen as the most powerful lobbyist in the country. Gordon, a lifelong friend of Lester Pearson, had been finance minister in the former prime minister's cabinet. He now served as a well-paid lobbyist, as well as an ardent advocate for using culture as a tool for the nation's political independence.[3] Walter Gordon had sipped sherry at the Château Laurier with every mandarin in Ottawa. For the construction of a landmark theatre, he would know the magic words to whisper in their ears—or so the Shaw Festival organizers thought.

In late 1969, the Shaw Festival group met with Gordon at his King Street West office, immediately feeling confident when they beheld this iconic figure with his signature black-framed glasses and dapper mustache. Gordon committed to making the funding requests, but weeks later, he brought them back sobering news. The federal government was planning budget cuts across the board, and couldn't grant them the funds they needed. The Shaw team smiled cordially: they presumed that his initial refusal was just part of the game. "Yes, we know," they replied, expecting advice on how to do the follow-up ask.

And then Walter Gordon bluntly set them straight: "No. This time it's different. Everything's changing."

As the entire North American economy slowed to a crawl, the public money stream dried up. Governments were shifting priorities, from qualitative—architecture and culture—to business and the bottom line.

The Shaw Festival team realized that their design ambitions would likely be limited. Just the same, they remained committed to securing one of the nation's best architects. The board made up a shortlist of five finalists, and then unanimously selected the Thom Partnership.

Ron drew up a conceptual design: a jogged volume with indents and projections and a curvilinear cedar-shingled roof, tucked into a space beside the city's courthouse as though it had been there since ancient times. Unfortunately, the hoped-for capital funding didn't materialize, and Ron had to revise his design, simplifying its complex form.

Meanwhile, some local citizens protested the building's proposed site in the downtown core, arguing that it would add too much traffic and density to the area. The site was then moved from behind the courthouse to a more remote area at the edge of town, and the design team had to overhaul their scheme yet again.

TOP Ron Thom with Peter Smith. BOTTOM The Shaw Festival Theatre, Niagara-on-the-Lake, Ontario.

As project architect, Peter Smith stickhandled much of the fraught process, along with Susan Black, one of the firm's first female architects, who worked on the interior design. They ultimately created a handsome building, with Ron's characteristic deep eaves and interplay of volume, a vaulted ceiling in the performance hall, and West Coast cedar producing superb acoustics. Upon its opening in 1973, the architecture pleased observers and critics. The design team had teased a sparse budget into a cohesive form.

The core massing of Ron's original design remains at the heart of its architecture. Ron privately lamented its mandated simplification, but the public still loved the building, and it sealed the reputation of Peter Smith as a masterful theatre architect.

"The Shaw Festival was a delicious building to do," Ron told the *Toronto Star* on the eve of its opening. He also alluded to the challenges that arise for the architect when a festival co-founder, a government, a board of directors, and an entire town all have conflicting demands. "From a business sense, it would be better to do one office building after another," he added. "But there are other things that are sweet to do. A house, for example, is strangely satisfying because the architect has a direct relationship with one person: the owner."[4]

RON'S REPUTATION for embedding architecture within nature positioned him well for a prestigious international secondary school to be built on Vancouver Island. Spearheaded by and named after a former Canadian prime minister, it would be called the Lester B. Pearson College of the Pacific.

The idea for the school had emerged in 1969, when Pearson visited the United World College of the Atlantic in Wales and spoke with its students. The school was part of the fledgling global network of post-secondary institutes that welcomed students from a variety of countries and demographics to focus on peace and international unity.

The concept resonated with Lester Pearson, a Nobel Peace Prize laureate, especially as the Cold War continued to rattle on the horizon. He returned to Canada having drafted a vision statement:

> Students will be welcomed without regard to race, religion or politics and we intend to establish scholarships so that the students who attend the College will be from all levels of society and will be genuine representatives of their own peoples.[5]

Sited on Vancouver Island near the town of Sooke, about twenty-five miles from Victoria, Pearson College would aim to draw bright adolescents from around the world with the broad goal of international relationship-building. And the former prime minister had tremendous fundraising clout to get the project off the ground.

Sadly, for both his loved ones and for the college, the former prime minister—its namesake—died in 1972, in the early days of fundraising. Despite the physical absence of its champion, the board of governors pressed onward, hiring the Thom Partnership to realize the former prime minister's vision.

At its forested site, Ron and his design team beheld what he called a "West Coast jungle."[6] He worked with Barry Downs, who had by then started his own firm, Downs Archambault. Together, the joint venture team created a village of small, charming buildings anchored by two dramatic larger structures: the administration building and the dining hall.

Working with Barry, Ron expanded on the concepts he played with in creating his hex-grid houses. The administration and dining hall buildings would expand on the pinwheel plan of the Case House in West Vancouver—mandala-like in form, a circular mass that characteristically appears low-profile from the outside, as though it's growing out of the earth, and then shocks the senses once a visitor steps inside its centrifugal spaces.

Pearson College offered Ron what he considered to be the perfect kind of site: a highly natural landscape. When he learned that

Barry Downs's photograph of Ron Thom (centre, facing camera) and officials on opening day at Pearson College.

the college's board of governors had commissioned Cornelia Oberlander as the project's landscape architect, he became apoplectic.[7] Cornelia had a high profile within the design community. But her ethos sprang from the hard-edged Bauhaus ideology of logic and functionalism, absorbed while studying at Harvard under Walter Gropius. Cornelia's rationalist approach worked well within more rigidly constricted sites, with streets and property lines laid out at right angles. For a secluded college on a sprawling site in the ragged wilderness of Vancouver Island, such an approach made little sense. And for an intuitive, organic designer like Ron Thom, it made no sense at all.

At one board meeting at the Empress Hotel in Victoria, he angrily protested the board's choice of landscape architect, which he felt was prompted by the personal connections of her spouse, Peter Oberlander. At any rate, Ron's noisy protest at the Empress Hotel cost him dearly—the board ejected Ron from the project team.

From that point on, Downs Archambault assumed responsibility for the project, and Barry led the remaining buildings to fruition. The Pearson College brass kept Ron's dismissal quiet and continued to publicly credit him as the principal designer. Ron Thom, after all, was still a marquee brand. When Ron and Barry attended the official 1974 opening, they watched and took photographs from the sidelines, as they were not invited into the VIP circle.[8]

With powerful architectural forms that seem to grow naturally right out of the site, Pearson College turned out to be a qualified success. It has suffered from lack of funding—for construction, maintenance, and renovation. On the positive side, it beautifully reflects Lester Pearson's goal of peace through education, nestled as a village in natural surroundings.

RON TRAVELLED around the contours of his own mind, but rarely elsewhere. His university scouting expedition for Trent had been his first trip overseas, at age forty. As he approached his fiftieth year, he still hadn't made the pilgrimage to Japan, which had been a rite of passage for so many of his West Coast peers, including Barry Downs and Arthur Erickson.

His world seemed to open up when the Tokyo-based Seibu Group approached him in 1972. The corporate overseers of the high-end Prince Hotels chain, the company wanted him to design their first overseas hotel, to be built in a northern suburb of Toronto.

Ron worked with Alastair Grant and Reno Negrin, devising several possible concepts. He presented three schemes: two of them mostly low-slung and horizontal, like the traditional Japanese inns known as *ryokans*; plus a high-rise concept with a ryokan-like base nestled into the site. The high-rise concept exhibited Ron's characteristic solid-and-void rhythm in the balconies that defined the facade, its four corners stepped back and recessed just like the tables at Trent University, all nestled into the forty-five acres of surrounding greenery.

The Seibu Group invited Ron and his team to present to their board of directors in Tokyo, offering them an all-expenses-paid fortnight in Japan.[9]

The invitation filled Ron with joy. So many of his mentors and colleagues had already travelled to Japan and drawn inspiration for their own work. Until now, Ron had only seen Japanese architecture in books, slides, and journals.

Ron and Alastair set off across the Pacific with Reno Negrin accompanying them. The team needed someone with hotel experience, and Negrin—who designed the 1961 Bayshore Inn on Vancouver's Coal Harbour waterfront—provided expertise in that realm.

After landing in Japan, they settled into their rooms at the Tokyo Prince Hotel. The next day, the Canadian architects presented their three options to the Seibu board, rattled only momentarily mid-presentation by the overhead chandelier tinkling ominously during a brief seismic tremor. Then the board unanimously accepted the team's preferred scheme, an eighteen-storey structure set on a large horizontal splayed plinth.

At the request of the Seibu Group, the design team then met and dined with architect Kenzō Tange, one of the most internationally celebrated architects. A leader of architecture's Metabolist movement, Tange agreed with the board of directors that they had selected the best scheme of the three.

The Seibu Group staff then toured the Canadians around Kyoto, the Japanese Empire's ancient cultural capital, which had much of its historic architecture still intact. They walked past *machiya*, the traditional wooden townhouses with deep eaves that had inspired Wright; they visited the Katsura Imperial Villa, which had so profoundly impressed Arthur Erickson; they visited Zen temples and saw fine wood joinery and millwork.

The older, traditional wood architecture of Kyoto enchanted Ron, but the contemporary concrete architecture of Tokyo interested him less—much like his pre-Trent research trip to England, where the medieval colleges of Oxbridge entranced him, and the stark new campuses left him cold.

Molly later joined Ron in Japan, and the couple took a side trip to the studio of ceramic artist Shōji Hamada. Hamada carved out personal time for a private visit with Ron and Molly, concluding with a gift of one of his own vases, which he invited Ron to pluck out from his not-for-sale "seconds" batch. Ron chose a hex-shaped vase, its earthen red glazing overlaid with a streak of light glaze resembling a checkmark or an acute angle of a hex-grid floor plan.

Ron had led the conceptual design of the Toronto Prince Hotel and seemed happy with the scheme. After he returned from Japan, he was plagued with second thoughts, which he shared privately with a friend.[10] Why, with their rich culture, did his Japanese clients just seem to want a typical North American high-rise? Although the design's horizontal base and jogged massing did embody some Japanese influence, Ron felt that had he been sent to Japan and seen its ryokans and temples *before* he designed it, in the way he had seen the universities of England before designing Trent, he would have designed the Prince Hotel much differently. Maybe like a ryokan— low-rise and melding into the landscape everywhere, not just at its base, and with more wood. By now, though, a "Western-style" concrete high-rise was precisely the type of building favoured by most corporate clients, international and otherwise.

At the office, Ron remained positive about the project, and construction proceeded apace. Two years later, in partnership with Reno Negrin & Associates, the Prince Hotel[11] opened its doors—not a groundbreaking masterpiece, but a handsome building that stood out like a lighthouse amid the suburban sprawl of North York.

When Ron next visited Morton and Irene Dodek, he told them that had he visited Japan first before designing their 1957 house, he would have designed it differently. Morton replied, "Well then, we're happy that you didn't go first, because we wouldn't want anything to be the slightest bit different."[12]

The Japanese-sponsored Prince Hotel in North York/Toronto.

Not long afterward, during one unfortunate evening at home, Ron accidently sent the Hamada vase sailing to the floor.[13] The vase broke cleanly into two pieces, and a bit of carefully applied glue fused the fragments back together. But from then on, a discernable crack meandered through it.

FOR THE MASTER PLAN and design of the new Metropolitan Toronto Zoo, Ron aspired to shift the conventional zoo design from visitor-centric to animal-centric. Earmarked for Toronto's verdant northeast periphery, the new complex would replace the city's century-old Riverdale Zoo. That structure had been designed in traditional zoo fashion, as a series of barred cages with no relation to the animals' natural habitat. The elephants, monkeys, lions, and other creatures sat behind bars, looking forlornly outward.

"I despise Riverdale Zoo," Ron had told a reporter. "I regard it as an animal jail. That ape lurching about in his cage has become an animal moron rather than an ecological link."[14] The conditions in which the animals lived horrified him. He hated their confined spaces, the leg shackles, the negation of their natural lives.

A 1968 feasibility study by architect Raymond Moriyama helped greenlight the new zoo. In partnership with two other Toronto firms— Crang & Boake and Clifford & Laurie—the Thom Partnership would plan the zoo's overall layout and design some of its major pavilions.

The zoo's director, a German zoologist named Gunter Voss, knew what he wanted and fought hard to get it. Instead of arranging animals taxonomically, Voss placed the groups of animals based on their natural habitat and range. Voss turned out to be a brusque micromanager, but fortunately his design ambitions for the zoo dovetailed with those of the architects.

Conventional zoo design had actually progressed by this time beyond the late-nineteenth-century Riverdale Zoo's animal prison, yet the modernist versions that had taken over in the twentieth century were often not much better. Architects could now use concrete and epoxy to mimic the look of rocks or bluffs, but even this half measure aimed to please humans more than animals, by creating a visual abstraction of the natural environment. The animals could usually tell the difference.[15]

Ron Thom and his joint-venture partners aspired for a truly animal-centric zoo. They created a series of small, amorphous zones

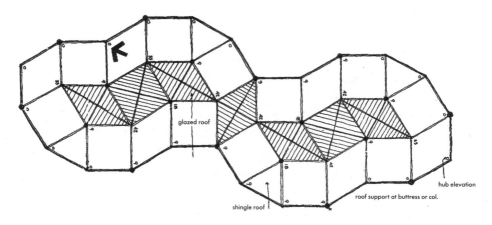

glazed roof

shingle roof

hub elevation

roof support at buttress or col.

TOP Roof structure of the African Pavilion.
BOTTOM Local kids cavort in front of the African Pavilion, still under construction.

that evoke the natural habitat of each animal. Ron's contributions, including the African and Indo-Malaysian pavilions, featured deep eaves and gently curving rooflines, both in keeping with Ron's aesthetic and with the innate needs of the resident creatures.

The interplay of different firms, along with the prickly disposition of Gunter Voss, made it difficult for Ron to exert the level of design control he craved. But he evidently impressed the chair of the committee overseeing the zoo project, Pamela Goh, since she had hired him to design her own home in Caledon.[16]

Gunter's wife, Anita Voss, sometimes joined the meetings and consultations. As a professional biologist, Anita had worked on several projects with her husband in the past. She found this one particularly stressful, however. Turf wars had broken out between the director and each of the three architectural firms. Sometimes she felt caught in the crossfire between Gunter and Ron. Gunter, she felt, was already treating her with the disdain that would eventually end their marriage.

As for Ron, he exasperated Anita. She found him to be stubborn, argumentative, and nasty when drunk.

That didn't stop her from falling in love with him, though.[17]

THE METROPOLITAN TORONTO ZOO opened on August 15, 1974, presenting a striking contrast to the jail-like Riverdale Zoo it had replaced. A year later, Seattle opened the Woodland Park Zoo, designed by Jones & Jones Architects, which replicates the animals' natural environments on an even grander scale. With no roofs or walls, the Woodland Park Zoo is like a zoological park or a wildlife conservation area with controlled visitor access. Woodland Park Zoo launched the term "habitat immersion" in the field of zoo design—but the Metropolitan Toronto Zoo team anticipated this revolutionary approach, where visitors can see animals freely roaming around in spacious structures that evoke their natural settings.

18

THE
ELUSIVE CONCEPT
OF HOME

JUST LIKE HIS client designs, Ron Thom's own headquarters at 47 Colborne exuded warmth, informality, and enclosure. Architect Ian MacDonald felt that warmth on his first day at the Thom Partnership. As a young co-op student in 1975, Ian stepped into the reception area at 47 Colborne and beheld the semiotics of home: "Comfortable leather couch with a phone; subdued light levels; low, intimately scaled ceiling of rough-sawn cedar; and a strategic panel between the visitor and the receptionist so that eye contact could be optional as opposed to obligatory."

Ian had spent his previous work placement at John C. Parkin's firm, Parkin Architects, Engineers & Planners, where he remembered the reception area as "a two-storey space with monochromatic white walls and furniture, very high illumination level, one lonely transparent acrylic chair sitting in the middle of the space for guests, and traffic moving through continuously and overviewed by a receptionist."[1]

There was no doubt in Ian's mind where he wanted to be. From institutional projects to private living space to the firm's public reception area, Ron Thom had transformed every space he inhabited into a kind of home. It was a cavern-and-cave home, with twenty-foot-high

The third-floor entrance to the Thom Partnership headquarters at 47 Colborne Street, with the iron gate pulleyed up.

ceilings and Ron's much lower cave of an office, "where he would hide in," recalls Jamie Smallwood. "You come to the door and you're amazed by what you're seeing: this big iron gate that would be either up or down, with a totally mechanical pulley system, no electric."

The office at 47 Colborne felt like a collective, and those working there treated it as such, working furiously and interactively on the firm's projects.

Except for one quiet youngish man named Andrew Binnie, a fixture at the Thom Partnership for several years, beginning in the mid-1960s.

Few people at 47 Colborne Street seemed to know where Andrew had come from. He arrived at the office very early most days, and he prowled around the studio without an obvious task at hand, even though the office was in the throes of handling the massive Trent project. Ron had taken in Andrew and given him a desk, and Andrew spent part of each day hunkered over it on cryptic projects of his imagination. Mostly, he remained quiet, staring out the window in silence. His expression suggested a perennial moodiness, but it was difficult to ascertain, because he spoke very little.[2]

In time, a few of the staff came to know Andrew and hear his story:[3] that he had worked for Frank Lloyd Wright at Taliesin; that he had attained the rare and coveted status of Apprentice; that he had married Wright's own daughter; that they had had a child together;

that after Wright died in 1959, he had been hounded out of Taliesin by Wright's famously eccentric third wife, Olgivanna.

Andrew's story seemed fantastical at first—but it was all true.[4] He had been Frank Lloyd Wright's son-in-law, and that marked the start of his troubles.

While still in high school at Trinity College School in Port Hope, Andrew had dreamed of a career in architecture, and most fervently wished to work for Frank Lloyd Wright. He had begun his studies at McGill University and did well enough as a freshman. But in 1956, his sophomore year, he decided to leave McGill and head to Taliesin in Wisconsin for a shot at working for the Great Man. At that time, Wright was approaching his ninetieth birthday, so Andrew knew that this opportunity could vanish any day.

After a requisite period of training at Taliesin, Wright conferred on Andrew the coveted position of Apprentice. When his brother Ian[5] visited him at Taliesin in the late 1950s, the adjoining studio thrummed with activity. Wright's final project, the spiral-shaped Guggenheim Museum, had broken ground in New York, and Taliesin's reputation—which had roller-coasted through peaks and valleys—now reached a new high. But Wright's ambition thrust even higher: working with his apprentices, he had configured a scheme for a conceptual project called "The Illinois"—a hypothetical Chicago skyscraper that would rise up 5,280 feet—literally a mile high.

In the spring of 1959, Frank Lloyd Wright died at age ninety-one. The mile-high skyscraper he had designed with the help of Andrew and other apprentices would never come to fruition. But in the interim, Andrew's creative spirit had caught the eye of Wright's free-spirited daughter, Iovanna.

A slim, dark-haired woman in her mid-thirties, Iovanna was the only child of Wright and his fiery third wife, Olgivanna. Andrew was nine years younger than Iovanna, but that didn't seem to matter. She noticed his talent and his taste in books, music, and poetry. They spent one afternoon at the edge of a nearby river together, drawing all shapes and figures in the sand until sunset. "A wonderful time," as she remembered it.⁶

Iovanna became pregnant, and she asked Andrew to marry her. "He was so kind and generous about it all," she recalled. Their daughter, Eve Lloyd Wright—Frank's grandchild— was born around 1960.

The splendour did not last long.

Both Olgivanna and Iovanna had studied with the Russian spiritual philosopher George Gurdjieff and aspired to transform all of Taliesin, launching every morning with "movements"—dance sessions expressing Gurdjieffian mysticism.⁷

Andrew wasn't interested in proto-New-Age dancing; he just wanted to design buildings. But now that he had married into the family, it was more important that he fit in. Olgivanna loathed Andrew for resisting her command to perform in the dance rituals. And in this power struggle, she had the upper hand. After the demise of Frank Lloyd Wright, interpretative dancing trumped architecture at Taliesin.

During this time, Andrew's family assumed he was carrying on with his upward trajectory. Then his brother Ian, who was at the time studying overseas at Cambridge University, received a middle-of-the-night telephone call from Andrew. Still half-asleep, Ian listened while his older brother unspooled a jumble of incoherent thoughts.

Ian correctly sensed that his brother might be having a nervous breakdown. Iovanna had effectively abandoned him, and Olgivanna had driven him out of Taliesin, angered by his refusal to embrace interpretative dancing and other tenets of her fiefdom. With both his architectural career and his mental health shattered, the former son-in-law of Frank Lloyd Wright returned to Toronto, where his worried family awaited to support him as best they could.⁸

At the Colborne Street office, Ron Thom provided Andrew with a sanctuary, giving him a desk and the freedom to do whatever he wanted to do. Andrew started off with some projects for the firm but seemed unable to complete them. This did not faze Ron, who let him stay on even when it seemed to other staffers that Andrew could not produce anything of value to the firm.[9] Ron appeared driven by no other motive than compassion, just like his mother when she had welcomed the rail-riders into their Marpole home forty years earlier.

Ron did glean something valuable from Andrew: the two men shared a strong interest in Northrop Frye. After his divorce from Iovanna, Andrew had married a woman named Patricia, a one-time doctoral student of Frye's, who now taught at Victoria College alongside Frye. As for Ron, he had been intrigued by Northrop Frye himself ever since hearing fragments of his Massey Lectures on CBC Radio a decade earlier. Ron spent several languid evenings in the company of Northrop Frye and his wife Helen, at the home of Andrew and Patricia Binnie.

Frye and Ron Thom had entirely different adult lives and professions, but similar backgrounds: Frye's parents had been devout Methodists like Ron's mother Elena, and Frye himself had spent five months in Saskatchewan as an itinerant student minister travelling from town to town before later switching career paths. With Frye's epic knowledge of the Bible and the poet William Blake, and Andrew's own passion for the latter subject, the evenings supplied Ron with a welcome intellectual diversion.

Meanwhile, back at Taliesin, Olgivanna was busy scrubbing away all traces of Andrew Binnie from the family's life stories, public face, and archives. But Iovanna never forgot him. Decades later, Frank Lloyd Wright's oft-married daughter recalled her attraction and marriage to that young Canadian architect:

> Certainly, he was the most talented of my husbands. He designed a house that would be floated in the air, connected to the earth by massive strong cables, held aloft by ingenious machinery and an arrangement of flaps. Andrew also recently designed a boat—an enormous kind of love boat. He said more people ought to have beauty in this life.

We divorced after about six months of official marriage, largely because I was worried that his family of lawyers might try to get custody of Eve if we stayed together till she was older. As it turned out, it was a friendly divorce though sad. Andrew set up practice in Ontario, married a charming woman, and has a handsome son, James. We still keep up with one another—he is the only husband I have had that I still love to hear from.[10]

RON STOOD READY to provide a sheltering space for Andrew Binnie and to design houses for others. He wasn't quite ready to buy a property in Toronto for his own growing family in Toronto, though, even after he and Molly welcomed their second child, Adam, in 1967. Their apartment on Washington Avenue had many virtues, being close to the centre of town in a vibrant community of artists and other creative-minded people. More pertinently, Ron hadn't been sure whether he could stay in Toronto forever. Throughout the 1960s, he had always had it in the back of his mind that he might return with his young family to the West Coast, by choice or necessity.

By 1970, with his name established and an avalanche of major new projects rolling in, he told Molly that now he knew: Toronto would be their lifelong home base. And so, they could finally start looking to buy their permanent family home.

Like most architects, Ron wanted to design his *own* house, on the kind of site that he was used to on the West Coast, with trees and craggy rock and water views. Finally, he decided to just drive until he found such a site. With Molly in the passenger seat, he launched his scouting journey on the western edge of Toronto and drove east, until eventually he entered the Scarborough Township.

Then he saw it: a "Lot for Sale" sign nestled in what looked like a small forest, on the edge of a steep hillside overlooking the Scarborough Bluffs. He pressed on the brakes. Even the street name—Meadowcliffe Drive—promised the kind of refuge he was seeking. This would be the one.

An architect's own self-designed home almost invariably presents something of a self-portrait, a catalogue of core values and life situation. Ron's design on Meadowcliffe reflected as much, for better and worse. He drew up a four-level origami-like structure that would be nestled in the greenery atop the bluffs, framed in cedar that he would import from the West Coast. The house would have niches and caves to retreat from the world, and huge expanses of glass to bring in the sweeping lake view. For his studio, Ron designed a mezzanine loft hovering over the living area, whose sharply sloped ceiling soared to double height where the mezzanine began. There he planned to work during evenings and weekends while remaining visually and audibly connected to his wife and two young children below.

Off the main living area, he designed a triangular bay jutting out of the facade—a dedicated space for the baby grand piano. As with several of his other house designs, he drew an outline of the piano—no other furniture—right onto the floor plan, as though the piano were part of the architecture. And then, just as Ron's mother had done with him, Ron exhorted his daughter to take piano lessons and to practise every day. Maybe *she* would become the concert pianist.

This architectural self-portrait also projected the problematic aspects of his wishes and circumstances. He seemed determined to replicate the site conditions of midcentury Vancouver, choosing an irregular slope to build on. His reluctance to remove even a single tree put an egregious constraint on the floor plan. Ron also wanted West Coast cedar as the main building material, and its cross-country journey on a flatbed truck devoured the construction budget.

While construction of their new home was under way, Ron received news from Vancouver: his eighty-nine-year-old father had died, on November 11, 1973. In a counterpoint to his loud anguish at his mother's death a decade earlier, he became extremely quiet for days, sober in every sense,[11] in reaction to the distant father who expired on Remembrance Day.

On the edge: Ron Thom in the mezzanine studio of his self-designed house on Meadowcliffe Drive, Scarborough.

BENDING TO THE various local and regional building codes delayed the home's construction and incurred more costs. To complicate matters further, the vendor had not legally severed it from the lot next door, triggering a bout of legal headaches.

The freewheeling building spree of Vancouver in the 1950s turned out to be a logistical and bureaucratic nightmare in 1970s Toronto. Upon its 1974 completion, Meadowcliffe projected uniqueness and drama, but the delays had compromised its size and design.

Still, the Thom family moved in with high hopes. Every window and door opened to a view of the nature that surrounded it—interacted with it, actually—since he designed walls and windows to bend in and jut out around the beech trees on the lot. He brought nature indoors as well—visually, by way of floor-to-ceiling windows, and literally, by way of hanging plants and Japanese wallpaper embedded with real leaves.

Ron moved his baby grand, which had already travelled from Beach Avenue in Vancouver, to Washington Avenue in central Toronto, to its new home in suburban Scarborough—in the triangular bay off the living room. And so from age four to fourteen, Emma took piano lessons and practised every day, just as her father had. She proved to be especially gifted at reading music. She entered the Kiwanis Music Festivals, followed the Royal Conservatory program, and performed all the exams.[12]

In media coverage, Ron Thom expressed perfect contentment with his self-designed home. "When I'm sitting in the living room looking out to the water and the trees, I find it hard to imagine I'm not in West Vancouver."[13]

At home, the configuration of the house posed challenges. His open-mezzanine work area—designed to keep him physically close to his family while working—exasperated them. Molly struggled to get to sleep while the shuffle of Ron's drafting pen jarred her ears late into the night.

During Emma's evening practice, her father worked on the mezzanine above. He could hear every note she played, and every time she hit the wrong one, he would shout his disapproval from above. Still, she stuck to it for ten years, plunking away on that well-travelled baby grand that now sat in its own custom-designed space in their suburban home. But she never felt like a classical-musician-in-training, and never aspired to be one. She would simply remember it as "the endless stupid piano playing—oh god, I just hated it!" Not until her late teens, when she delved into a stint as a rock musician, would Emma shed her reflexive dread of making music.[14]

In both his first and second families, Ron—a firstborn child—had been especially harsh on his own firstborn children—Robin in his first marriage, and now Emma in his second.[15] Since the age of six,

Emma had a propensity to blink frequently, which prompted her father one morning to holler: "Stop that fucking blinking! What do you want people to say when you go to school? 'There goes the Thom girl, always blinking!'" Many years later, they would learn that an undiagnosed medical condition had been prompting her involuntary blinking. But at the time, what disturbed the young girl most about her father's tirade was his great worry about what other people might think about *him*—about the Thom name.[16]

And Meadowcliffe's biggest drawback? Its location. Just as Chris Thom had felt marooned many years ago in North Vancouver, Molly Thom felt exiled in Scarborough. They now lived far away from their friends and the big-city attractions, and public transit to Scarborough was minimal. Ron, after acquiring a stack of impaired-driving citations, eventually lost his driver's licence permanently, and so a Thom Partnership staffer showed up at his door every morning to drive him to work and back.[17]

Not long after they settled in, their new home became the site of an ambitious family reunion. The four kids from his first marriage—plus their partners, a toddler, and a baby—travelled from their verdant West Coast homes to join their father and his second family. All four led free-spirited lives on or near Hornby Island. They bused, drove, and hitchhiked across the country, arriving at Meadowcliffe days later.

Molly struggled with the influx of eight additional houseguests in their open-plan three-bedroom house. The West Coast visitors scrounged around the suburban outskirts for food, but the closest thoroughfare—Kingston Road—had little to offer.[18] Later, the blended family gathered outside the house for a group photograph, projecting the very look of bucolic harmony, even if tensions simmered below the surface.

Aaron, who worked in logging en route to his eventual career as an arborist, noticed that his father had not heeded his advice to remove at least some of the trees on the site.[19]

Bronwen's husband Jim McLeod shot this photo of Ron's blended family and their partners convening at the Meadowcliffe house, 1975. *Back row, left to right*: Bronwen, Robin, Robin's girlfriend Patti, Sidney's boyfriend Ron, Sidney. *Middle row, left to right*: Ron, with Robin's infant son Steele on lap; Molly; Aaron's then-wife Donna-Sue; Aaron. *Front row, left to right*: Emma, Aaron's son Ace, Adam.

Sidney stood in the living room, admiring the huge triangular window that offered a sweeping view of Lake Ontario, until a sickening thud shattered the moment. A hawk had soared straight into the expanse of glass and then, with a *whump*, plunged lifelessly to the ground.[20]

FOR MOLLY, the move to this challenging new home marked a watershed year in their marriage, where Ron's alcohol dependency began to overwhelm their domestic life. At the advice of a colleague who had successfully beaten the bottle, Molly coaxed Ron into agreeing to a month-long stint at the Donwood Institute, a rehabilitation centre in the north end of the city. He relapsed shortly afterward. After more coaxing, he tried some pharmaceutical interventions, including a chewing gum designed to make liquor taste unpalatable. One friend recommended Alcoholics Anonymous; another recommended a psychiatrist—he had no faith in either option.[21]

Alastair Grant, one of Ron's partners at the Thom Partnership, contacted Molly to tell her how concerned the office staff all were about Ron's deteriorating condition. The conversation relayed nothing that Molly didn't already know, but it showed his colleagues' sincere and collective concern for his well-being.

WITH HIS YOUNG Toronto family, Ron did manage to get away from the office for the occasional fortnight into nature. They tried camping, driving all the way to Nova Scotia one year—but Ron became too obsessed with pitching their tent on *just the right spot*—not the designated campsites, but right on the beach. A man approached them in their tent in the middle of the night to warn them a storm was coming and that they had to move their tent. Ron demurred, and so the next morning, they awoke to waves crashing into their tent.[22] He just had to be close to nature—sometimes too close.

Happier memories derived from their outings to Georgian Bay, a sublime stretch of Precambrian rock face off Lake Huron, about a hundred miles north of the city. Normally, Ron would pack a briefcase with work and then, mercifully, not even open the briefcase during the whole trip. After a few days on the secluded lakefront, he would seem to forget about the madness of work and the burden of a big name.

19

ART VERSUS
THE CORPORATE
WAVE

EVEN AS THE CULTURE and the clients around him changed, Ron maintained aspects of his *modus operandi* that were either essential, endearing, or exasperating—depending on one's perspective. He persisted in prioritizing hand-drawing, for instance, and well beyond his initial schematic scribbles. His artistry drew like-minded clients to his door.

His work drew the admiration of a dentist named Murray Frum and his wife Barbara, a journalist. In his spare time, Murray was an avid art collector and aspiring real-estate developer. It seemed a propitious time to expand their small, unassuming bungalow into a place for showcasing his art and entertaining the city's elite.

Meanwhile, Barbara had just been named one of the first hosts of CBC Radio's new current-affairs program, *As It Happens*. The show quickly became a mainstay in households across the country and transformed Barbara Frum into a star. She sat in front of a mic almost every weekday evening, broadcasting to a million listeners. She yearned for her home to be a sanctuary: creative, restorative, private—inward-looking.[1]

While sipping sherry at a Massey College reception one evening, Murray felt awestruck by the beauty of the surroundings. He had already met Ron at previous social gatherings, so he felt embold-ened to phone the next day to ask him to recommend an architect who worked in his idiom.

"Well, what's the matter with *me*?" Ron retorted.

Ron's response left Murray speechless. This award winner, this great architect of Massey College—why would he want to bother taking on something as small as a house addition for a dentist? How insulting it would be, he had thought, to ask the great Ron Thom himself to do it.[2]

But Ron wanted very much to do it. And with that, Ron began yet another epic project: the Frum residence.

Their house stood at the edge of a ravine in what was then the borough of North York, just north of Toronto. On his initial visit, Ron sat down on a patch of grass on the slope, and spent over an hour looking intensely at his surroundings. He decided to reorient the small bungalow to face the ravine behind it rather than the street in front of it. This simple re-siting would connect the house to its natu-ral setting rather than the banal built landscape out front.

Ron designed the new main component of the house with heavy timber beams filled in with glass and raw unpainted cedar. Follow-ing the Wrightian concept of cavern-and-cave, he designed a double-height living room conjoined with a lower-height niche for more intimate conversations and seclusion.

When Murray—who stood six-foot-four—saw the elevations for the living room, he balked. He knew enough about architecture to grasp the cavern-and-cave concept, and he had no qualms about speaking his mind bluntly. "The idea was that you pressed down on the person when they entered, and then you exploded up, so that you got the feeling of the space. And so I said, 'Terrific idea, Ron, but you know how tall Frank Lloyd Wright was? He was about five-foot-two—a midget!' Five-seven for him would be a tall space. Five-seven for me means that I'm going to have welts on my head every time I walk into the room. That can't be."[3]

Ron begrudgingly added a few extra inches of height, but Murray still felt a bit claustrophobic every time he walked in. Barbara, on the other hand, absolutely loved this cozy nook-like space off the living room. She loved the shadows, the poetic darkness, the light seeping into their home through strategically placed windows. Her workdays were filled with the stress of interviewing and jousting with program guests. Her new home became her refuge.

The Frum's house addition turned into a decade-long series of incremental additions and modifications, and Ron felt a strong bond with these two clients—especially Barbara. He and she would spend hours enthusiastically discussing stair details, material options, lighting effects, the distinct qualities of different kinds of stone, the poetics of space. Like his lifelong friendships with Molly Bobak and Irene Dodek, Ron's affection for Barbara was platonic and profound. As Murray Frum put it, "Everyone loved Barbara. But Ron *loved* Barbara."

Upon the completion of their home's main expansion and transformation, the Frums enlisted Ron for repeated refinements, furniture, and fittings. Assisted by Jamie Smallwood, Thom designed a new bathroom, complete with a concrete tub custom-fit to Barbara's form. Like tailors to royalty, Ron and Jamie instructed Barbara to sit on a chair while they traced the outline of her hips and back and shoulders on a board behind her back. Using a cardboard cutout made with a plastic French curve, they calibrated the concavity of the lumbar curve and fashioned the tub to cradle her almost as closely as a plaster cast.[4]

RON CONTINUED TO prioritize artistry over business, believing the former better served his clients and the world at large. He had enlisted Bob Montgomery, a West Coaster on his staff and a highly gifted artist, to create beautiful drawings of the firm's work. To the more practical-minded staff like Stan Sota, the drawings amounted to a waste of resources. Stan had felt that way ever since he'd started

244 · RON THOM, ARCHITECT

at the firm back in the late 1960s, when Montgomery was making hand-drawn renderings of Champlain College. "He spent all his time drawing the foliage," laughed Stan. "The focus was on all the romantic stuff, not precision. And that drove me crazy, because I like precision. He would start his drawing in one corner with a fuzzy pen, and then you'd come back and it would be two inches larger on Tuesday, and then on Wednesday it was another two inches larger, and then in two weeks you'd have the whole drawing."[5]

Trying to maintain the primacy of art within architecture became ever more difficult, especially when Ron began losing his most important friends and mentors in the arts. In March of 1976, Ron's lifelong mentor Bert Binning died of heart failure. A year later, during a national travelling retrospective of his graphic art, Allan Fleming suffered a stroke. By the time the show opened at the Art Gallery of Ontario in June, he could barely speak. By the end of the year, Allan was dead of heart disease, at the age of forty-eight.

As the artists of Ron's prime creative period died off, it seemed to reflect the simultaneous demise of an overall creative spirit in architecture across the country. In a speech prepared for the Royal Canadian Academy of Arts in November of 1979, Ron warned against what he saw as a trend within architectural schools to segregate the art and the science of building, of dividing future architects into boutique names or technicians, with neither group understanding or caring about the other. "There is no need for these attitudes to exclude each other," he averred. "Structures can be understood and qualities felt in a single, balanced perception of order, in an experience which has characteristics of scientific and artistic activity both."[6]

AS THE 1970s rolled on, the Vitruvian triad of *firmitas, utilitas,* and *venustas* made way for the fourth pillar of *lucrum*—profit. Developers always wanted to make money, but now the mandate to wring every possible cent out of a project pervaded the profession.

By the late 1970s, Murray Frum had grown wealthy as a prolific shopping mall developer. Ron hoped that he would become his business client as well as his house client, and suggested that he design something for the Frum Development Group. It might seem obvious: Why shouldn't Murray enlist his favourite architect to design not just his family home but also these acres of commercial projects cropping up all over Ontario?

Ron's proposal got as far as a few verbal entreaties and some exchange of office correspondence, but Murray squelched that idea as best as he could tactfully manage. A realist, Murray knew that whether or not suburban shopping malls could be made architecturally beautiful was irrelevant. They existed to make money, period. "They're all wham, bam, thank you ma'am," said Murray, "You just want to get in and you want to get out. Time is money. And you're working with regional firms—Loblaws, Kmart, Hudson's Bay—that know exactly the building they want. They'll *maybe* let you fool around with the colours of the building. If I gave him a set of drawings and said, 'Here's what The Bay's gonna look like,' or 'Here's what Loblaws is gonna look like,' he'd have said something like, 'I don't wanna do that; I wanna put a window there.' And I'd have to say something like, 'You *can't* put a window there; there's a *fridge* going there!' And he would have argued, 'No, no, I gotta put a window there.' It would have driven him mad."

ACROSS THE ENTIRE CITY, the pressure to design fast and build fast ramped up considerably.

Meetings became more officious. The tools of the trade changed: instead of hand-drawing, clients wanted to see precise line drawings, machinelike. So the crew prepared slews of camera-ready art—big negatives of their renderings, with the black negative film taped together like a collage, and the scratched parts and errors painted over. No matter: the photomechanical reproduction process would then transform them into clean, high-contrast black-and-white renderings, with the austere precision that only a machine could reliably perfect.

Aware of the need to reinvigorate the firm, Ron brought in new blood throughout the 1970s, including architects Stephen Quigley and Peter Berton. They were both young, energetic, and seemed at first to enjoy protégé-mentor relationships with Ron. He recognized both of their family names by way of their big-shot fathers. Peter, the son of the famously prolific author Pierre Berton; Stephen, whose father owned that posh Vancouver menswear shop Arnold & Quigley on Granville Street in Vancouver.

Stephen and Peter became key players at the Thom Partnership and, eventually, full partners. In terms of business prowess, however, the benchmark hire was Murray Beynon, who came on board in 1976. Clearly a neck-up kind of architect, Murray focused on design efficiency, pragmatics, and good relationships with power mongers. "Murray was the person that everybody was waiting for," recalled Stan Sota. The existing partners and associates were skilled designers, "but Murray was a shark. Murray talked the language of developers."[7]

Almost immediately after joining, a major project fell into Murray's lap. Marathon Realty had allotted a parcel of land in suburban North York[8] for an office-building complex, and Ron had drawn up a schematic design. Ron's scheme showed a block with a hollowed-out centre for an atrium—essentially, a square doughnut. The atrium would be filled with over eight thousand square feet of tropical foliage that office employees could look out onto. That approach was vintage Ron Thom.

Ron had not yet found a way to resolve the issue most important to the clients: how to make it rentable in practical terms. The square-doughnut design had a huge footprint—seventy-five-thousand square feet—which would be fine if the developers knew for sure they'd have one or two big tenants, and therefore only need a few entrances. Back in the mid-1950s, men like Dal Grauer could commission entire buildings solely for the needs of their own companies. Now, in 1979, society's economic matrix had changed so that the emphasis would no longer be on a building's permanence but rather its adaptability. "You have to be able to have the flexibility to change the configuration, because you don't know if you'll have three tenants or thirty tenants," said Murray. "If you can't find three big companies to rent it, then you have to make it into thirty doctors' offices or something of that scale."⁹

Murray set to work to salvage the project, first setting up a meeting with the client. He explained where contingent entrances and exits would be situated, how interior walls could be installed and reconfigured. At this stage he would use a soft-lead 2B pencil to create thick, dark lines on vellum paper, "because you want to do something very quickly, and you want the lines to be bold and hard to show your confidence."

These business-minded presentation drawings—so different from the intricate landscape renderings by Ron Thom and the firm's other artisans—worked perfectly for this client, and for the new corporate era. Murray managed the project from then on, and Marathon remained on board for the project, calling it Atria North and later expanding it to include additional buildings. Despite further amendments in response to economic gyrations, Atria North opened to wide praise and accolades, including an award for energy efficiency—since its windows were inward-looking—and a Governor General's Medal in Architecture. Its success propelled Murray to a partnership at the firm.

By now, the dawn of the 1980s, a high-rise had emerged as the most financially worthwhile building type for a firm to take on. That posed a great challenge for an architect like Ron Thom, who loved wood, brick, and stone—none of which could be used structurally to make tall buildings.

As for the four-storey-high Atria North complex, its aluminum-plank cladding features subtly different colourations in the different planks, creating a visual effect that evokes the texture of wood. "That was pure Ron Thom," said Murray.

OPPORTUNITIES FOR Ron's kind of artisanal design approach shrivelled up along with his circle of intimates. The provincial government coffers that had once opened wide for academic and cultural buildings now opened just a sliver. The Thom Partnership won the commission for the new building for the school of architecture at Ryerson Polytechnical Institute (later known as Ryerson University). An architecture school might have been a landmark in another era, but provincial austerity measures limited its construction budget to $4.75 million—roughly $15 million in today's dollars. The funding did not allow for much artisanal arm-stretching.[10]

Partner Michael Miller took the design lead after Ron's primordial drawing. To create an effective teaching facility on a tight budget, he kept the materials bare and unfinished. It worked; in a backhanded compliment, columnist Leon Whiteson of the *Toronto Star* wrote a column titled "Ryerson designer defies temptation for rare grandeur," noting the fraught semiotics of designing a school of design. "The temptation to be brilliant must be overwhelming," he wrote. "But Ronald Thom, designer of the new $4,750,000 building for the Ryerson School of Architecture,[11] has avoided all such temptation to be too clever."[12]

The critical assessment reflected how much times had changed. In architecture, being "clever" and creating "rare grandeur" had now become suspect. Governments and clients had become more cautious. On certain kinds of public projects, a visible show of "brilliance" in architecture morphed from an asset into a liability, as though it were evidence of a waste of taxpayers' money.

At the Thom Partnership, other partners and senior associates now stickhandled most of the client relationships and logistics, while ensuring that Ron Thom's design ethos, if not always his actual hand, ruled the project. For the Transport Canada Training Institute in Cornwall, Ontario, Ralph Bergman served as the project architect. He proposed dark grey brick and wanted the project to shine—literally—with a shimmering exterior: either steel or clear

Dick Sai-Chew and Ron Thom with a model of the Transport Canada Training Institute on the wall.

anodized panels. Ralph knew that an inorganic-looking metallic cladding was "off-brand," but wanted to expand the firm's colour and material palette. Alastair Grant, who along with Dick Sai-Chew was the partner in charge of the huge commission, rejected the dark grey brick and clear metal in favour of reddish-brown brick and a chocolate-brown porcelain enamel on the steel panels. They had to keep faith with the Thom Partnership's earthy colours.[13]

Ron Thom had evolved from an architect into a brand. Prospective clients wanted to believe that this man who had created Massey College and Trent University would bestow the same magic upon them.

Phil Goldsmith, one of Ron's more artisanal associates, noticed that the Thom Partnership seemed to have cleaved off into two distinct groups—"not overtly, but in terms of spirit."[14] One group wanted to stick with Ron's architecture-as-art approach, and the other group focused on getting and keeping new business. To members of the first group, it seemed wrong that the other, more corporate-minded architects in the firm would use Ron's name and reputation to win a contract; it seemed like a denial of the firm's history—a betrayal, even.

The reality, however, is that times had changed. From the mid-1970s onwards, most of the country's business titans had to defer not only to economic hard times but also to shareholders. The balance sheet now ruled everything.

IN A NOD to that new reality, the firm hired graphic designer Shauna Haugen as its first staffer devoted full-time to marketing and communications.[15] A recent university graduate who had been studying part-time at the Ontario College of Art, Shauna was short on experience but in tune with contemporary culture. She was aware of the importance of promoting the firm's "brand"—something Ron and his coterie had never bothered with, perceiving it almost as a vulgarity.[16]

Shauna reviewed the firm's marketing materials: photocopies of random projects with typed bits of text here and there, as amateur as a school yearbook. No sense of the illustrious past and current power of this firm—and confusing dual images of cultural identity. Half the projects looked like woodsy, artisanal architecture—designed by Ron, or in the spirit of Ron. The other half looked like glass and steel corporate buildings. For her first meeting with the partners and staff, she asked the pertinent question: *Who are you?* A boutique studio that specializes in artisanal design? Or a slick firm that's all about efficiency?

Nobody could properly answer. In truth, the Thom Partnership had cleaved off into two camps by now. There was the neck-down

Winnifred Copp stands by Ron Thom in Ottawa, after Ron formally received his Order of Canada from the governor general. Harold Copp, who took the photo, was promoted to Companion in the same ceremony.

artisanal camp and the neck-up business-minded camp. Each group relied on the other to stand out from the competition and survive.

WONDERFUL NEWS arrived in the early months of 1980: the federal government named Ron Thom to the Order of Canada for his contributions to architecture. The same investiture bumped Harold Copp—the client of Ron's first officially signed house, and a lifelong friend—from his original Order of Canada to the higher tier of Companion. They convened at Government House in Ottawa to accept their honours.

At the post-investiture ceremony, he basked in his newly earned honour, standing alongside Winnifred Copp while Harold snapped a photo. Ron now wore a red and white livery collar with the enameled silver insignia as its pendant, a tiny wheel of white chevrons encircling a stylized maple leaf topped with the Royal Crown. The narrow red band that circumscribes the maple leaf is inscribed, in letters almost illegibly tiny, with a simple three-word Latin motto: *desiderantes melioriem patriam*—they desire a better country.

AS RON'S PARTNERS at the firm became more business-minded, they tried to follow the money, opening a satellite office in booming Calgary in 1979. Two years later, the partners at Montreal-based Arcop[17] approached the Thom Partnership with an enticing offer: the merging of their Calgary branch plants and the joint venture establishment of a West Coast satellite operation. For the Thom Partnership, the partnership would bring new opportunities, along with a chance for Ron to spend more time in the place he loved most. For Arcop, one of the largest firms in the country, the partnership would bring them Ron's name and, they hoped, some business in British Columbia. Arcop-Thom Architects & Planners officially launched in October that same year.

The newly amalgamated firm opened a small Vancouver office in Gastown, and for a short while, the future looked promising. At the very least, it provided Ron with a means and excuse to head back to the West Coast more often. But it didn't take long for the senior partners at 47 Colborne to realize that the mash-up of two very different firms carried its own challenges.[18] For the Arcop brass, the West Coast was less about designing in nature and more about chasing clients in the burgeoning economies of the Pacific Rim.

Through its affiliation with Arcop, Ron could more easily extend his reach right across the country, working with Lydon Lynch in Halifax to help design North American Life Centre, comprising two office buildings near the Citadel.[19] The sleek office buildings were not the kind of work Ron liked to be involved with. But the project afforded him a chance to reconnect with his old friend Doug Shadbolt, who now ran the architecture school at the Technical

University of Nova Scotia (now the Dalhousie School of Architecture). What's more, that kind of corporate project now paid the bills at the Thom Partnership, as everywhere else. "The seventies and the eighties—pah! What's left?" he lamented to design critic Adele Freedman in 1983.[20]

As the country lurched toward recession, Arcop-Thom desperately needed to look beyond regional and even national boundaries. The firm vied for the kind of massive corporate and commercial projects that were completely out of keeping with Ron's talents and interests, but which other partners could successfully pull off to keep things afloat.

One such megaproject heaved into view the following year: a forty-storey harbourfront building in Hong Kong, with a massive shopping mall, exhibition hall, and convention space. "Frankly it scares the pants off me just thinking about doing it from North America," Ron wrote to his daughter Sidney. The huge scale of that project might have secured the financial future of the firm—but they did not get the job.[21]

It now seemed to Ron that his career had switched from creating meaningful architecture to chasing giant corporate projects, the kind that were once anathema to him. "Honestly—in my next life I am going to be a doctor!" he wrote in one of his lengthy handwritten letters to the Dodeks. "Or a typist."[22]

The firm's senior partners grew to realize that for everyone's sake, especially Ron's, he should stick to designing houses. Project management had never been his strength or interest. Anything bigger than a house, like an office building or institution, brought nothing but headaches.

And so the other partners dealt with the larger-scale corporate projects, and Ron took refuge in the design of single-family homes. Here, in this compact design brief, he could deal with a structure that he could feel out from one end to the other. Small-scale, enclosed, and personal—that, he could still do.

Perspective drawing of the Thom Studio at the Banff Centre for Arts and Creativity.

Ron had the opportunity to indulge in his beloved small-scale artistry when an invitation arrived from the Banff Centre in Alberta. The well-regarded cultural and educational institution enlisted him to design one of the studios in its new Leighton Artists' Colony. He would join a team of seven other prominent Canadian architects,[23] each of whom would design a stand-alone studio for an individual visiting writer, musician, or visual artist. The Thom Studio for visual artists at Banff is small and relatively simple, but emphatically Ron. Its steeply sloped roof is half skylight, and deep eaves hang over its front and back entrances. Along with the other artists' studios, it still stands there to this day, housing sequences of artists in an idyllic wooded enclave.

20

FEAR HAS
A LONG,
LONG TALE

BY 1980, Ron's addiction had begun to engulf him. In the morning, he could present the gentle and charismatic persona that so many people loved and admired. And then, too often, he would return from lunch in an altered state, "shouting like a crazy man,"[1] as Frank Hamilton and many others at the office remember. Ron's stalwart and compassionate assistant, Angela Cadman, took on the responsibility of helping him up the stairs and calming him down. Frank and others nicknamed her "the lion tamer" for her exceptional ability at this crucial task.[2]

Ron's inner circle struggled to determine how to respond and how—if at all—they could help. Leslie Rebanks, who so enjoyed his languid lunches drinking and conversing with Ron, concluded that he was enabling him, and had to distance himself for Ron's sake.[3]

In a similar but far more momentous realization, Molly recognized that she had run out of options—that for the sake of their children and for both her and Ron's own lives as well, she had to leave. She petitioned for a formal separation.[4]

Ron remained in their Meadowcliffe Drive property after his split with Molly, but his dwindling financial resources compelled him to sell it a few years later. He then moved into a small apartment on Adelaide Street in downtown Toronto. His new home would be walking distance to his office—a huge plus—but the arid concrete surroundings contrasted harshly with the leafy surroundings of Meadowcliffe. He hauled over his paintings, some furniture, the plywood built-ins and panels that had been shipped from the West Coast all those years ago, and the piano.[5] He then reverted to a bachelor's existence.

As his Toronto social circle shrank, Ron struggled to keep the bonds of his earlier important friendships intact. Doug Shadbolt had moved back to Vancouver the year before to head UBC's architecture school, severely reducing their opportunities to get together. All his revered teachers from art school were now dead, except for Jack Shadbolt, who still lived in the house in Burnaby that his brother Doug had designed for him. "I'm afraid the one thing I don't like about this country is the vast distances between places and the effect that has on keeping in touch with so many people that you really want to keep in touch with,"[6] Ron wrote in a letter to Jack.

He returned to the West Coast whenever he could find the opportunity: for design "crit" sessions at the University of British Columbia, guest lectures, big projects, small projects. He designed a weekend cabin in Roberts Creek for Morton and Irene Dodek—a ridiculously small commission for an architect of his stature, but he nonetheless enlisted four staffers and engineer Morden Yolles for the 1,200-square-foot cabin.[7] Like so many of his commissions, that one would be a labour of love rather than any kind of moneymaker.

IN TORONTO, Ron relied heavily on a handful of old and new friends who could tolerate his situation and offer compassion. Dorothy Irwin offered one such friendship. A renowned medical illustrator for journals and textbooks, Dorothy worked out of a studio at 47 Colborne, one flight down from the Thom Partnership. She frequently offered Ron the couch to spend the night when he worked or indulged too late to make it back to his home.[8]

Dorothy and Ron shared a passion for drawing, art, and heritage buildings. She helped lead an activist group called the Draper Street Residents' Association, fighting to keep a block of unique nineteenth-century rowhouses from the wrecker's ball.

With Ron's driver's licence now permanently revoked, Dorothy drove Ron everywhere. They would occasionally drive north of Toronto for an hour to reach a favourite architectural landmark: the Sharon Temple. Built in the early nineteenth century by a Quaker breakaway group, the temple is animated inside by ziggurat tiers and a symmetry meant to relay a spirit of equality. The surrounding village had transformed it from a house of worship into a public museum in 1918.

Ron had been agnostic most of his life and rarely entered a church, but he relished his visits to the Sharon Temple. Strolling around and inside the temple seemed to restore his sense of calm.[9]

Dorothy struggled to support Ron and extract him from the tightening vise of alcoholism. She recognized Ron as a good man, a genius, whose drinking stemmed from internal struggles and insecurities. She began writing a book about addiction, about and for Ron. An early draft conveys its wistfully childlike tone, illustrated with a drawing of a menacing dragon with an elongated tail.[10] "Fear has sharp teeth and a long, long tale," she wrote, the odd spelling of that last word evoking a double meaning: the menacing tail on the metaphorical dragon, and the long story of how fear and insecurity slowly grew to overwhelm their victim.

AS HIS FINANCIAL pressures intensified, Ron poured out his worries to his progeny on the West Coast, in prolific letters written in longhand and signed with love. All four children from his first marriage had remained in British Columbia. Ron accepted every proposal for any Vancouver-based talk, consultation, or crit session, catching up when time allowed with his four West Coast offspring scattered along the coast.

Narod House on Jericho Beach, Vancouver.

Solicitations of his design expertise continued to trickle in from across the country, partly on the basis of his reputation, and partly on the bedrock of friendships he had established among his many clients. The White Rock home he had designed for Phil and Mairi Narod in the early 1960s had befriended him not only to them but also to Phil's brother Alvin, an engineer turned developer. Alvin Narod became a great fan of Ron's and, a decade later, enlisted him to help him design his waterfront house near Vancouver's Jericho Beach. Working in collaboration, the former engineer and the architect created a highly unusual house: a series of inverted A-frame forms that buttress a cantilevered upper deck jutting over the shore.

Alvin Narod was evidently pleased with his house, for in 1980, he summoned Ron to Vancouver for input on a major new structure about to transform the city. The province's then-premier Bill Bennett[11] had appointed Alvin to develop an astonishing 224 acres of prime downtown real estate. The flagship project on this giant swath of land would be a multipurpose sports stadium on the north side of False Creek. It would be part of the infrastructure for the upcoming Expo 86, and the largest air-supported domed stadium in the world. They planned to call it BC Place.

After commissioning an engineering firm to design the stadium, Alvin enlisted Ron and architect Bruno Freschi as consultants after the fact. Ron flew to Vancouver and checked into the Sylvia Hotel, his usual Vancouver accommodation. The next morning, Bruno arrived at the Sylvia to whisk Ron to the downtown meeting with the government officials of the B.C. Pavilion Corporation, known as PavCo, the Crown corporation bankrolling and managing the stadium. Ron seemed in no condition to meet with anyone, let alone a client group.

Bruno grew even more apprehensive when he and Ron arrived at the BC Place headquarters and saw the conceptual design. In his eyes, the stadium model looked like "a big ugly drum,"[12] with a huge off-white inflatable roof bulging out of the top.

With Bruno leading the way, he and Ron worked hard to find ways to enliven and humanize the giant drum. They managed to add large areas of glass at the concourse level, which improved it significantly, but there wasn't much they could do to change the roof scheme at that stage.

One of the few design elements they could change was the colour of the cloudlike dome, from its pallid greyish-white to a softer light blue. Bruno and Ron prepared to relay their design input at a meeting of the PavCo board.

Unfortunately, Ron—now in the grips of a monstrous hangover—was in no mood for tact. Before the roomful of corporate brass, he stood up and bellowed out his evaluation: "This roof looks like a used condom!"[13]

The board fell momentarily silent. Bruno inwardly groaned at Ron's lack of diplomacy, which he knew would undermine their sway with the board. Just the same, he thought that Ron's comparison was apt.

The PavCo team did not adopt the Freschi-Thom recommendation of the "northern sky" hue for the inflatable roof, though they did decide to alter the colour slightly. Decades later, after the condom-like roof started leaking and spontaneously deflating, it was replaced by a cable-supported retractable roof. But Bruno would long wonder how much more effective their advice could have been, had Ron not been so openly ravaged by his addiction.

Ron's colleagues realized that although Ron could still be a superb designer and critic, his alcoholism now threatened to bulldoze his entire career, along with everything else that mattered to him. His team at the Thom Partnership could no longer rely on him to chair meetings or deliver client presentations, let alone provide the oversight on the large and complex projects. Murray Beynon took charge and attempted to lay down the law, informing Ron that all client meetings would need to be scheduled for the morning—never in the afternoon, a time of day when his state of sobriety would be much more unpredictable. And under no circumstances, asserted Murray, could Ron meet clients on his own; another partner or senior associate at the firm needed to be present.[14]

Ron accepted those terms and tried to adhere to them. He didn't have much choice—and, however constricting, these terms were in everyone's best interest, including his own.

The partners consulted with Toronto's Centre for Addiction and Mental Health. The experts there told them that Ron could overcome his addiction only if he deeply wanted to, and if he worked at it full-time.

As a last resort, Ron agreed to a surgical implant in his stomach that would induce nausea upon ingestion of alcohol. That worked for about a week.

His loyal support staff helped manage his mood swings and smooth over his absences to clients. With each volley of bad news, Ron would thunder at his associates, leaving it to assistants Angela Cadman and Daphne Sherrard to calm him down and get resettled in his office.

Angela Cadman with Ron at the Colborne Street headquarters of the Thom Partnership.

As the incoming projects dwindled, Ron lost some of his most reliable senior associates. Among them was Ralph Bergman, who fled the chaos at 47 Colborne to work at Arthur Erickson's Toronto office. Sequestered on the seventh floor of a high-rise at Bloor and Bay Streets, Arthur's workplace offered just the respite Bergman needed, at least on the surface. The calm atmosphere and the ambiance of a well-managed, high-functioning office reassured him in his early weeks.

Then Ralph noticed other distinctions at the Erickson office, not all of them positive. Unlike Ron, for example, Arthur hardly ever showed his face at the office. For much of the time, Arthur was away travelling or at one of his other houses, even when key project deadlines loomed. Bergman pondered the stark differences in these two men: Ron was accessible, inviting Bergman and other staffers to his home for informal visits and parties. Arthur lived in a coach house in the city's posh Rosedale neighbourhood, and the only visits Bergman made were strictly for business. Ron's Christmas parties

transpired at the office, in an air of jovial and warmhearted bac-
chanalia. Arthur held his Christmas parties in the elegant but staid
atmosphere of high-end commercial restaurants.

At Arthur's office, Ralph sat near the bookkeeper's office, and
could hear the remonstrations from the office manager. The firm
was hemorrhaging money to fund Arthur's exotic travels, homes,
and offices in New York and Los Angeles—and the whims of his
senior interior designer and life partner, Francisco Kripacz. When
Arthur did make it to the office—every three weeks or so during
Bergman's time there—he was focused, lucid, neat, and well-
organized. Like an absentee parent, he partly made up for his extensive time away from the office by offering quality time when he
returned.

Still, Arthur Erickson Associates struggled financially. Not even
his senior staff could curtail the expenditures of Arthur and, especially, Francisco. On one occasion, Arthur and Francisco were
planning one of their typically elaborate dinner parties at their
Manhattan townhouse, and wanted Francisco's favourite vase for
the table. Unfortunately, the vase was in Toronto—so they enlisted
a young staff member to catch the next flight to New York and
hand-deliver it to Francisco for the party. That, thought Bergman
and others, was "a microcosm of the problem."[15]

It had become apparent that what drinking was to Ron Thom,
spending was to Arthur Erickson. Both Arthur and Ron had fallen
under the spell of their respective addictions, which would eventually bring each of them crashing down to earth.

RON'S LETTERS to his four children on the West Coast grew ever
more plaintive. "At this moment, I don't know what I'm doing—or
should be—or where anything is going," he wrote to Sidney. "I'd just
like to get a job at Thompson Berwick Pratt and move back to Vancouver. Ha! That's it—when you grew old with a <u>name</u>, you have two
things against you—age and name. I should have kept on through
life as a good little draftsman."[16]

That was the paradox that both reassured and tormented him: even as alcoholism tightened its grip, his name endured. Universities still gratefully flew him across the country. He continued to draw and scribble rough designs and spend restorative weekends with those remaining friends, like Dorothy Irwin or Anita Voss, who felt they understood him and could help him.

Ron spent long lunches and evenings with friends bemoaning the state of things and berating the people who he felt brought it to that state. In the small hours of the morning, he would occasionally dial up people like the Frums to further unload. "When the phone would ring at three in the morning, we'd know who it was," sighed Murray Frum. The outbursts eroded so many relationships that his once-enormous pool of friends and admirers shrank to a puddle.

Ron usually found social salvation during annual trips to the West Coast. He would visit friends like Doug Shadbolt and enjoy the ocean-view lounge at the Sylvia Hotel. He would also reconnect with Morton and Irene Dodek at the Vancouver home he had designed for them. Then, whenever possible, he would side-trip to Vancouver Island and Hornby Island, visiting his offspring who lived there, and take in the islands' sublime beauty.

In 1981, Ron travelled to Hornby to undertake a small but highly personal commission: a permanent home for his ex-wife Chris. In recent years, Chris had stabilized emotionally and—thanks to an inheritance from an aunt—financially. She had purchased a waterfront acreage that she would later subdivide. Ron designed the house, and their son Robin built it: a light-filled one-bedroom home with a large room for painting and craft-making—"my playroom," she called it.[17] Clad in cedar, art studio at its core, and looking out over a beach of dark volcanic stone toward a vast expanse of ocean—a catalogue of everything Ron himself loved.

Chris Thom's Hornby Island house would not be destined for the architectural-history books, and it exhibited more than a few construction quirks. But it turned out to be a light, bright, art-centric home that made Chris very happy in the final decades of her long life. Designed twenty years after their ugly and hostile breakup, the small and simple house expressed something unique to their situation: reconciliation through architecture.

"WELL, THE TIME has finally come to resurface in Vancouver," he wrote to his old friends Morton and Irene in the fall of 1981.[18] Resurfacing was an apt verb; Ron was allegorically underwater in many ways. His firm lurched from one tenuous contract to another, with revenues often lower than his overhead. When he escaped from Toronto, he felt free—for a while.

The reconnections with family and old friends would shore up his spirits for a while, but the surge of self-confidence from his Order of Canada seemed to have collapsed. When Irene Dodek pointed to his investiture pin as something to be supremely proud of, Ron scowled and said, "What, this little thing? It's nothing."[19]

His architectural mind would never leave him, even when far away from the workplace. He visited his eldest daughter, Sidney, on Vancouver Island one year just as she and her two young daughters were resettling in the town of Royston. He took it upon himself to design her fence, breaking the inert line with jogs at semi-regular intervals. "You can't have a straight-line fence," he told his daughter. "It would feel too unnatural."[20]

IN A LOSS to him and to the entire staff, Ron's assistant Angela Cadman reluctantly left the firm in 1982 to move to Picton, Ontario, with her husband. Daphne Sherrard left shortly afterward. Both remained concerned about his well-being, however. Daphne continued to check in on Ron even after she left the firm, and they remained close and mutually supportive. And in summers, Ron had the extra help and company of his teenage son Adam, who ran prints, put Letraset text on drawings, made deliveries, organized documents, washed coffee cups, and hauled up cases of beer for the staff on Friday afternoons.[21]

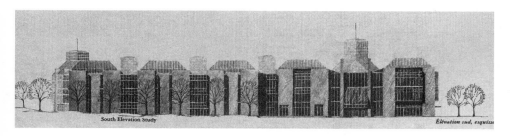

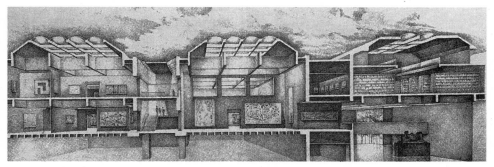

National Gallery of Canada competition renderings, as published in the August 1984 edition of Montreal-based *Section A*.

That same year brought an invitation to compete for the design of the new National Gallery of Canada. The country's existing gallery stood forlornly and anonymously, embedded in a nondescript office building on Ottawa's Elgin Street. The National Gallery competition, part of Prime Minister Pierre Trudeau's plan for a series of legacy buildings, promised to be one of the most momentous commissions in decades.

Jean Boggs, the chair and CEO of the Canada Museums Construction Corporation, invited a group of five architectural firms to submit proposals. Boggs wielded massive power to reshape the nation's cultural landscape. Back in 1966, she had become the first female director of the Gallery and logged a decade at its helm. Now, she carried with her the respect and open wallet of the Trudeau government. Ron felt confident that he would be handed the National Gallery; he was friends with Jean, after all.[22]

In the end, none of the five firms received that plum commission; it was handed to Moshe Safdie, a McGill-trained, Boston-based architect who had originally gained his fame as the designer of the Habitat housing complex at Expo 67 in Montreal. Ron felt utterly cheated. The competition guidelines had stated that any of the invited entrants might well be chosen for another category instead, but Ron remained livid. "This issue of 'Section A' just arrived about that dreadful National Gallery competition—the one we got ripped off in—and they gave it to Safdie who didn't compete for it," he wrote.[23]

IN 1983, a recession ravaged the entire national economy. At 47 Colborne Street, jobs dried up and the partners struggled to meet payroll every month. Several of the partners and staffers at the Thom Partnership had grown deeply concerned about Ron's health and well-being. Ron shambled through the office by day, and staggered home to his Adelaide Street apartment at night. Or he would spend the night at Colborne Street, either on his office couch or at Dorothy Irwin's studio one flight down. His once-expansive social circle contracted further, as more friends retreated, disturbed to realize they might have been enabling him—or just plain disturbed.

BY 1984, Ron had reconnected with Anita Voss, whose marriage to Metropolitan Toronto Zoo director Gunter had imploded years earlier. Anita now lived in Sooke, and she welcomed him into the oasis of her home. Ron found a creative refuge during his stays with

Anita. He designed a table for her, and he sat quietly for hours, painting the waterfront view outside her living room window. Days later, he would return to the mainland, and then back to Toronto, leaving Anita longing for him. Despite the ephemeral nature of their relationship—or possibly because of it—Ron turned out to be one of the greatest loves of her life.[24]

THE YEAR 1984 brought some key staff changes. Ron welcomed another promising young designer to the firm, Howard Sutcliffe, who had just graduated from the University of Waterloo School of Architecture. Howard shared Ron's sensibilities and turned out to be a natural collaborator with Ron on the ongoing furniture design projects for Barbara and Murray Frum. With Howard, Ron seemed capable of designing closer to the top of his form. He certainly behaved better.

That same year, however, also saw the departure of Murray Beynon, who left to co-launch his own practice with two other founding partners. Regardless of how much Ron differed from Murray in his approach to architecture and practice, he had needed him to keep the business side of things afloat. But Murray could no longer tolerate Ron's erratic behaviour. Like Bill, Peter, Alastair, and so many other architects who revered Ron but eventually reached a breaking point, Murray knew when it was time to go.[25]

THE FOLLOWING SUMMER proved to be a scorcher. On one of its most sweltering days, Ron penned an update to Sidney and her partner, apologizing for delaying his trip west to visit them. "The office is a loony bin right now—with half the people off on summer holidays and the place busier than it has been for a year."[26]

Life and work seemed to offer nothing but trouble. In March of 1986, the chief curator at the McMichael Canadian Collection, an art museum in Kleinburg, Ontario, asked Ron if he could prepare a talk to complement a solo exhibition of the work of his mentor, Bert Binning. Ron unpacked his ordeal in a letter to Sidney and several others:

> Naturally I said sure. Ha! You can't believe the amount of work. I had to analyse three books—all written by different people at different times—and full of contradictions—and I had to talk to dear old Jessie Binning—who is still alive and living in the house they built in West Vancouver in 1940—and spend a bundle on long-distance phone calls to people like Don Jarvis. Work piled on work—days and nights and weekends to sort it all out.[27]

Ron had arrived an hour early. The auditorium seated three hundred, but only twelve people showed up. It turned out the museum had not advertised the talk in advance, and the curator himself was a no-show. The apathy so enraged Ron that he sent a transcript of his lecture to friends and family members, bemoaning the "sick/funny story" of his talk.

The transcript of the talk conveyed an eloquent appreciation of art in general, and Binning's art in particular: "Abstracted anchors, towers, weather stations and pennants become geometric motifs and linear rigging forms a counterpoint to coloured masses. Contrasts and complexities continually engage the eye." Ron concluded his lecture wistfully: "Binning espoused a philosophy of cultured civilization in which the arts played a central role. We can only conjecture where Binning's genius might have led him, had he more time."

AT THE THOM PARTNERSHIP, the financial problems worsened. One day, Dick Sai-Chew approached the other four partners with a grim edict: "Guys, if we're going to make payroll, we have to all put in some money." And then four of the five partners—Dick, Peter Berton, Paul Nevins, and Steve Quigley—walked to the bank that day and each transferred $10,000 to the firm. Just enough so the staff cheques wouldn't bounce.

Ron, the fifth partner, didn't have any money to put in.

By this point, his partnership stake was slipping out of his hands. "I'm going crazy here with what is going on in the office," he wrote to Aaron. He complained that "two young turks wanted to take it over—and have. One is Peter Berton—Pierre Berton's son—and the other is Stephen Quigley—from the Arnold & Quigley bunch. The two of them were working on the one big job the office had—a large shopping centre—and they threatened to quit if I didn't back out of the partnership and they take over. We would have lost the job if they did—and the office would have gone belly up. So how could I turn them down?"[28]

The answer to his rhetorical question would be: he couldn't. The shopping centre and other projects brought in and carried out by the other senior partners kept the firm afloat.

In September, Ron closed a letter to Sidney on a brighter note: "It looks as though I will be out in dear B.C. in mid-October to give some lectures to the students at UBC." He had been invited to be the guest speaker in their periodic lunch hour presentations.[29] In exchange for his lecture, he would receive a one-hundred-dollar honorarium and—far more enticing to him—round-trip travel to Vancouver.

A few weeks later he received a letter signed by the other four partners: "Under the circumstances, we have no alternative but to relieve you of your duties, effective Oct. 17, 1986," it stated.[30] The letter added that he could stay six more months in the office while receiving a monthly cash stipend, and that he could stay on longer than that if he could manage his "personal problems," referring to his alcohol dependence. If he could recover, then he could officially rejoin the firm.

But he must have known what an untenable request that was.

THEIR LETTER was accurate; there was no alternative. Ron had run out of options for managing the deleterious effects of his addiction, and the Thom Partnership was slithering into bankruptcy. "He was incredibly depressed at that time," recalled Peter Berton, "because although he was still in the firm, he couldn't manage money, and he lost control of it. So we said, 'Okay, Ron, you stick around, you be the grey-haired experienced one, the advisor; you do what you want to help us, and we'll pay you.' And he didn't like that, and he told everyone out west that we booted him out, which wasn't true. We kept him on; we just saved the firm."[31]

Ron didn't see it that way. "I am as of now no longer a partner. I am a 'consultant'—which to me is just another word for employee," he fumed to Sidney. "The game is over. I won't be in the firm after March. They've made the final push (blackmail)—and—even though I don't know what I'll be doing then, I'll be glad to be out. So—don't worry about me."[32]

The final push wasn't "blackmail," of course, by any standard definition of the term. And his offspring *did* worry about him. Sidney and Bronwen both urged him to come back to the West Coast for good, and just design houses. He'd have plenty of clients.

He had thought about that idea before. But some kind of invisible chains seemed to shackle him to the firm that bore his name.

21

THE
LAST TRIP HOME

STILL REELING FROM the announcement of his impending ouster, Ron prepared for his trip to British Columbia. He alerted a few close friends that he hoped to see them while he was in town. To his children from his first marriage, who were now all settled in various regions of the West Coast, he sent a different kind of message—he stressed that he *must* see them. He made plans for post-lecture trips to the west coast of Vancouver Island to visit his son Aaron; to the island's east coast, where Sidney lived; and finally to Hornby Island, to see Bronwen.[1]

On the eve of his flight, he phoned his youngest daughter, Emma, at her apartment in Toronto. "Where's Adam?" he demanded. He had tried to telephone his youngest son—her brother—without success. "Well, how should I know? I don't live with him!" Emma replied.

And then she wondered, as she hung up the phone, *Why is he asking me that?*[2]

ON FRIDAY, October 17, Ron Thom woke up to his first day of expulsion from the firm that bore his name. Then he headed out to the Toronto airport, boarded a morning flight to Vancouver, and flew across the country to give his scheduled midday lecture.

Ron arrived at the Frederic Lasserre Building at UBC shortly before the designated hour. He then met with Stephanie Robb, the student who had extended the invitation, in the staff room to discuss the imminent lecture. Stephanie suggested to Ron that he talk to the students about his design process.[3]

"What do you mean by that?" he asked.

"Well, how you generate ideas and form, and then how you develop them throughout the course of the project," replied Stephanie.

"Hmm," he replied, as though he had never heard of such a thing before. Ron's intuitive mind defied the need for a conscious, rational, and explicable design process.

Then they headed over to Room 202 and set up the slide projector, slotting images of his life's work inside the plastic carousel.

He looked pale. He spoke quietly and listlessly while the slide projector clicked and whirred, ticking down his allotted hour.[4]

AFTER THE PRESENTATION, Ron didn't stick around the Lasserre Building for long. He told Stephanie that he was looking forward to visiting his family and to seeing Hornby Island again.

Ron visited with his eldest son, Robin, in Vancouver. He crossed Burrard Inlet to visit his friend of over forty years, Fred Hollingsworth, at his North Vancouver home.

He headed to the Horseshoe Bay ferry terminal to begin his series of visits to the rest of his West Coast offspring. His son Aaron picked him up at the Nanaimo terminal and drove him to his Port Alberni home, on the west coast of the island, where Ron stayed the night. From there, Aaron drove him to Sidney's house in Royston. She hosted her father there for a day and a night, and then drove him to the Buckley Bay ferry terminal. Bronwen waited on the other side of the water for him, to transport him to nearby Hornby Island.

As he walked through Bronwen's home, she could hear bottles clank inside his suitcase, which he carted around like a patient tethered to an oxygen tank. The entire family were well aware of the severity of their father's addiction, so the suitcase jammed with bottles was no surprise. What was unusual and gratifying to Bronwen was that on this trip, her father took great care to *present* himself as sober. By this point, the high-proof liquor was not bacchanalian but medicinal. Even temporary abstinence no longer seemed viable; he needed to avoid obvious withdrawal symptoms that would sully this precious visit. He kept his self-ministrations as discreet as possible. And then he met his daughter, his son-in-law, his grandchildren—and they beheld him as perfectly well-behaved, kind, attentive, and—to all appearances—sober.[5]

Then Ron headed back to Vancouver to visit his former protégé, who now ran his own eponymous firm: Paul Merrick Architecture. Paul had a storefront office in Gastown, in a nineteenth-century brick building at the corner of Carrall Street and Blood Alley. The address—1 Gaoler's Mews—bespoke its history as the site of the city's first jail. Paul's office comprised the horse stable, evidenced by the swale of the floors.

Ron looked around, and then said to Paul, "I've got to get back to the coast."

On the spot, Paul offered him a space in his office, where he could come in on his own time, do his own work—no need to pay rent. He could leave Toronto behind and make a fresh start in Vancouver.

Ron hesitated. "Maybe just a desk in the corner," he replied. He told Paul that he didn't want to make things complicated, didn't want anything high-profile—that if he came back, he would want to do it in a simple way, if possible, and he'd want to stay in the shadows.

That night, Paul drove Ron to the airport for his overnight red-eye flight back to Toronto. Paul reminded Ron of his offer, and then they said their goodbyes.[6]

Early the next morning, Ron arrived boozy and bleary-eyed in Toronto. Dorothy Irwin and another friend[7] met him at the airport and drove him around the city until he sobered up. The next day, he walked to 47 Colborne Street, up the stairs, under the medieval-like industrial iron gate, past the gargoyle-like lion's head. He joined Peter Berton, Dick Sai-Chew, and Paul Nevins at a meeting; the fourth partner, Stephen Quigley, was on vacation out of the country.

When Ron disrupted the meeting with a stream of angry heckling, the other partners asked him to leave.[8]

By this point, his afternoons routinely included sipping spiked coffee or tapping into the bottle in his desk drawer, until he would inevitably slump into oblivion. So it was not particularly alarming when, toward the end of the day, Dick and Paul found Ron collapsed in the corridor, halfway inside the elevator. Dick pulled him up and urged Ron to let him escort him back to his Adelaide Street apartment. Ron declined; he wanted to hole up in his office. When Dick tried to insist, Ron more forcefully refused to return to his apartment. Dick was mystified: Why wouldn't Ron want to go home?

What the partners did not yet know, but would soon find out, is that Ron's home was occupied by others that night. He had recently begun offering shelter to acquaintances and even strangers in need— at his office, at his home, or both. This time, Ron had offered up his apartment to a homeless couple.[9]

Dick and Paul left the Colborne Street office around 6:30 PM, pulleying down and locking the iron front gate of the office. Berton remembers working later, till about 8:30 PM, and leaving by the back door. "I stayed late at the office that night," recalled Berton.[10] "At eight o'clock, I said to myself, *Well, he's still asleep; I won't bother him.* And so I went home. I sat down and said to my wife, 'It's so depressing, because Ron wasn't well today and he's still asleep in his office.' And my wife said, 'Don't be surprised if he just drops dead one day, Peter.' And I said, 'Oh god, don't say that!'"

"The next morning," Berton continued. "I went into the office, and our receptionist was saying, 'The door's still shut and he's still in there, and I'm just wondering if he's okay.' I went to talk with Paul Nevins and we said okay, let's leave it for now. But about an hour or so later we decided we'd better check on him, and we did, and we opened the door, and he was on the floor, and he was clearly—dead. I freaked! I dialed 9-1-1, but I could barely touch the numbers on the dial. So the fire department and the police department came up within two minutes; they came running up the stairs with all their defibrillator equipment. They came in, the guy opened the door—the fireman—and he said, 'He's a goner.' And then he shut the door."

THE POLICE INTERVIEWED all the partners and staff separately, ruling out homicide. The coroner's report described the manner of his death as "natural," and its medical cause as "acute alcoholism/cardiac arrest."[11]

Around the design community, the news shocked everyone and surprised no one. It did traumatize most of the Thom Partnership staff, including Peter Berton. He had watched so many colleagues join the firm out of reverence for Ron, and then leave before that reverence had a chance to evaporate. "Now, let me tell it totally straight here: I liked Ron—*loved* Ron," said Berton. "We stuck with him, and at the end we were paying him. We could have all walked out the door. But *we* didn't leave. I tried to talk to Ron a million times, said, 'Ron, you'd be so much happier if you quit drinking.' But there's nothing we could have done."[12]

ON WEDNESDAY, November 5, 1986, several hundred people from all corners of Toronto headed to St. James Cathedral, a Gothic Revival church that stands in the middle of a manicured garden, one block away from Colborne Street. Politicians, tradespeople, planners, clients, academics, critics, and friends filed in. Architects from all over showed up: Paul Merrick, Howard Sutcliffe and his partner Brigitte Shim, Dick Sai-Chew, Paul Nevins, Peter Berton, and so many others. John C. Parkin hobbled in slowly, his own health eroded by the same kind of hard-driving life that had ravaged his late colleague.

Visitors received a booklet listing the speaker lineup. On the booklet cover was Paul Merrick's sketch of the chapel where Ron's body had been cremated a few days earlier. By the time the public service commenced at 2 PM, the cathedral was packed right to its nineteenth-century stone walls. "He thought that he wasn't worth a nickel and that nobody cared about him anymore," observed Paul. "And then seven hundred people showed up."[13]

The eulogies began. Doug Shadbolt described the forces that had shaped his genius: "From his music, he had learned order, structure, composition, and the discipline of technique. From Bert [Binning] and Jack [Shadbolt] he learned to love line drawing, and he developed the eye of the artist, that sensitivity to the field of vision and to form, colour, material, texture, and surface that is at once highly selective and critical."[14]

Denis and Dawn Smith, the Trent University professors and friends, summarized Ron's creative provenance: "He was a romantic—a man inspired equally by the tall trees of his native British Columbia, the delicacy and light of Japanese design, and the strong enduring qualities of the great European builders of the past. Yet, while he was touched by a number of influences—as is the way with great artists—he was able to blend them into his own unique style, a style which is also especially Canadian."[15]

Alastair Grant then spoke, lauding his drawing skill, creativity, dedication, and innovation: "Ron showed us a new way of doing things, a new way of thinking. There was no other office to compare with it and we responded with a total commitment in the pursuit of an ideal."[16]

Barbara Frum took the lectern and delivered the most riveting tribute of the day:

> I speak on behalf of those fortunate few who were privileged to work with Ron on the creation of the most personal of projects—their own home. And I hope what I say does justice to their love for Ron too and their respect as well.
>
> Shortly after Massey College was completed, Murray [Frum] called Ron on the telephone to ask if he would recommend to us

someone who worked in his idiom to do a project for us. We loved Massey College—knew before the scaffolding came down it was a masterpiece—and wanted to live in a house with that same spirit and serenity, though we were terribly timid about asking the genius architect who produced that marvel to do a mere house addition for us.

The person Ron recommended was himself, and that was the beginning of a fifteen-year-long association and friendship, in which just about every spring Ron would be at our house where some new project was being entertained. Sometimes the project was as large as a room, sometimes as small as a table. We did the landscape together. We built the furniture together. As he told us at that first meeting, he loved doing houses, enjoyed working closely with clients on the intimate sum of personal details that a house is.

Our kids soon learned it was truly spring not when the robins arrived in the garden, but when Ron arrived at the front door—the buzz saws not far behind him.

Ron was an artist who made a refined aesthetic out of unrefinement, a master of the difference between complexity and fussiness. He taught us to love raw surfaces and the natural, to recognize harmonious proportions—how good it is to sleep and eat close to the floor, to be wrapped at night in the cocoon of a dark room punctuated by a sparkle of tiny beams of light, how everything went together if you knew what you were doing—how many steps made a walk inviting, how many made a destination too far, and how broad and deep these treads must be, which he'd dance out for us to teach the difference, striding up and down across the floor.

Ron loved solving riddles and we sometimes felt he built problems into his drawings so he could be summoned in desperation by anxious clients to dazzle them with the brilliance of his remedies.

Ron was never happier than when he could place some British Columbia mood down on a Toronto street—sometimes with an excess of wishful thinking, which produced occasions like

Murray's discovery that Ron's specs called for single glazing throughout the house against the Ontario furies; or the morning when Murray—who revered Ron's talent—called rather apologetically about two corners of the living room without any glazing called for at all and asked if that was Ron's intention. He—Murray—was prepared to try it for one winter, though he doubted it would work for two!

With clients—certainly with us—there was a sense of partnership. You were needed to work problems through with. And workmen, they loved him—because he knew their craft and because he loved materials so.

And yet he resolved the endless articulations of boards and joints involved in a hand-made house, all that was genius in him he downplayed: "Oh that! That's nothin', Frum! Just one of my tricks."

The big room he built for us remains to my mind one of the finest, most humane spaces he ever produced: an enormous, deceptively simple square, above which he slung an overhanging triangle, both levels cantilevered off an unornamented slab of caramel brick, the whole hunkered down under a shallow hill and married to the landscape through the mediation of suspended trellises.

Ron produced the sketch from which the room was built after four hours of just sitting by himself looking at the problem, and then drew a sketch that was perfect—perfect on completion as the first day he sketched it on his notepad, and perfect to this day. His space is never austere, it is for human beings. And we have never had a visitor yet who didn't smile in recognition of the embracing comfort he envelops you in and didn't leave saying: "I'd love to live here."

Ron achieved greatness without ever knowing his greatness, though we never, ever failed to tell him of our love and admiration.

Did he hear us? I don't know. I do know that we respected him and, I think, understood him. And we want his children to know how grateful we will always be to him, for what he was and what he gave us.[17]

Among Ron's colleagues and friends in attendance, Barbara's eulogy prompted a unanimous reaction in their minds: *She nailed it.*

A RECEPTION at Massey College followed the memorial service. Ron's Toronto family and his closest colleagues filed to the head table in the dining hall. Paul Merrick settled into his high-back leather chair at the centre of the head table and gazed around the perimeter of the room: the planes of brick, the columns, the grid of glass shot through by a strip of magenta, the huge concrete hearth with protruding vertical forms that echoed the hanging lanterns. Every form, every colour and texture seemed perfectly in harmony with everything else in the room.[18]

By god, thought Paul, *that bugger really did know how to design a space.*

The dining hall at Massey College.

TEN DAYS AFTER the Toronto memorial, a selection of Ron Thom's West Coast contingent of family and friends filed into the basement of Marpole United Church. In contrast to Toronto's large and dramatic send-off, Ron's two sisters had arranged for a dry afternoon with a handful of guests. The pastor affirmed the Presbyterian belief in God's power over death.

Five of his six children from his two marriages attended. The core contingent of his West Coast architects was there, including Barry Griblin, Bud Wood, and also Paul Merrick, who attended both east and west services. A reception of coffee, sandwiches, and cigarettes followed, and then Bud invited the men to the nearest bar to get "gassed up." Bronwen vetoed the gender-exclusive suggestion and the family repaired instead to the Shaughnessy home of Robin and his wife Elizabeth, to share beers and roll Drum tobacco in their attic rec room.[19]

Ron had loved nothing more than the trees, ocean, and shores of the coast. Hence, the following day's trek—to take his ashes to their final resting place in the waters of Burrard Inlet near Lighthouse Park.[20]

From a family friend, Robin had borrowed a vintage sixty-five-foot-long halibut packer called the *Annie Tuck*. They launched the oak-ribbed vessel from the Granville Island marina. On the other side of False Creek stood the remains of Expo 86, which had closed a month earlier. They sailed in the opposite direction, away from the Expo lands, and then tacked north in English Bay.

Beside them were two urns and a bouquet of carnations. One urn held Ron's ashes; the second held the ashes of his mother, Elena. The container of her long-cremated ashes had been stored away for so long that some family members hadn't even been sure of their whereabouts. Now it seemed fitting to have her accompany her only son on his final send-off.

With Point Atkinson Lighthouse looming high above them, they poised the urns on the edge of the boat and opened the lids. Sidney marveled at the different textures of the two cremains: the ashes of her father, cremated by modern methods, were much finer and smaller than the ashes and bone fragments of her grandmother.

First went Elena.

And then Ron.

As they were tipping the second urn over the side of the boat, a sudden gust of wind grabbed some cremains and flung them right back at them, like a ghostly ambivalence about his ultimate return home. Momentarily flustered, the family brushed off the stray ashes of their father and then returned to the task at hand. They picked up the bouquet of white carnations and lobbed it overboard where they had poured out the contents of the urns.

The flowers tumbled into the water and bobbed up and down for a few moments before fanning out and vanishing under the waves.

Slate plaque on the bell tower of Massey College.

ACKNOWLEDGMENTS

GREATEST THANKS go to Ron Thom's family, whose collaborative spirit has made this book possible. In British Columbia: Chris Thom, Robin Thom, Sidney Thom, Aaron Thom, and Bronwen Thom McLeod. In Ontario: Molly Thom, Emma Thom, and Adam Thom. They have gifted this project with their time, personal letters, vintage photographs, and memories.

My interviews with former Thompson Berwick Pratt and Thom Partnership staff were also crucial, and I am particularly grateful to Dick Sai-Chew, Barry Downs, Paul Merrick, Geoff Massey, Bill Lett, and Peter Smith. I also thank Paul Barnard, Alan Bell, Ralph Bergman, Peter Berton, Murray Beynon, Wyn Bielaska, Susan Black, Shanna Fromson, Phil Goldsmith, Alastair Grant, Barry Griblin, Paul Halpern, Frank Hamilton, Daphne Sherrard Harris, Shauna Haugen, Fred Hollingsworth, Brian Kilpatrick, Zoltan Kiss, Ian MacDonald, Paul Martel, Bill McCreery, Michael Miller, Jim Nelles, Paul Nevins, Stephen Quigley, Jamie Smallwood, Stan Sota, Angela Cadman Strachan, and Howard Sutcliffe.

Additional insight has come from interviews with Ron Thom's friends and colleagues, or their relatives: Bruno and Molly Bobak,

Morton and Irene Dodek, Dawn and Denis Smith, Bob Dawson, Eberhard and Jane Zeidler, Morden Yolles, Peter Pratt, Selwyn Pullan, Leslie Rebanks, Ian Anderson, John Andrews, Emily Aspell, the Right Honourable Ian Binnie, Douglas Buck, Harvey Cowan, Jack Diamond, Marya Fiamengo, Bruno Freschi, Murray Frum, Bo Helliwell, Ann, Jill, Jane, and Susan Irwin, Jamie Kennedy, Janis Kravis, Phyllis Lambert, Mel Lauder, Andy Lynch, Mary MacDonald, Jim McLeod, Michael McMordie, Patty Copp Montpellier, David Mooney, Tim Murray, Cornelia Hahn Oberlander, Joseph Pliss, Stephanie Robb, Bob Rowland, Richard Sadleir, Anny Scoones, John Scott, Sidney Shadbolt, Gordon and Marion Smith, Sheila Southworth, John Stubbs, Jim Sykes, Tom Symons, Anne Tait, Bing Thom, Anita Voss, Joe Wai, Erica Warrington, and Diane Wood.

Colleagues in the art, architecture, and writing communities who have assisted me include Jim Ferguson and Jan Pidhirny, Brigitte Shim, Angie Abdou, Nancy Bendtsen, Anne Ferries, Bernard Flaman, John Flanders, Steve Gairns, Michael Geller, Sascha Hastings, Odile Hénault, Alexi Hobbs, Maggie Hunter, Jane Kinegal, Henning Knoetzele, Naomi Kriss, Hilary Letwin, Janna Levitt, Laura Lind, Don Luxton, John Mackie, Eva Matsuzaki, Sherry McKay, Carol Moore-Ede, Josh Nychuk, Jan Redford, Gary Ross, Kim Smith, Michael Smith, Kathleen Staples, Andy Sylvester, Peeroj Thakre, Leslie Van Duzer, Alex Waterhouse-Hayward, Scott Watson, Howard White, and Harold Zellman. Extra thanks to Adriana Barton and Hal Wake for their crucial commiseration. I also owe much to the late Doug Shadbolt, whom I never met but whose 1995 book *Ron Thom: The Shaping of an Architect* established a foundation for other writers and scholars to build upon.

My 2013–2015 travelling exhibition, *Ron Thom and the Allied Arts*, provided a wellspring of opportunities for the cross-country research and interviews that inform this book. For this I extend special thanks to Brigitte Desrochers, Steven Evans, John Fraser, Linda Fraser, Rachel Gotlieb, Helena Grdadolnik, Lee Hays, John Leroux,

Raymond Massey, Tony Robins, Kiriko Watanabe, Public: Architecture + Communication, the Massey Foundation, the Canada Council for the Arts, and the BC Arts Council. For this current book, the BC Arts Council has also provided me with funding for the final intense months of research and writing.

My hat is off to the staff and associates of Greystone Books, especially Derek Fairbridge, James Penco, Jessica Sullivan, and Jennifer Stewart, for their patience and skill in transforming an unruly swarm of information and images into a beautiful final product. I thank Maggie Hunter and the rest of the diligent staff of the Canadian Architectural Archives at the University of Calgary, West Vancouver Art Museum, Massey College, Trent University, Emily Carr University of Art and Design Library and Archives, Banff Centre for Arts and Creativity, University of British Columbia Archives, Library and Archives of the Vancouver Art Gallery, City of Vancouver Archives, and Toronto Reference Library. A huge thanks to the many residents and owners of Ron Thom houses across the country who have generously allowed me access to their homes. To all my other colleagues and friends who have helped me in so many ways, please know how much I appreciate you.

As ever, I remain deeply grateful to Julia, Natalie, and Jamie Chrones, who have advised and supported me throughout this and so many other epic challenges.

ADELE WEDER, *March 2022*

ENDNOTES

PROLOGUE · THE ROYAL BLESSING

1 Douglas Shadbolt, *Ron Thom: The Shaping of an Architect* (Vancouver: Douglas & McIntyre, 1995), 73.
2 Robertson Davies, *A Celtic Temperament: Robertson Davies as Diarist* (Toronto: McClelland & Stewart, 2015), 222–223.
3 Davies, *A Celtic Temperament*, 210.
4 Among other sources, see W.H. New, *A History of Canadian Literature* (New York: New Amsterdam Books, 1992), 142.
5 Davies, *A Celtic Temperament*, 192.

1 · A FOUNDATION IN MUSIC

1 Shadbolt, *Ron Thom*, 4.
2 See George Emery, *The Methodist Church on the Prairies, 1896–1914* (Montreal: McGill-Queens University Press, 2001). Also see: www.thecanadianencyclopedia.ca/en/article/methodism.
3 See Emery, *The Methodist Church*. Confirmed by the Law Society of Saskatchewan archives.
4 See Mary Jane Mossman, *The First Women Lawyers: A Comparative Study of Gender, Law and the Legal Professions* (London: Hart Publishing, 2006). Mossman relays that in the early twentieth century the first women were finally allowed to enter law school or, alternatively, become a lawyer via the apprenticeship system—in theory; the societal impediments and expectations of the era, however, meant that many of the nation's first female lawyers ceased practising law upon marriage or shortly thereafter.
5 Information and images of historic Weyburn sourced online from the Provincial Archives of Saskatchewan and the website www.prairie-towns.com, published by the DGL Historical Foundation.
6 Ibid.; confirmation and further details provided in dossier compiled by Mavis Thom, "A History of the Thom Clan," sec. 1.

7 A "journeyman" in 1800s Scotland would have completed his apprenticeship but not yet attained the title of Master. See J. Brinsden, *Regional Furniture*, vol. 18 (2004).

8 Mavis Thom, "Thom Clan."

9 Mavis Thom, "Thom Clan."

10 Mavis Thom, "Thom Clan."

11 Sidney Thom, telephone interview, June 4, 2020.

12 Shadbolt, *Ron Thom*, 5; and Mavis Thom, "Thom Clan."

13 Shadbolt, *Ron Thom*, 5; and Mavis Thom, "Thom Clan."

14 In over a dozen of the roughly one hundred interviews conducted in the course of writing this book, friends and colleagues mentioned that Ron Thom spoke often of his mother, including memories of how she raised him, but rarely or never of his father.

15 Mavis Thom and Ron Thom, relayed by S. Thom and B. McLeod.

16 R. Thom's memories of his mother's hosting of itinerants were relayed in Shadbolt, *Ron Thom*; by S. Fromson in a telephone interview, Feb. 7, 2021; and Molly Thom by email, Feb. 9, 2021.

17 "Ronald Thom tops all piano contestants," *The Review*, April 8, 1936 (photocopy of clipping from Thom family archive).

18 Musical evaluations, 1934–1938, Thom family archive.

19 Bob Rowland, interview, White Rock, June 19, 2015.

20 D. Shadbolt reported Ron Thom's high school art teacher as Jessie Faunt, who has also been cited as Arthur Erickson's teacher, and who later became one of the Vancouver Art Gallery's first docents.

21 Shadbolt, *Ron Thom*, 7; confirmed by Thom family members and archive.

22 Adele Freedman, "Thom: 'A man of tall timbers,'" *Globe and Mail*, March 12, 1983; confirmed by S. Thom, telephone interview, Feb. 9, 2021.

23 Shadbolt, *Ron Thom*, 5–7; Molly Thom, interview.

2 · BUILDING A CULTURE

1 Information on Thom's early days at Vancouver School of Art is sourced from D. Shadbolt book and Thom family archive; description of VSA's physical form and syllabus is sourced from photography in the City of Vancouver Archives and Emily Carr University of Art and Design library and archives.

2 Passage describing the art scene sourced from R. Amos, *Harold Mortimer-Lamb: The Art Lover* (Vancouver: Touchwood Editions, 2013); S. Watson (ed.), *Vancouver: Art and Artists 1931–1983* (Vancouver: Vancouver Art Gallery, 1983); Peter Varley, *Frederick H. Varley* (Toronto: Key Porter, 1983); and multiple other sources.

3 Passages relating to the history of the B.C. Art League and Charles Scott, art school, and art gallery were sourced from documentation

in the City of Vancouver Archives, ECU Archives, and the private family archive of John Scott—grandson of Charles.

4 Charles Scott was likely referencing the 1898 landmark book designed by Frank Lloyd Wright, titled *The House Beautiful*.

5 Notes for a speech by C. Scott, J. Scott family archive.

6 See *Vancouver School of Art: The Early Years, 1925-1939* (Vancouver: Charles H. Scott Gallery and Emily Carr College of Art, 1980); and Varley, *Frederick H. Varley*.

7 See *Vancouver School of Art* and Varley, *Frederick H. Varley*.

8 Abraham Rogatnick, "A Passion for the Contemporary," in A. Rogatnick, I. Thom, and A. Weder, *B.C. Binning* (Vancouver: Douglas & McIntyre, 2006), 6.

9 The cultural history of the Binning House and its exceptional optical qualities are relayed in Rhodri Windsor Liscombe, *The New Spirit: Modern Architecture in Vancouver, 1938-1963* (Cambridge, MA: MIT Press, 1997); Rogatnick, *B.C. Binning*; and Matthew Soules, *Binning House* (Novato, CA: ORO Editions, 2017).

10 Memories of the social scene at the VSA at that time were collected from Molly Bobak, Gordon Smith, Chris Thom, and from the books by A. Brown and J. Plaskett.

11 Emily Aspell recollected to this author that her father, Peter Aspell, spoke of Christine Millard's exceptional beauty. Photographs of her during that time confirm that assessment.

12 This passage is sourced from interviews with C. Thom and other family members, and M. Bobak.

13 M. Bobak, interview.

14 M. Bobak, interview.

15 M. Bobak, interview.

16 Transcript of McMichael speech, multiple copies in Thom family archive. Many of Ron Thom's thoughts on B.C. Binning are found in the transcripts of his 1986 public talk given at the Kleinburg, Ontario, gallery then known as the McMichael Conservation Collection of Art.

17 See Rogatnick, *B.C. Binning*.

18 B.C. Binning, "The Artist and the Architect," *Royal Architectural Institute of Canada Journal* 27, no. 9 (September 1950), 320-321.

3 · THE SHADOW OF CONFLICT

1 Sidney Thom, interview, Royston, July 13, 2011.

2 William Lyon Mackenzie King, "Canada at the Side of Britain," broadcast speech, Sept. 10, 1939, CBC Digital Archives, www.cbc.ca/archives/entry/1939-canada-at-the-side-of-britain.

3 S. Thom, interview.

4 Aaron Thom, interview, Port Alberni, June 25, 2019; Bronwen Thom McLeod, interview, Hornby Island, July 15, 2011.

5 Chris Thom, interview, Hornby Island, July 16, 2011.

6 A. Thom, interview.

7 This information, and that of subsequent paragraphs, was retrieved from military records archived at the National Library and Archives, Ottawa.

8 Griffin, D.F., *First Steps to Tokyo: The Royal Canadian Air Force in the Aleutians* (Toronto: J.M. Dent & Sons, 1944), 25.

9 Thom family archive.

10 C. Thom, interview.

11 For a comprehensive understanding of the Vitruvian triad and theory of architecture, see Vitruvius, *The Ten Books on Architecture*, trans. Morris Hicky Morgan (New York: Dover Publications, 1960).

12 Following the death of Harold Mortimer-Lamb's wife, he did not marry Molly's mother but instead married the decades-younger Vera Weatherbie, a former art school classmate of Molly's and the longtime muse and lover of Frederick Varley.

13 Among other books and documents, Andy Sylvester provides a concise history of G. Smith's experience at the VSA in *Gordon Smith: Don't Look Back* (London: Black Dog Publishing, 2014).

14 C. Thom, interview; G. Smith, personal communication, West Vancouver, 2013.

15 Gordon Smith turned out to be the most prominent and acclaimed visual artist of the VSA class of 1947, with solo retrospectives at several major galleries, and paintings in the collections of the National Gallery, Smithsonian, and Victoria & Albert Museum.

16 Jack Shadbolt, "A Report on Art in British Columbia," *Canadian Art*, Nov./Dec. 1946, 4.

17 Ron Thom, "Art and Architecture in Society," *Behind the Palette*, 1947, Vancouver School of Art, Emily Carr University of Art and Design archives.

18 Ron Thom, "Art and Architecture."

19 G. Smith, interview, West Vancouver, March 9, 2008.

20 Ron Thom, transcript of McMichael Gallery talk, Thom family archive.

21 M. McMordie, interview, June 7, 1978, transcript, Canadian Architectural Archives, University of Calgary.

4 · REBUILDING

1 "Directions in British Columbia Painting," *Canadian Art*, Oct./Nov. 1947, 3–6.

2 *Seated Figure* is now in the permanent collection of the Vancouver Art Gallery.

3 Frederic Lasserre, "Regional Trends in West Coast Architecture," *Canadian Art*, Oct./Nov. 1947, 7–9.

4 Raymond J. Cole and Sherry McKay, *Good Times: 70 Years of Architecture at the West Coast School* (Vancouver: University of British Columbia, 2019), 37–39.

5 Bob Dawson, email communication, Feb. 16, 2021; promotional poster, Thom family archive.

6 University of Toronto School of Architecture course catalogue, 1939.

7 For a comprehensive account of the region's post-settlement

architectural history and Sharp & Thompson's role within it, see Donald Luxton (ed.), *Building the West: The Early Architects of British Columbia* (Vancouver: Talonbooks, 2007).

8 David Monteyne, "Sharp & Thompson" in *Building the West*, edited by Donald Luxton, 352: "Thompson... had some trouble adapting to the modernist aesthetic that his firm—particularly Berwick and Ned Pratt, both of whom became partners in 1945—championed in the postwar period. Indeed, when the UBC administration, wanting an image of progress, insisted that Pratt be the chief designer of the 1951 War Memorial Gymnasium, Berwick recalled that Thompson cried at the loss of control over his pet project."

9 The passage describing the mid-century ambiance in Vancouver and activities at TBP is informed by Dick Sai-Chew, Barry Downs, Zoltan Kiss, and Geoffrey Massey.

10 Shadbolt, *Ron Thom*.

11 "Architecture and Town Planning," in chapter 15 of *Royal Commission on National Development in the Arts, Letters and Sciences 1949–1951* [a.k.a. "the Massey Report"], 218, no. 7. Library and Archives Canada, viewable online at www.collectionscanada.gc.ca/massey/index-e.html.

12 Among other sources, the under-reported history of Indigenous architecture is relayed in Edward Mills and Harold Kalman, "Architectural History of Indigenous Peoples in Canada," *Canadian Encyclopedia* online, last modified April 27, 2020, www.thecanadianencyclopedia.ca/en/article/architectural-history-early-first-nations.

13 Rudy Kovach, videotaped interview by Michael Smith, c. 2005.

14 Barry Downs, Dick Sai-Chew, Zoltan Kiss, Geoff Massey, interviews.

15 Rogatnick, *B.C. Binning*, 16, 28–30.

5 · ACROSS THE WATER

1 For a comprehensive account of the bridge's complex negotiations and construction, see Lilia D'Acres and Donald Luxton, *Lions Gate* (Vancouver: Talonbooks, 1999).

2 Adele Weder, "Reconsidering the Binning House" (master's thesis, University of British Columbia, 2004), 21.

3 The racially discriminatory stipulation remained in effect for three decades and remained in print in the historic archives for five more decades after that. In 2020, West Vancouver District Council moved to have article #7 officially erased from the British Properties' land title act.

4 Bruno and Molly Bobak, interview, Fredericton, June 13, 2011. See also Bernard Riordon (ed.), *Bruno Bobak* (Fredericton: Goose Lane Editions, 2006).

5 Bruno and Molly Bobak, interview.

6 Erica Warrington, interview, Vancouver, Nov. 25, 2019.

7 B. Bobak, interview.

8 Ron's indifference to money was cited by Bruno and Molly Bobak, Irene and Morton Dodek, and by several frustrated colleagues.

9 Sidney Shadbolt, interview, Vancouver, May 23, 2011.

10 C. Thom et al., interviews.

11 B. and M. Bobak, interview.

12 Rogatnick, *B.C. Binning;* Jessie Binning, interview, West Vancouver, March 7, 2002.

13 See Elspeth Cameron, *Earle Birney: A Life* (Toronto: Viking, 1994) for a comprehensive account of Birney's interactions with the Vancouver visual arts community.

14 Richard Neutra, *Mystery and Realities of the Site* (New York: Morgan & Morgan, 1951), 62.

15 The Royal Architectural Institute of Canada hosted these conferences at the Banff Centre and invited a select group of architects for a multi-day retreat. In 1956, both Thom and Neutra participated.

16 B. Downs, interview.

17 C. Thom, B. Thom McLeod, and S. Thom, interviews.

18 M. Fiamengo, interview, Sechelt, Oct. 19, 2012.

19 M. Fiamengo, interview.

20 M. Bobak archive, letter from J. Plaskett to M. Bobak.

21 C. Thom, interview. Chris Thom spoke openly with the author of her mental health challenges during those difficult years.

22 C. Thom, S. Thom, M. Bobak, interviews.

23 M. Fiamengo, interview.

24 Marya Fiamengo, *The Quality of Halves and Other Poems* (Vancouver: Klanak Press, 1958).

25 B. and M. Bobak, interview.

26 The pre-stressed plywood panels were part of the "Silverwall" infill system, co-developed by the forestry giant MacMillan Bloedel in consultation with Ned Pratt, and were used by Pratt himself in the design of his 1950 plywood-panel family home in West Vancouver.

27 "Experimental House Proves Versatility of Plywood Panel Construction," *Western Homes and Living,* Feb. 1956, 11–14.

28 C. Thom, interview.

29 Adele Weder, "Repositioning the New," in Kiriko Watanabe et al. (ed.), *Selwyn Pullan: Photographing Mid-Century West Coast Modernism* (Vancouver: Douglas & McIntyre, 2014), 124.

6 · BOLD BOYS ON BLUEPRINTS

1 Margaret Ecker Francis, "Bold Boys on Blueprints," *Saturday Night,* April 18, 1950, 5–9.

2 Description of office activity and culture at Thompson Berwick Pratt sourced from interviews with Geoffrey Massey (West Vancouver, Dec. 14, 2010; April 11, 2014; April 7, 2017; July 4, 2019), Barry Downs (West Vancouver, Dec. 10, 2010; Dec. 1, 2012; July 25, 2017), Zoltan Kiss (June 30, 2012), and Dick Sai-Chew (Feb. 15, 2011; Oct. 21, 2015; Jan. 9, 2016).

3 G. Massey and B. Downs, interviews.

4 Examples of such projects are the Stittgen House in West Vancouver, owned and inhabited by artist/writer Douglas Coupland, and the McLellan-Saddy House in Vancouver.

5 G. Massey, B. Downs, D. Sai-Chew, interviews; Freedman, "Thom."
6 Coincidentally, his father had co-starred with Gary Cooper in *The Fountainhead*, the 1949 movie version of Ayn Rand's novel about a trailblazing modernist architect.
7 G. Massey, interview, 2014.
8 Gropius and Breuer designed the 250-unit Aluminum City Terrace housing with facades sheathed in brick and cedar slats, windows of various sizes and shapes, wooden sunshades, and an open interior layout with kitchens separated from living areas by a half-wall.
9 The first Smith House was an architectural failure, according to Gordon and Marion themselves (interview, 2008). They nonetheless hired Arthur Erickson to design their second home, known as Smith House II, which is an internationally recognized landmark.
10 G. Massey, interview.
11 B. Downs, P. Merrick, interviews.
12 This passage informed by Shadbolt, *Ron Thom*, 15–17; plus interviews with G. Massey, B. Downs, Z. Kiss, and D. Sai-Chew.
13 B. Downs, interview.
14 Selwyn Pullan, interview, North Vancouver, April 18, 2012.

7 · HIGHER LEARNING
1 Sherry McKay, "Western Living, Western Homes," SSAC Bulletin 14, no. 3 (Sept. 1989), 71.
2 The house still stands today, nestled in its verdant—albeit overgrown—landscape.

3 Undated draft notes, probably for a student or public talk; Thom family archive.
4 P. Copp and M. Macdonald, interviews, Vancouver, Oct. 31, 2012.
5 Wolfgang Gerson, a German-born, London-educated recruit from the University of Manitoba's architecture school, had shown a defiance of shoebox modernism in the barrel-vault design of his own 1958 family home in West Vancouver, and the 1964 Unitarian Church on Oak Street and 49th Avenue.
6 G. Massey, interview.
7 Ron Thom's frequent presence at the North-Shore and art school parties, and his lack of presence at the Harris residence, were noted by M. Bobak, G. Massey, and G. Smith, in interviews.
8 Paul Merrick, phone interview, Nov. 14, 2019.
9 Bruno Freschi, interview, Vancouver, April 24, 2012; Joe Wai, interview, Vancouver, June 25, 2015.
10 B. Downs, interview.
11 "Lakeland Death Fall Inquest," *Liverpool Echo*, April 8, 1961.

8 · ELECTRIFYING THE WEST
1 For a full account of the rise of Dal Grauer and B.C. Electric, see David J. Mitchell, *W.A.C. Bennett and the Rise of British Columbia* (Vancouver: Douglas & McIntyre, 1983), and Gordon Shrum with Peter Stursberg, *Gordon Shrum: An Autobiography* (Vancouver: University of British Columbia Press, 1986).

2 The passages on the procurement, construction, and public reception of the substation and tower were informed by R. Liscombe, *The New Spirit*, and by interviews with G. Massey, D. Sai-Chew, B. Downs, and Z. Kiss.

3 D. Sai-Chew, interview, 2011; and B. Downs, interview, 2010.

4 D. Sai-Chew and B. Downs, interviews.

5 D. Sai-Chew, interview.

6 B. Downs, interview.

7 The account of the procurement, design, and construction of the B.C. Electric Building is derived from multiple sources, including R. Liscombe, *The New Spirit*; B. Downs, G. Massey, D. Sai-Chew, and Z. Kiss, interviews; plus correspondence and documents at the Thompson Berwick Pratt archives at the Canadian Architectural Archives, University of Calgary.

8 "New Architecture Abroad: High Buildings in Canada," *The Times*, Feb. 2, 1962.

9 Nikolaus Pevsner, "Canada," *Architectural Review* 126, no. 752 (October 1959), 155.

10 The Hotel Vancouver has just seventeen storeys, but because of its massive steeply pitched roof, it rises 369 feet; the B.C. Electric Building is twenty-one storeys but just 293 feet high.

11 B. Downs, interview.

12 Barry Downs and Geoff Massey expressed awareness of others' murmured accusations of "copying." Downs, who was working at TBP at the time, recalls the *Domus* edition with the cover story on the yet-to-be-built Pirelli Tower arriving at the office before the design team had decided on the elevator location and lozenge shape. Although he was not part of the core team deciding the B.C. Electric Building's shape, he presumes that the Pirelli renderings served as a logical inspiration for the team.

13 D. Sai-Chew, interview.

14 Pierre Berton, "A Native's Return to B.C.," *Maclean's,* May 10, 1958, 15.

15 Ron Kenyon, "Here's What's Wrong With Your City," *Star Weekly*, June 11, 1960, 15.

16 Kenyon, "Here's What's Wrong," 6.

17 Rudy Kovach, Ron Thom, and Bill Leithead, "Street Decoration and Street Improvement," project report, City of Vancouver Archives, 1960.

18 After temporarily expanding during the 2010 Winter Olympics, the street banner program was permanently dismantled by then-mayor Gregor Robertson.

19 D. Sai-Chew et al., interviews.

20 Mitchell, *W.A.C. Bennett*.

9 · THE ALLURE OF THE WOODS

1 Undated, unpublished draft for talk or essay, Thom family archive.

2 Fred Hollingsworth, interview, North Vancouver, April 20, 2008.

3 For a comprehensive account of the Taliesin operations and business model, see Roger Friedland and Harold Zellman, *The Fellowship: The Untold Story of Frank Lloyd Wright and the Taliesin Fellowship* (New York: Harper Collins, 2006).

4 F. Hollingsworth, interview.

5 S. Thom, interview.

6 Ron Thom spent an evening showing slides of Taliesin to the Dodeks (Dodek interview), and he told some family members that he discovered that an architect had to pay to work for Frank Lloyd Wright, which gave both the Dodeks and some offspring the impression that Ron once physically travelled to Taliesin. However, there is no evidence in private or professional correspondence, or collegial conversations, including with his close confidante Paul Merrick, that he ever made the multi-day journey.

7 The passage describing the Lynn Valley Road house is primarily sourced from Bob Dawson (interview, Vancouver, Dec. 15, 2010) and S. Thom (interview, Royston, July 13, 2011), plus photographs in the Thom family archive.

8 These passages largely sourced from interviews with Robin Thom, partly corroborated by Sidney and Aaron Thom and Bronwen Thom McLeod.

9 C. Thom and B. Thom McLeod, interviews.

10 Sheila Southworth, interview, Duncan, June 26, 2019.

11 S. Southworth, interview.

12 Bob Dawson, interview, Vancouver, Dec. 15, 2010.

13 Adele Weder, "Ron Thom's Carmichael Residence heads to market," *Globe and Mail*, Aug. 5, 2011.

14 This passage sourced from Morton and Irene Dodek, interview, Jan. 10, 2011, fact-checked by email interview with M. Dodek on Jan. 28, 2020.

10 · THE HOME FRONT

1 G. Massey, D. Sai-Chew, B. Downs, interviews.

2 C. Thom, interview.

3 C. Thom, F. Hollingsworth, interviews.

4 Vancouver Art Gallery Library and Archives. Reconfirmed in email correspondence, Nov. 15, 2021.

5 B. Dawson, F. Hollingsworth, interviews.

6 On April 1, 1963, Chris Thom's lawyer in Victoria sent the final settlement terms for "Thom and Thom" to the Hastings Street law firm engaged by Ron Thom.

7 B. Dawson, interview, C. Thom, interview, legal document, and diary notes in Thom family archive.

8 Terms sourced from the formal petition to divorce, Thom family archive.

9 B. Dawson, interview.

10 B. Dawson, interview.

11 Personal letter from M. Fiamengo to M. Bobak, Molly and Bruno Bobak Archive, National Archives of Canada, call no. MG 30 D 378. Cited with permission.

12 Davies, *A Celtic Temperament*, 279.

11 · DIGNITY, GRACE, BEAUTY, AND WARMTH

1 Canadian Architectural Archives at the University of Calgary, Accession 2A/75.02.

2 The surviving stack of his early Massey College conceptual sketches are now archived at the

CAA at the University of Calgary, Acc. 2A/75.02.

3 The firm itself—Thompson, Berwick, Pratt & Partners—was formally engaged as the "architect," but Ron Thom was formally named as the principal designer.

4 B. Downs, interview.

5 G. Massey, interview, West Vancouver, Dec. 14, 2010; Shadbolt, *Ron Thom*. For a comprehensive account of the architectural selection process, see Judith Skelton Grant, *A Meeting of Minds: The Massey College Story* (Toronto: University of Toronto Press, 2015), 34–42.

6 G. Massey, interview.

7 Ron Thom, "Massey College," *Canadian Architect*, Dec. 1960, 41.

8 G. Massey, interview.

9 Davies, *A Celtic Temperament*, 156.

10 Letter from TBP, July 26, 1962, Canadian Architectural Archives at the University of Calgary.

11 This paragraph and the preceding four paragraphs are sourced from Molly Thom, interview.

12 Molly Thom archive.

13 Letter from Ron Thom to Molly Golby, undated, c. early 1963.

14 Shadbolt, *Ron Thom*, 40, excerpted from interview with Ned Pratt, April 26, 1991; G. Massey, D. Sai-Chew, interviews.

15 The tune of "St. James Infirmary Blues" can be found on YouTube. Hear Louis Armstrong at www.youtube.com/watch?v=yKt5wzcbmbo or Cab Calloway at www.youtube.com/watch?v=fEyEcHX8WLo.

16 Undated letter, Molly Thom archive.

17 Ned was referring here to Zoltan Kiss, one of the firm's architects who moonlighted on his own projects after-hours.

18 Thom family archive; B. Downs, interview.

19 Thom family archive.

20 Lew Crutcher was a then-prominent architect, artist, and printmaker in Portland, Oregon.

21 Molly Thom archive.

22 Northrop Frye, "The Educated Imagination," part 1, CBC Radio, November 8, 1962, radio broadcast, www.cbc.ca/ideas/episodes/massey-lectures/1962/11/09/massey-lectures-1963-the-educated-imagination/

23 Molly Thom archive.

24 D. Sai-Chew, B. Downs, G. Massey, interviews.

25 Davies, *A Celtic Temperament*, 278.

26 Davies, *A Celtic Temperament*, 284; Molly Thom, email correspondence, March 5, 2020.

12 · THE GREAT TRANSITION

1 Letter from Ron Thom to Molly Golby, undated, Molly Thom archive.

2 Letter from Ron to Molly.

3 This passage sourced from Tom Symons, interview, Peterborough, April 19, 2013; and A.O.C. Cole, *Trent: The Making of a University, 1957–1987* (Peterborough: Trent University, 1992).

4 Robertson Davies, "The Architect and His Community," *Canadian Architect*, April 1956, 32–36.

5 Eberhard and Jane Zeidler, interview, Toronto, March 24, 2016.

6 Cole, *Trent*, 12.

7 E. and J. Zeidler, interview; Eberhard Zeidler, *Buildings Cities Life: An Autobiography in Architecture*, vol. 1 (Toronto: Dundurn Press, 2013).

8 T. Symons, interview.

9 Molly Thom archive.

10 Richard Sadleir, interview, Toronto, April 19, 2013.

11 Letter from Elena Thom to Molly Golby, dated July 3, 1963. Thom family archive.

12 Denis Smith, interview, Ottawa, June 9, 2011.

13 R. Sadleir, interview.

14 D. Smith, R. Sadleir, interviews.

15 Molly Thom email, Dec. 28, 2020.

16 D. Smith and Tom Symons, interviews.

17 Thom family, interviews. Though all family members were aware that Elena Fennell Thom was killed in a car accident, not all of them were aware of the assumption that James Thom had fallen asleep while driving.

18 Original CN telegram, dated Aug. 9, 1963, Molly Thom archive.

13 · RISING IN THE EAST

1 Davies, *A Celtic Temperament*, 313.

2 Molly Thom, interview.

3 Ron Thom, "St. Lawrence and Old York," in Annabel Slaight (ed.), *Exploring Toronto* (Toronto: Architecture Canada, 1972), 14.

4 Peter Smith interview, Massey College, Toronto, Dec. 6, 2010; Molly

Thom, copy of fax to Doug Shadbolt dated Dec. 19, 1994.

5 John Andrews, telephone interview, Aug. 17, 2015; Jim Sykes, telephone interview, July 26, 2019; Jack Diamond, interview and draft memoir, Oct. 20, 2020. Diamond would leave John Andrews's office within the year, frustrated at not being offered a partnership.

6 Jim Sykes, telephone interview.

7 P. Smith, interview.

8 P. Merrick, P. Smith, B. Lett, et al., interviews.

9 Executed while he was in the employ of the firm Page and Steele.

10 While designing the TD Centre in Toronto, Mies van der Rohe, in response to Phyllis Lambert's question to him about how to keep the two Parkins straight, advised: the "B" stands for Business and the "C" stands for Creative, a nod to their respective roles and talents.

11 J. Andrews, interview.

12 The firm was Shore & Moffat Architects.

13 Bill Lett, interview, Toronto, Dec. 6, 2010.

14 Letter from Alan Jarvis to Ron Thom, May 17, 1963, Canadian Architectural Archives at the University of Calgary.

15 Molly Thom, interview.

16 Leslie Rebanks, interview, Toronto, June 9, 2012. Rebanks averred that Ron Thom's complete description of Three Small Rooms was "a place where you can sit quietly and listen to your wife talk while you admire her boobs," though others said it

would be uncharacteristic of Ron to speak of his wife this way.

17 Jamie Kennedy, telephone interview, March 16, 2017.

18 When the Lacharitys rejected Thom's unusual plan, he revised it to a more conventionally orthogonal floorplan. Both versions are now at the Canadian Architectural Archives at the University of Calgary.

19 Letter to Phil and Mairi Narod, July 23, 1965, Thom family archive.

20 For example, an undated invoice to the Dodeks, formally stamped and signed reads: "Amount: One evening of good conversation and good whiskey—when we can all make it." Canadian Architectural Archives at the University of Calgary.

21 CAA at the University of Calgary.

22 Davies, *A Celtic Temperament*, 316.

23 Letter from Hart Massey to Ron Thom, dated April 1, 1964, Canadian Architectural Archives at the University of Calgary.

14 · THE BIG TIME

1 John C. Parkin, "The Design of an Architect," *Perspective*, 1956, 13–17.

2 Ron Thom, "Houses in Vancouver," *Canadian Architect*, March 1962, 37–39.

3 For a comprehensive account of J.C. Parkin's architecture and personal design values, see Linda Fraser, Michael McMordie, and Geoffrey Simmins, *John C. Parkin, Archives and Photography: Reflections on the Practice and Presentation of Modern Architecture* (Calgary: University

of Calgary Press, 2013). Parkin was as fastidious in daily life as at the drafting table, ensuring his furnishings and even reference books on display were black and white, and instructing his housekeeper to ensure the positioning of the telephone at a clean ninety-degree angle on the table.

4 Angela Cadman Strachan, telephone interviews, Feb. 8 and 19, 2020, et al.

5 Morden Yolles, interview, Toronto, June 14, 2010.

6 Frank Lloyd Wright, *The Natural House* (New York: Horizon Press, 1954), 63.

7 Paul Halpern, interview, Toronto, March 14, 2012.

8 In John C. Parkin's archival correspondence at the Canadian Architectural Archives at the University of Calgary, he refers derisively to an unnamed prominent architect who displayed the social ineptitude of wearing "wool ties."

9 D. Sai-Chew, interview.

10 T. Symons, interview.

11 Paul Barnard, interview, Long Beach, California, June 9, 2014.

12 Paul Martel, interview, Toronto, April 18, 2013.

13 Letter from James Thom to Ron Thom, 1965, Thom family archive.

14 B. Lett, email communication, April 3, 2021.

15 D. Smith, T. Symons, P. Barnard, P. Martel, interviews.

16 Paul Merrick, telephone interview, Feb. 22, 2021; Barry Griblin, interview, West Vancouver, April 6, 2012.

17 T. Symons, interview.

18 P. Merrick, interview.

19 Morden Yolles, interview, Toronto, Nov. 28, 2012. See Beth Kapusta and John McMinn, *Yolles: A Canadian Engineering Legacy* (Vancouver: Douglas & McIntyre, 2002) for a comprehensive account of the rubble-aggregate process at Trent University.

20 Several colleagues cited Thom's disdain for concrete; this specific quotation is recalled by Murray Beynon, email communication, Feb. 15, 2021.

21 T. Symons, D. Smith, interviews; correspondence at the Canadian Architectural Archives at the University of Calgary.

22 L. Rebanks, Ed Cowan (Jan. 18, 2013), D. Smith, M. Frum, interviews.

23 D. Smith, interview.

24 The master's residence at Champlain College has since been converted to an administrative building.

25 "Trent University: Architecture for a Special Curriculum," *Architectural Record*, September 1969, 151–162.

26 Arthur Erickson, "Trent University," *Canadian Interiors*, June 1969, 29.

27 Freedman, "Thom."

15 · HIGH FLYING

1 Among other sources, see John Mackie, "This Week in History: 1956: 'Flying Phil' shows off his highway program," *Vancouver Sun*, July 30, 2021; "A side trip: Gaglardi under fire again," *Globe and Mail*, March 21, 1968; and Mitchell, *W.A.C. Bennett.*

2 Canadian Centre for Architecture, Arthur Erickson Fonds, ARCH257571, collection number APO22.S2.SS1.D6.

3 Fifty years later, the whole composition of Simon Fraser University is still part of the mountaintop, but the once-forested mountain slopes are now encrusted with condo developments built and sold to pay for the ongoing expansion and operations of the university.

4 Ron Thom, paper presented at the International College and University Conference and Exposition, Atlantic City, New Jersey, March 16–18, 1970. Canadian Architectural Archives at the University of Calgary.

5 Peter Smith, Alastair Grant, interviews.

6 Letter, Ron Thom to Dennis and Adele Case, Nov. 25, 1964, Canadian Architectural Archives at the University of Calgary.

7 Peter Smith, interview.

8 As well as Ron, Merrick had assistance from Thom Partnership architect Brian Kilpatrick in designing the Fraser Residence.

9 P. Merrick, telephone interview, Feb. 13, 2021.

10 Thomas J. DiCiccio, Mary E. Thompson, and Donald A.S. Fraser, "A Conversation With Donald A.S. Fraser," *Statistical Science* 19, no. 2 (May 2004), 376.

11 Mitchell, *W.A.C. Bennett*, 414–415.

16 · ROILING FAME

1 Frank Hamilton, interview, Toronto, April 26, 2014.
2 Notable examples include the 1910 Penn Station in New York by McKim, Mead & White, demolished in 1963 despite widespread protests.
3 Examples include Jane Jacobs, *The Death and Life of Great American Cities* (New York: Random House, 1961); and Peter Blake, "The Folly of Modern Architecture," *Atlantic Monthly*, Sept. 1974, 59–66.
4 Office handout, courtesy of Peter Smith.
5 Multiple sources, including Hamilton and Halpern.
6 By 2008, the Vancouver School of Art had evolved into the Emily Carr University of Art and Design.
7 D. Sai-Chew, B. Downs, et al., interviews.
8 Jamie Smallwood, interview, Toronto, Feb. 16, 2012.
9 J. Smallwood, interview.
10 B.C. Binning, "The Teaching of Drawing," *Canadian Art*, Autumn 1947, 21.
11 Alastair Grant, interview, Toronto, Feb. 16, 2011.
12 J. Smallwood, interview.
13 Marathon Realty was the real-estate arm of Canadian Pacific Railway Ltd.
14 David Folster, "Will 'development' make Fredericton the home town you want to leave?," *Canadian Panorama*, May 20, 1972, 2.
15 Molly and Bruno Bobak, interview, Fredericton, June 13, 2011.
16 Folster, "Will 'development'..."
17 M. and B. Bobak, interview.
18 David Mooney, telephone interview, March 11, 2021.
19 Thom family archive.
20 Robert Fulford, "Leaving a Mark on Canada: The Career of Ron Thom," *Saturday Night*, June 1975, 24–29.
21 Fulford, "Leaving a Mark."
22 Saskatoon RAIC 70th Assembly panel discussion: "Toward Design"; Vancouver speech, "Rethinking My Architecture," November 1976; Toronto at the Ontario General Contractors Association Annual Meeting, Sept. 23, 1977. Thom family archive.
23 Italics/emphasis are Ron Thom's.
24 Thom family archive.
25 The Vancouver School of Art later expanded its name to Emily Carr College of Art and Design and then, in 2008, to its current name: the Emily Carr University of Art and Design.
26 Paul Halpern, interview, Toronto, March 14, 2012; reiterated and confirmed by several colleagues.
27 This and preceding paragraph: B. Lett, P. Smith, et al., interviews.
28 P. Smith, interview.
29 Tim Murray, telephone interview, Sept. 12, 2019.

17 · CULTURALLY DEFINING

1 Molly Thom, email, Oct. 28, 2021. Ron's love of Inuit culture was evidenced in his first Christmas present to Molly: a large soapstone sculpture of a walrus, which they nicknamed "Uncle Vince," after Vincent Massey.

2 The project's engagement with the local community could not make up for the contempt harboured by many residents for the very concept of a church, and in 2005 the cathedral was destroyed by arson.

3 Walter Gordon, *Walter L. Gordon: A Political Memoir* (Toronto: McClelland & Stewart, 1977); Molly Bobak archives. In the fall of 1970, Gordon launched the Committee for an Independent Canada, approaching not only political and business leaders but also Molly Bobak and other nationally renowned artists for their public support.

4 Ron Thom, quoted in Sid Adilman, "Shaw festival builders first-nighters," *Toronto Star*, June 11, 1973.

5 Lester B. Pearson, 1969. On "Our History" section of Pearson College's official website, accessed Nov. 24, 2021, www.pearson college.ca/who-we-are/our-history.

6 Fulford, "Leaving a Mark."

7 Adele Weder, "The Many Layers of Cornelia Oberlander's Landscapes," *Azure*, June 1, 2021, www.azuremagazine.com/article/the-many-layers-of-cornelia-oberlanders-landscapes.

8 B. Downs, interview.

9 Alastair Grant, interviews, Feb. 16, 2011, and Feb. 2, 2021.

10 Murray Frum, interview, Toronto, March 17, 2012.

11 Reflecting subsequent changes of ownership, the hotel later became the Westin Prince and in 2019 was renamed the Pan Pacific Toronto Hotel.

12 M. Dodek, telephone interview, Feb. 21, 2021.

13 Thom family archive.

14 Kay Kritzwiser, "Designing a zoo to please the animals," *Globe and Mail*, July 10, 1971.

15 An early example is Berthold Lubetkin's 1934 Penguin Pool at the London Zoo, whose curvilinear ramps provide a conceptual abstraction of the shoals of Antarctica and a long path for the birds to strut upon, but no place for them to copulate in comfort and privacy. The Penguin Pool was closed in 2004, after the resident penguins developed bacterial infections from the concrete surfaces.

16 Margaret Mironowicz, "Zoo experience has taught Pamela Goh how to be tough," *Globe and Mail*, Nov. 1, 1976.

17 Anita Voss, interview, Sooke, B.C., Jan. 6, 2015.

18 · THE ELUSIVE CONCEPT OF HOME

1 Ian MacDonald, email interview, Feb. 21, 2021. Smallwood also described at length the uniquely warm, comfortable, homelike atmosphere of the Thom Partnership reception and office.

2 P. Smith, M. Thom, interviews.

3 Among others, Peter Berton, Stan Sota, and Paul Nevins had heard the story of Andrew Binnie's Taliesin experience.

4 H. Zellman, interview, Los Angeles, June 11, 2014; Ian Binnie, interview, Toronto, Feb. 7, 2014.

5 Andrew's brother Ian Binnie would later become one of the Supreme Court justices of Canada.

6 Notes from an unpublished interview with Iovanna Wright by R. Friedland and H. Zellman, c. 1997, cited with permission.

7 See Friedland and Zellman, *The Fellowship*, for a comprehensive unpacking of the culture and activities at Taliesin.

8 This and preceding info regarding Andrew Binnie sourced from Ian Binnie, interview.

9 Paul Smith, Peter Berton, Jim Nelles, Stan Sota, Molly Thom, interviews.

10 Friedland and Zellman, unpublished interview of Iovanna Wright.

11 M. Thom, email communication, Nov. 25, 2020.

12 M. Thom, interview; E. Thom, interview.

13 Bernadette Andrews, "A 'sweet, satisfying house' for Ron Thom," *Toronto Star*, March 22, 1976.

14 E. Thom, interview, Ottawa, June 9, 2012.

15 Robin Thom, interview, Vancouver, Jan. 25, 2011; E. Thom, interview; M. Bobak, interview; Sidney Shadbolt, interview, Vancouver, Oct. 10, 2011.

16 E. Thom, interview.

17 J. Smallwood, interview, and M. Thom, interview.

18 S. Thom, B. Thom McLeod, M. Thom, interviews.

19 A. Thom, interview.

20 S. Thom, interview.

21 M. Thom, A. Grant, P. Berton, D. Sai-Chew, interviews; letters, Thom family archive.

22 E. Thom, interview.

19 · ART VERSUS THE CORPORATE WAVE

1 M. Frum, interview.

2 M. Frum, interview.

3 Though Murray Frum commented in the spirit of rhetorical irreverence, reliable reports of Wright's height range from 5'6" to 5'8". Scholars—and Wright himself—have indeed attributed his penchant for low heights in part to this fact.

4 J. Smallwood, interview.

5 Stan Sota, interview, Toronto, June 14, 2014.

6 Text of RCAA speech.

7 S. Sota, interview.

8 Now part of the City of Toronto.

9 Murray Beynon, telephone interview, Feb. 13, 2021.

10 By way of comparison, the final construction costs of University of Toronto's 2018 architecture school, designed by NADAAA with Adamson Associates, clocked in at 52 million dollars.

11 Its full name at the time was Ryerson School of Architectural Science and Landscape-Architecture. It is now in the process of changing its name entirely.

12 Leon Whiteson, "Ryerson designer defies temptation for rare grandeur," *Toronto Star*, Oct. 31, 1981.

13 Ralph Bergman, interview, Chatham, Ontario, Sept. 15, 2014. Alastair Grant does not recall this

event, though he allows it might have happened this way. Even for the firm's projects in which Ron Thom had no direct involvement, the Thom Partnership had a product to sell: the design values of Ron Thom. The Training Institute ended up with a chocolate-brown baked-enamel tiling.

14 Phil Goldsmith, interview, Toronto, Sept. 11, 2014.

15 The Thom Partnership's first female designers included architect Susan Black and interior designers Shanna Fromson and Linda Lewis.

16 Shauna Haugen, telephone interview, April 3, 2020.

17 The Montreal architectural practice Arcop (sometimes spelled ARCOP) is an acronym for Architects in Co-Partnership. Founded in Montreal in the early 1950s as Affleck, Desbarats, Dimakopoulos, Lebensold, Sise, it changed its name to Arcop in 1970.

18 Stephen Quigley, interview, Vancouver, April 27, 2011.

19 Andy Lynch, telephone interview, July 25, 2019.

20 Freedman, "Thom."

21 S. Quigley, interview.

22 Letter, Dodek family archive.

23 The other seven architects were Douglas Cardinal, Ian Davidson, Michael Evamy, Peter Hemingway, Richard Henriquez, Guy Gerin-Lajoie, and Fred Valentine.

20 · FEAR HAS A LONG, LONG TALE

1 F. Hamilton, interview, reiterated and confirmed by several other Thom Partnership associates.

2 S. Quigley, S. Sota, A. Cadman, interviews.

3 L. Rebanks, interview.

4 Molly Thom, interview.

5 A. Thom, D. Sai-Chew, interviews; Shadbolt, *Ron Thom.*

6 Thom family archive.

7 M. Dodek, S. Quigley, interviews.

8 Ann, Jill, Jane, and Susan Irwin, Zoom interview, Oct. 26, 2020.

9 Ann, Jill, Jane, and Susan Irwin, interview.

10 Irwin family archive.

11 Elected premier of B.C. in 1975, Bill Bennett was the son of W.A.C. Bennett.

12 B. Freschi, Z. Kiss, interviews.

13 This passage is largely informed by B. Freschi, interview, Vancouver, September 20, 2020.

14 M. Beynon, email and telephone interview, Feb. 15, 2021.

15 Arthur Erickson filed for bankruptcy in Vancouver in 1989.

16 Thom family archive. The word "name" is underlined in the letter.

17 C. Thom, interview.

18 Letter from Ron Thom to Morton and Irene Dodek, Dodek family archive.

19 I. Dodek, interview.

20 S. Thom, interview.

21 Thom family archive.

22 Paul Nevins, interview, Toronto, Oct. 1, 2021; also mentioned by D. Smith and S. Quigley.

23 Letter, Thom family archive.

24 A. Voss, interview.
25 M. Beynon, interview.
26 Letter, Thom family archive.
27 Letter, Thom family archive.
28 Letter, Thom family archive.
29 The invitation was extended by Stephanie Robb, Canada's 2006 co-representative at the Venice Biennale of Architecture, who was at that time a UBC architecture student and member of the school's lecture series committee.
30 Letter dated October 10, 1986, Thom family archive.
31 Peter Berton, interview, Toronto, December 6, 2010.
32 Letter from R. Thom to S. Thom, Thom family archive.

21 · THE LAST TRIP HOME

1 D. Shadbolt, *Ron Thom*, 151; B. McLeod, interview.
2 E. Thom, interview.
3 Stephanie Robb, telephone interview, Dec. 30, 2020.
4 S. Robb, interview, and Jane Kinegal, email communication, Dec. 28, 2020. Both attended the lecture.
5 Bronwen and Jim McLeod, telephone joint interview, Dec. 28, 2020.
6 P. Merrick, telephone interview, Feb. 4, 2021.
7 Sourced from Ian Anderson, the other friend who drove around with Ron that day, telephone interview, Nov. 12, 2020.
8 D. Sai-Chew, P. Berton, P. Nevins, interviews.
9 D. Sai-Chew, interview, Toronto, Sept. 29, 2021. Sai-Chew cited George Miller, a lawyer for both Ron Thom and the Thom Partnership, who entered Ron's apartment the next day and found the couple inhabiting the premises. They told Miller that they were homeless, that Ron Thom said they could stay there, and that they had no place else to go. Miller told them they had to leave, and then gave them some cash to send them on their way.
10 D. Sai-Chew and P. Nevins recalled leaving around 6:30 PM and believing they were the last to leave out the front entrance; Berton recalls working later and leaving by the back entrance.
11 Coroner's Investigation Statement, Ministry of the Solicitor General, Government of Ontario, case no. 24094, Oct. 30, 1986 (retrieved Feb. 23, 2022).
12 P. Berton, interview.
13 P. Merrick, telephone interview, Nov. 14, 2019.
14 D. Shadbolt, handout, Thom family archive.
15 Denis and Dawn Smith, handout, Thom family archive.
16 Alastair Grant, handout, Thom family archive.
17 Barbara Frum, handout, Nov. 5, 1986, Thom family archive.
18 P. Merrick, interview.
19 P. Merrick, B. McLeod, interviews.
20 This passage is sourced and confirmed from interviews with P. Merrick, S. Thom, B. McLeod, R. Thom, and A. Thom.

IMAGE CREDITS

Note: Unless otherwise noted, most of the photos in this book have been sourced from historical archives, and the photographer is unknown.

ii Courtesy of the District of West Vancouver archive.

2 *Toronto Star* photograph archive. Courtesy of Toronto Public Library; Eddy Roworth.

4 Courtesy of the Massey College archive.

6 Courtesy of the District of West Vancouver archive.

10 From the Victoria College Archives. Reprinted from Douglas Shadbolt, *Ron Thom: The Shaping of an Architect* (Vancouver: Douglas & McIntyre, 1995).

13 Courtesy of the Thom family archive.

14 Courtesy of the Thom family archive.

15 Courtesy of the Thom family archive; Tony Archer.

16 Courtesy of the Thom family archive.

21 Courtesy of the Vancouver School Board.

23 Jack Long.

24 Graham Warrington, courtesy of the Warrington family.

25 Courtesy of the Thom family archive.

30 Courtesy of the Thom family archive.

33 Courtesy of the Thom family archive.

37 Courtesy of the Thom family archive.

42 Ron Thom, courtesy of the Vancouver Art Gallery.

45 Graham Warrington, courtesy of the Warrington family.

52 Courtesy of the Bobak family archive and Anny Scoones.

53 Courtesy of the Thom family archive.

56 Courtesy of the Thom family archive.

59 Courtesy of Marya Fiamengo.

62 Courtesy of the Thom family archive.

70 Courtesy of the West Vancouver Art Museum. © Selwyn Pullan.

72 Courtesy of the West Vancouver Art Museum. © Selwyn Pullan.

74 Courtesy of the West Vancouver Art Museum. © Selwyn Pullan.

76 Canadian Architectural Archives at the University of Calgary, Peter Varley.

77 Canadian Architectural Archives at the University of Calgary, Peter Varley.

80 Courtesy of Dick Sai-Chew.

81 Courtesy of the Massey family archive, Tony Archer.

89 Courtesy of the West Vancouver Art Museum. © Selwyn Pullan.

93 Jack Long photo, reprinted from Pierre Berton, "A Native's Return to B.C.," *Maclean's*, May 10, 1958, 15.

98 Courtesy of the West Vancouver Art Museum. © Selwyn Pullan.

99 Courtesy of the West Vancouver Art Museum. © Selwyn Pullan.

101 Fred Hollingsworth.

107 *top left* Courtesy of the West Vancouver Art Museum. © Selwyn Pullan.

107 *top right* Courtesy of the West Vancouver Art Museum. © Selwyn Pullan.

107 *bottom* Courtesy of the District of West Vancouver archives.

108 Courtesy of the West Vancouver Art Museum. © Selwyn Pullan.

110 Courtesy of the West Vancouver Art Museum. © Selwyn Pullan.

111 Courtesy of Josh Nychuk.

112 Courtesy of the Vancouver Art Gallery Library & Archives and the Dodek family archive.

119 Canadian Architectural Archives at the University of Calgary, Ron Thom.

121 Canadian Architectural Archives at the University of Calgary, Ron Thom.

123 Canadian Architectural Archives at the University of Calgary, Ron Thom.

133 Canadian Architectural Archives at the University of Calgary, Ron Thom.

134 Courtesy of the Thom family archive.

143 Courtesy of John Reeves.

145 Courtesy of the Thom family archive.

146 Canadian Architectural Archives at the University of Calgary, Ron Thom.

150 Courtesy of the Thom family archive, Robert Montgomery.

156 Courtesy of the West Vancouver Art Museum. © Selwyn Pullan.

157 Courtesy of the West Vancouver Art Museum. © Selwyn Pullan.

158 Courtesy of the West Vancouver Art Museum, R.J. Thom, Architect.

159 Adele Case (attrib.), courtesy of Anne Ferries.

163 Canadian Architectural Archives at the University of Calgary, Peter Varley.

164 *top* Canadian Architectural Archives at the University of Calgary, Peter Varley.

164 *bottom* Canadian Architectural Archives at the University of Calgary, Peter Varley.

171 Canadian Architectural Archives at the University of Calgary, R.J. Thom Architect (Paul Barnard, Alastair Grant, Paul Merrick attrib.).

176 Canadian Architectural Archives at the University of Calgary, Robert Montgomery.

177 Canadian Architectural Archives at the University of Calgary, Ron Thom.

178 Courtesy of Steven Evans.

180 Courtesy of Steven Evans.

182 Courtesy of Steven Evans.

189 Courtesy of Fred Schiffer.

191 *top* Canadian Architectural Archives at the University of Calgary, Ron Thom (attrib.).

191 *bottom* Courtesy of Carol Moore-Ede.

195 Canadian Architectural Archives at the University of Calgary, Ron Thom.

207 Courtesy of John Leroux.

216 Ron Thom (attrib.).

218 *top* Courtesy of the Peter Smith family archive.

218 *bottom* Canadian Architectural Archives at the University of Calgary, John Flanders.

221 Courtesy of Barry Downs.

225 Canadian Architectural Archives at the University of Calgary, John Flanders.

227 *top* Courtesy of the Thom family archive.

227 *bottom Toronto Star* Photographic Archive/Getty Images: Bob Olsen.

230 Courtesy of the Thom family archive.

236 *Toronto Star* Photographic Archive/Getty Images: Colin McConnell.

239 Courtesy of the Thom family archive; Jim McLeod.

249 Fiona Spalding-Smith.

251 Harold Copp.

254 Canadian Architectural Archives at the University of Calgary, Ron Thom.

258 Courtesy of Steve Gairns.

261 Fiona Spalding-Smith.

265 Courtesy of Odile Hénault, editor, *Section A*.

279 Canadian Architectural Archives at the University of Calgary, Peter Varley.

283 Courtesy of Adele Weder.

SELECTED BIBLIOGRAPHY

The 75th Anniversary of Thompson, Berwick, Pratt & Partners. Vancouver: Thompson, Berwick, Pratt & Partners, 1983. Brochure.

Alfoldy, Sandra. *The Allied Arts: Architecture and Craft in Postwar Canada.* Montreal: McGill-Queen's University Press, 2012.

Amos, Robert. *Harold Mortimer-Lamb: The Art Lover.* Victoria: TouchWood Editions, 2013.

Art in Our Time. New York: Museum of Modern Art, 1939. Exhibition catalogue.

Bellerby, Greg, ed. *The West Coast Modern House: Vancouver Residential Architecture.* Vancouver: Figure 1 Publishing, 2014.

Bellerby, Greg, Barry Downs, Kiriko Watanabe, Alan Bell, Hilary Letwin, Adele Weder, and Darrin Morrison. *Design for Living: West Coast Modern Homes Revisited.* West Vancouver, B.C.: West Vancouver Museum, 2019.

Birney, Earle. *David and Other Poems.* Toronto: Ryerson Press, 1942.

Brown, Adrienne. *The Life and Art of Harry and Jessie Webb.* Salt Spring Island: Mother Tongue Publishing, 2014.

Cameron, Elspeth. *Earle Birney: A Life.* Toronto: Viking Canada, 1994.

Cole, A.O.C. *Trent: The Making of a University 1957–1987.* Peterborough: Trent University, 1992.

Cole, Raymond, and Sherry McKay. *Good Times: 70 Years of Architecture at the West Coast School.* Vancouver: University of British Columbia School of Architecture and Landscape Architecture, 2019.

Davies, Robertson. "The Architect and His Community." *Canadian Architect,* April 1956, 32–36.

Davies, Robertson. *A Celtic Temperament: Robertson Davies as Diarist.* Edited by Jennifer Surridge and

Ramsay Derry. Toronto: McClelland & Stewart, 2015.

Emery, George. *The Methodist Church on the Prairies, 1896–1914*. Montreal: McGill-Queens University Press, 2001.

Erickson, Arthur. "Trent University." *Canadian Interiors*, June 1969, 29–30.

Fiamengo, Marya. *The Quality of Halves and Other Poems*. Vancouver: Klanak Press, 1958.

Francis, Margaret Ecker. "Bold Boys on Blueprints." *Saturday Night*, April 18, 1950, 29–33.

Fraser, Linda, Michael McMordie, and Geoffrey Simmins. *John C. Parkin, Archives and Photography: Reflections on the Practice and Presentation of Modern Architecture*. Calgary: University of Calgary Press, 2013.

Freedman, Adele. *Sight Lines: Looking at Architecture and Design in Canada*. Toronto: Oxford University Press, 1990.

Freedman, Adele. "Thom: 'A Man of Tall Timbers.'" *Globe and Mail*, March 12, 1983.

Friedland, Roger, and Harold Zellman. *The Fellowship: The Untold Story of Frank Lloyd Wright and the Taliesin Fellowship*. New York: Regan Books, 2006.

Gordon, Walter. *A Political Memoir*. Toronto: McClelland & Stewart, 1977.

Grant, Judith Skelton. *A Meeting of Minds: The Massey College Story*. Toronto: University of Toronto Press, 2015.

Griffin, D.F. *First Steps to Tokyo: The Royal Canadian Air Force in the Aleutians*. Toronto: J.M. Dent & Sons, 1944.

Hume, R.M., ed. *100 Years of B.C. Art*. Vancouver: Vancouver Art Gallery, 1958. Exhibition catalogue.

Iglauer, Edith. *Seven Stones: A Portrait of Arthur Erickson, Architect*. Madeira Park, B.C.: Harbour Publishing, 1981.

Kapusta, Beth, and John McMinn. *Yolles: A Canadian Engineering Legacy*. Vancouver: Douglas & McIntyre, 2002.

King, James. *Inward Journey: The Life of Lawren Harris*. Toronto: Thomas Allen Publishers, 2012.

Kiss, Zoltan S. *Without a Blueprint: Surviving in a Changing World*. West Vancouver: Sandor Press, 2005.

Lasserre, Frederick. "Regional Trends in West Coast Architecture." *Canadian Art*, Autumn 1947, 7–9.

Lindberg, E. Theodore. *Vancouver School of Art: The Early Years, 1925–1939*. Vancouver: Charles H. Scott Gallery, 1980. Exhibition catalogue.

Lindberg, E. Theodore, Daina Augaitis, and Elsa Schamis. *Vancouver School of Art: The Growth Years, 1939–1965*. Vancouver: Charles H. Scott Gallery, 1983. Exhibition catalogue.

Liscombe, Rhodri Windsor. *The New Spirit: Modern Architecture in Vancouver, 1938–1963*. Vancouver: Douglas & McIntyre, 1997.

Luxton, Donald, ed. *Building the West: The Early Architects of British Columbia*, 2nd ed. Vancouver: Talonbooks, 2007.

Massey Commission. *Royal Commission on National Development in the Arts, Letters and Sciences 1949–1951* [a.k.a. "the Massey Report"]. Ottawa: Library and Archives Canada, 1951. www.collectionscanada.gc.ca/massey/index-e.html.

Mitchell, David J. *W.A.C. Bennett and the Rise of British Columbia*. Vancouver: Douglas & McIntyre, 1983.

Mossman, Mary Jane. *The First Women Lawyers: A Comparative Study of Gender, Law and the Legal Professions*. Oxford: Hart Publishing, 2006.

Neutra, Richard. *Mystery and Realities of the Site*. New York: Morgan & Morgan Publishers, 1951.

Plaskett, Joseph. *A Speaking Likeness*. Vancouver: Ronsdale Press, 1999.

Riordon, Bernard, ed. *Bruno Bobak: The Full Palette*. Fredericton: Goose Lane Editions, 2006.

Rogatnick, Abraham, Ian Thom, and Adele Weder. *B.C. Binning*. Vancouver: Douglas & McIntyre, 2006.

Russell, Paul. "Ron Thom's Architecture for Trent University." *artscanada*, June 1969, 29–30.

Scott, Charles H. *Vancouver School of Art Prospectus, 1945–46*. Vancouver: Vancouver School of Art, 1945. Brochure.

Shadbolt, Douglas. *Ron Thom: The Shaping of an Architect*. Vancouver: Douglas & McIntyre, 1995.

Shadbolt, Jack. "Recent British Columbia Painting and the Contemporary Tradition." *Royal Architectural Institute of Canada Journal*, December 1951.

Shadbolt, Jack. "A Report on Art Today in British Columbia." *Canadian Art*, Autumn 1946.

Shrum, Gordon and Peter Stursberg. *Gordon Shrum: An Autobiography*. Vancouver: University of British Columbia Press, 1986.

Single, Michael, dir. *The Aleutians: Cradle of the Storms*. Natural History New Zealand in collaboration with Oregon Public Broadcasting and NHK (Japanese Broadcasting Corporation), 2011.

Slaight, Annabel, ed. *Exploring Toronto*. Toronto: Architecture Canada, 1972.

Soules, Matthew. *Binning House*. Novato, California: ORO Editions, 2017.

Stacey, Colonel C.P. *The Canadian Army, 1939–1945: An Official Historical Summary*. Ottawa: Edmond Cloutier, 1948.

Stouck, David. *Arthur Erickson: An Architect's Life*. Vancouver: Douglas & McIntyre, 2013.

Sylvester, Andy. *Gordon Smith: Don't Look Back*. London: Black Dog Publishing, 2014.

Taylor, Jennifer, and John Andrews. *John Andrews: Architecture, a Performing Art*. New York: Oxford University Press, 1982.

"Trent University, Peterborough, Ontario." *Architecture Canada,* October 1966, 44–47.

Vancouver Art Gallery. *Vancouver: Art and Artists 1931–1983.* Vancouver: Vancouver Art Gallery, 1983.

Varley, Peter. *Frederick H. Varley.* Toronto: Key Porter Books, 1983.

Vitruvius Pollio, Marcus. *The Ten Books on Architecture,* trans. Morris Hicky Morgan. New York: Dover Publications, 1960.

Watanabe, Kiriko, Adele Weder, Donald Luxton, and Barry Downs. *Selwyn Pullan: Photographing Mid-Century West Coast Modernism.* Vancouver: Douglas & McIntyre, 2012.

Watson, Scott. *Jack Shadbolt.* Vancouver: Douglas & McIntyre, 1990.

Watters, Reginald Eyre. *British Columbia: A Centennial Anthology.* Toronto: McClelland & Stewart, 1958.

Weder, Adele. *Copp House.* Novato, California: ORO Editions, 2017.

Whiteson, Leon. "Ryerson designer defies temptation for rare grandeur." *Toronto Star,* Oct. 31, 1981.

World War II National Historic Landmarks: The Aleutian Campaign. Booklet 458022784-796. Washington D.C.: National Park Service.

Wright, Frank Lloyd. *The Natural House.* New York: Horizon Press, 1954.

Wright, Olgivanna Lloyd. *Frank Lloyd Wright: His Life, His Work, His Words.* New York: Horizon Press, 1966.

Zeidler, Eberhard. *Buildings Cities Life: An Autobiography in Architecture,* vol. 1. Toronto: Dundurn Press, 2013.

ADDITIONAL ARCHIVAL SOURCES

Bruno and Molly Lamb Bobak. Library and Archives Canada, Ottawa, Ontario; restricted papers, call number MG 30 D 378. Cited with permission.

Emily Carr University of Art and Design Library and Archives, Vancouver, B.C.

Military Service Records, R-192943, Ronald James Thom. ATIP and Personnel Records Office, Library and Archives Canada, Ottawa, Ontario. Retrieved February 19, 2018.

Jack Shadbolt fonds, 1934–1996, RBSC-ARC-1493, University of British Columbia, Vancouver, B.C.

Ron Thom Archives, Canadian Architectural Archives at the University of Calgary, Calgary, Alberta.

Thompson, Berwick, Pratt and Partners fonds; Ron Thom fonds; Michael McMordie fonds; John B. Parkin/NORR fonds; John Flanders photography collection, Canadian Architectural Archives at the University of Calgary, Calgary, Alberta.

Trent University Archives, Peterborough, Ontario.

City of Vancouver Archives, Vancouver, B.C.

West Vancouver Archives, District of West Vancouver, B.C.

INDEX

*Photographs and illustrations indicated
by page numbers in italics*